The Laughs and Times of a Sheffield Dee Dah

Eric Boocock

First published in the United Kingdom by Arc Publishing and Printing 2023

To my beautiful wife Dawn

You are my lady and I will cherish every second of our time together. With all my heart I thank the Lord for bringing you into my life and I promise I will love you forever.

In loving memory of my Dad Cliff, Mum Vera and my Grandparents Reg and Winnie

It was your undying love that gave me such a wonderful childhood. You taught me to show respect for everyone and how to enjoy life and I wouldn't be the person I am today without your love and guidance. God Bless you all and I hope and pray we will meet again one day.

Acknowledgements

My thanks to Ray Bruce of Ray Bruce Productions, who suggested I complete my story and have it published. Ray also offered to turn my story into a sitcom for the BBC, but unfortunately I simply couldn't complete it before Ray retired. I offer him my sincere thanks for his belief in me, and best wishes for the future.

My thanks also to Chris Keeling of Arc Publishing and Printing for not only getting this book out into the public domain, but also for his advice and support along the way.

I would also like to thank our good friend Sheila Vickers for proof reading the book and for her advice in relation to deleting certain elements of the book which she considered to be either boring, irrelevant or worse still, offensive.

A big thank you goes to my good friend Tajul Azwa Bani Hashim of Malaysia, for making sure my recollections of our time in Kuala Lumpur, Northern Peninsular Malaysia and Borneo are not offensive to our wonderful Muslim friends and colleagues.

Thanks also to the many friends and acquaintances who gave up a little time to read through certain elements of the book and to provide me with honest feedback in the hope of ensuring my story remains interesting and humorous as originally planned.

A special thank you to my wonderful wife Dawn, for her undying love and for giving me the space and quiet time I so desperately needed to write the story of my life.

Booey.

Contents

Chapter One

Welcome To My World

Saturday 10th March 1951 turns out to be a pretty special day for two reasons. First of all, Newcastle United are playing Wolverhampton Wanderers in the FA Cup semi-final at Hillsborough. No doubt you already know the game ends in a 0-0 draw and then after winning the replay, Newcastle waltz off with the Cup after beating Blackpool 2-0 in the final.

If you didn't know, then you only needed to Google it, didn't you?

The second reason however, is much more important to the history of mankind, as at sometime around nine-thirty in the morning, Booey decides to put in his first public appearance. As an incoming Dee Dah, I'm supposed to be entering this world somewhere within the seven hills of Sheffield. Unfortunately, Dad Cliff works on a shift system at Victoria Station, so he might not be around when Mum Vera needs somebody to sort out the obligatory bowl of warm water, can of WD40 and a clean towel, to help clear the ever-growing blockage that's been kicking around in the upper echelons of her reception area for the last nine months or so. So the debut performance will be delivered in the front room of grandparents Reg and Winnie Cope's house at 146 Model Village in Creswell, almost within spitting distance of Sherwood Forest and all that Robin Hood stuff.

As the action kicks off, and I don't mean the big game at Hillsborough, Winnie grabs a pair of scissors to hammer on the kitchen wall to alert next-door neighbour Mabel, who shoots round to assess the situation before instructing husband Charlie to hurtle up Elmton Road and drag the village midwife back down to 146. It's not long before the special delivery lady is parked-up in the vicinity of Ma's lower half, doing whatever she needs to do to drag Booey out into daylight to take his first breath of fresh air.

Rather disappointingly, nobody's given a thought to buying me a ticket for the semi-final, so I guess I'll just have to stay home. I won't be watching it on TV either, because just like most other folk in the early 1950s, Reg and Winnie don't have one. On the other hand, a one-all draw sounds a bit boring, so no doubt those gathering round in the front room are in for a more entertaining couple of hours than the footie match spectators. Anyway, I'm hoping my arrival will cheer everybody up a bit, as there's been little to smile about in the village lately, due to the horrific after-effects of last year's Creswell Pit Disaster.

It occurs some three months into Ma's pregnancy in the early hours of Tuesday 26th September 1950, when towards the end of the night shift, somewhere in the bowels of the earth a damaged conveyor belt gets caught-up in some machinery, causing it to overheat and burst into flames. Eighty men are trapped underground and it costs them their lives, but miraculously one miner manages to avoid the raging inferno, and that just happens to be Grandpa Reg.

As news starts to filter out from the colliery and around the village, Winnie is woken by the sound of someone hammering ferociously on the back door. She jumps out of bed and bolts downstairs to come face-to-face with one of her neighbours, who's spluttering something about a fire down the pit, and that the entire night shift is trapped in the mayhem. Her husband is one of them, and as he always works with Reg, she and Winnie need to get to the colliery to find out what's going on, and whether their hubbies are OK. It only takes a couple of seconds for the news to sink in, but the information Winnie is being given isn't quite correct, as Reg is tucked-up safe and sound in bed, but not for much longer, as she races back up the staircase to desperately shake him out of his slumber.

The three of them leg it across the village green towards the colliery pithead, and by the time they arrive a few minutes later, the whole village is beginning to congregate in the pit yard. Then, after waiting, worrying and praying for what seems an eternity, details start to emerge from the coalface and sadly, they're told that Winnie's friend and neighbour has lost her husband. The lady is clearly devastated, but she's also somewhat perplexed as to how she could possibly be comforted by Winnie and the man who should have been working side-by-side with her old man at the coalface.

Forward to September 2010, and on my way to visit Mum in her little sheltered-housing flat in Chapeltown on the outskirts of Sheffield, I pick up a copy of the Worksop Guardian which dedicates a number of pages to the disaster, and includes the names of the miners who lost their lives exactly six decades ago. After the usual exchange of greetings, I make us a brew and then she starts to read out each miner's name and goes on to tell me something about his family and where they lived in the village. As she comes to one particular name, I'm completely gobsmacked to hear that although they worked on different shifts, he and Grandpa were close friends, and the man lost his life because he'd asked Reg to swap shifts with him that week. If he hadn't have asked, or if Reg had refused, it would have been Grandpa's name in today's Worksop Guardian rather than his friend's.

Apparently, the man's daughter was due to be married on the Saturday prior to the disaster, and understandably her Dad didn't fancy working five night shifts at the coalface, ending on the Saturday morning and then having to play his role at the wedding a few hours later. Reg agreed to work his friend's night shifts leading up to the wedding day, and in return his friend was planning to work Reg's night shifts the following week, but tragically for him and his family he didn't even make it through the first night. There's no doubt Grandpa would have been absolutely gutted that his friend lost his life when it should have been Reg himself. Sadly, the remains of several miners remained underground for almost a year, my Great Uncle George being one of them. God bless them all.

Over the years little was ever said about the Cope family history, until Mum's older brother provided us with a few rather surprising details, shortly after Grandpa's passing. It turns out that during the mid-1800s, a family of Irish tinkers by the name of Ferguson were on the run from the authorities and for reasons known only to themselves, they made their way to Alfreton, where they settled and somehow managed to change the family name to Cope.

Shortly after his 17th birthday in 1914, Reg found himself holed-up in the trenches of Belgium's Western Flanders, fighting in the Battles of Ypres. He never spoke of his unimaginable experiences, but it was noticed that from the day he returned from serving King and Country until the day he died, he never allowed a single baked bean or slice of corned beef to pass his lips. We didn't even know he'd fought on the Western Front, until shortly after his passing, when a member of the local British Legion called round to ask if his coffin could be draped with the Union Jack whilst a bugler played the Last Post at his funeral. That was no more than Reg deserved after everything he went through in his late teens and early twenties, and there's no doubt in my mind he would have seen it as a tribute, not to himself, but to the countless thousands who gave up their lives and never returned home to their loved ones.

Grandma Winnie was born in Godstone Surrey in 1895, and during her younger days she worked 'in service' for a posh family. During the Great War, two of her brothers were sadly killed in France within a week of each other. Her third brother remained in Surrey throughout his life, but he wasn't best pleased when Tesco acquired the land adjacent to his. He refused to sell up and the last time I visited, the house was surrounded by a 100 vehicle capacity car park, umpteen shopping trolley parking bays a rather large pantry resembling a supermarket.

I've absolutely no idea as to how, where or when Reg and Winnie met, but they did and they had two children, namely Vera and Edwin. Edwin, aka Uncle Eddie, married Marian and they went on to have five offspring, Trevor, Neil, Peter, Christine and Sylvia. In the meantime, Winnie did what all wives did in those days, keeping house and looking after the family's health and welfare. Reg was devoted to her, and during the last few years of her life, he looked after her every need until she eventually lost her long battle with dementia in September 1971.

Now I suggest you grab a stiff drink before we move on to the Boocock clan.

The name of Boocock gets out of the starting blocks in Anglo-Saxon times. It's first heard of somewhere in the Durham area, where we apparently have a family seat, although the only family seat I ever knew about was the cracked wooden one we had in the outside loo in Pitsmoor, but maybe we're talking about something completely different here. Anyway, the family tree goes back to the mid-1700's, although the first Boocock doesn't actually appear until Thomas pops out in 1779.

Somewhere along the line, we find ourselves with a family crest and a motto that reads 'Regi Regnoque Fidelis', or 'Faithful to King and Kingdom' to the likes of you and me. There are a few variations of the name, such as Pecok, Pacok, Pocok, Pehen and Pohen, all deriving from Peacock, so that's probably why most of us tend to be a bit raucous, gaudy and brazen, and no doubt it's why many of the family's male members come across as being a bit cocky.

Oh, for goodness sake! Yes, I know using the terms 'male members' and 'cocky' in the same sentence sounds a bit iffy, but it's the best I can do right now, so can we just crack on as I've got loads of other things I want to tell you about.

Anyway, the Boococks have been kicking-around Yorkshire, Lancashire and Northumberland since the mid-1800's. A few of us even reside in America, mainly along the route taken by the early settlers, although I very much doubt any member of the family would have been known as a Pilgrim Father. Australia and New Zealand are also home to some of the clan, but that'll probably be due to one or two dodgy ancestors being shipped out there some time ago.

I must admit that my personal knowledge of the clan's more recent history is somewhat limited, so much of what you're about to hear is based on Ma and Pa's recollections and as we all now, recollections can differ.

So let's kick-off with Herbert, otherwise known as Grandpa Boo. He was wounded in the head during the First World War, and was left with a load of shrapnel lodged in his brain, so I guess that proves at least one member of the family had one, although it doesn't mean the rest of us were quite so lucky. Anyway, as a result of the injury, Herbert suffered from some kind of seizures, which could render him unconscious at any time, and sadly during one episode in 1939, he fell bum-over-elbow into the local canal and drowned.

His wife Agnes, known as Nan Boo provided shelter for Irish lodgers. She wasn't very good with the housework, so that's probably why the house always seemed to be a bit scruffy, and it didn't help that the Christmas decorations were still hanging from the walls and ceiling the following August.

I remember she had long, jet-black hair and she performed a somewhat bizarre hairdressing routine every evening, which almost killed her during one of our weekend visits. As usual, the process kicks off when she parks herself in the tatty old armchair by the fireplace and picks up the hair brush. She then lowers her head toward her knees, and once comfortable she brushes the hair up from the back of her head and down over her face, allowing it to come to rest over her knees. She continues brushing away, whilst peering down towards the floor and chatting away to whoever she thinks is listening. After a few minutes, her voice starts to fade into a whisper and her head gradually lowers further as she enters the land of nod. By now her hair is hanging precariously close to the coal-fire, so inevitably it's not long before her entire head goes up in flames, and she only realises what's happening when a dripping-wet towel slams across her scalp, courtesy of Pa.

Herbert and Agnes had quite a few offspring, possibly due to them being at a loose end every night, as television and t'internet hadn't been invented at the time. One of the babies was named after Herbert, but he sadly died shortly after birth. I don't recall anything about Uncle Robert, other than always being instructed to refer to him as Uncle Robert and never as Uncle Rob, Robbie or Bob. However I do recall visiting Dad's oldest brother Alfred, but it was on the same evening that Brazil beat Italy 4-1 in the 1970 World Cup, so I was only interested in watching the match on TV and enjoying Pele's performance.

No, you don't need to start Googling again. Just take my word for it.

I'm sorry to say Uncle Alf had a habit of attempting to commit suicide, but only when he knew someone would be around to save him.

Unlike his Dad, who didn't do it on purpose, he decided to chuck himself into the canal one summer's afternoon, but only because there were dozens of people around enjoying the sunshine, so he knew some do-gooder would risk life and limb to pull him out. Then one evening he decides to stick his head into the oven and turn on the gas, but only after checking that the rest of the family just arriving home from the pub. Of course, they're just in time to turn the gas off before either the fumes kill him or the oven explodes and blows his head to smithereens.

His final prank is when he writes a suicide note and mails it to one of his siblings, knowing it'll shoot through the letter-box 48 hours later. Alf writes to say he's about to attempt suicide yet again, this time by downing a load of tablets with the help of a couple of bottles of booze. He doesn't actually swallow the tablets right now though, as the plan is to hang onto them until around the same time the postman is due to deliver the suicide note. Then there'll be time for an ambulance to be called to get him to hospital for his stomach to be pumped-out before the damage is done. Unfortunately, the plan isn't up to scratch on this occasion, as he's failed to take into consideration the possibility of the mail being delivered later than expected, and by the time the letterbox is finally flicked open four days later, the tablets and booze have already put a stop to all the buggering about.

I promise I'm not making this up!

I only remember visiting Pa's youngest brother, Norbert briefly on one occasion, when he was living in a very posh bungalow in the Midlands area. It took us several hours to get to Nobby's by train and bus, but due to the fact he saw himself as being in a different league from Pa and the rest of the family, we were heading back to Dee Dah Land just minutes after strolling through the front door. He seems to have forgotten that when they were kids, weekday meals often consisted of a huge communal bowl of chips and a pile of bread and margarine, and that made it a racing certainty that anyone trying to get a bit above themselves in later life would be treated with little respect by the rest of the clan. That proves to be the case as 'Captain Upper Crust' hangs up our coats in what he refers to as the External Attire Storage Facility, and then he asks Dad in a rather pompous manner, if we would prefer to take afternoon tea in the lounge or on the patio, which apparently enjoys a glorious view of the private lawn and well-stocked fish pond, each bordered by a wonderful array of gladioli and climbing roses.

You just wouldn't believe the look on Dad's face.

"Afternoon tea? Lounge? Patio? Private Lawn? Fish Pond? Gladioli? Are we in a bloody garden centre or what? Who the hell do you think you are? What's wrong with us having a sarnie and a mug of tea in the front room or in the back yard? You can stick your afternoon tea and just fetch the bloody coats back," screams Pa, before dragging me and Mum back to the bus stop, never to see Nobby again.

Dad's older sister Edith, lived on the edge of the Derbyshire Peak District with husband Ted and daughter Margaret. Edith was one of the original Tiller Girls, and remained in the entertainment business throughout her working life, until retiring from her final job as an usherette at the local cinema. I remember being fascinated by her daily ritual of placing a line of tablets along the table before proceeding to swallow the lot with the aid of a jug of cold water, and once she'd downed the lot, she'd then start plucking her eyebrows out before painting them back in with something resembling a marker pen.

Pointless if you ask me, but I'm just a bloke, so what do I know?

In her later years, Edith started walking around the house stark naked, knowing the net curtains would prevent anyone from looking in, although at her age I would think anyone who actually managed to get a glimpse of her through the curtains, would just assume she was wearing a tatty old white frock in need of ironing.

One day, which turns out to be our final visit, we're strolling along the street towards the house, when Ma suddenly lets out a scream as she glances towards the window and realises the curtains aren't up to the job they've been purchased for. I can only assume she unexpectedly caught sight of Edith's 'tatty old frock', so I'm instructed to walk down the garden path and into the bungalow with my hands planted firmly over my eyes.

I never asked why and I was never offered an explanation, I'm glad to say, so let's just forget about it and move on to Mum Vera and Dad Cliff.

Dad told me that one day during the Second World War, whilst doing his bit for King and Country in Belgium, he and his mate were instructed to check-out a farmhouse, and they ended up having a bit of an altercation with the German Army. Then as they enter the farmhouse, they come across the bodies of the farmer and his wife, who look as though they were shot in the head quite some time ago, as they're now completely covered in ants.

They're still deciding what to do, when a German shell unexpectedly blasts straight into the farmhouse and explodes as it slams into the wall right right next to Cliff and his mate. The pair of them dive headlong onto the floor to avoid being hit by the lethal shrapnel, and as he's only five feet tall, Cliff hits the deck a split second before his pal lands on top of him. Cliff is hit in the thigh by a load of shrapnel, but his colleague takes the rest of it all the way down his back, and dies in screaming agony in shortly afterwards in the back of an ambulance, having unsuccessfully begged Cliff to put an end to the pain by bayoneting him.

I don't know why I'm telling you this, because shortly after Dad's passing, I was describing the incident to some friends when Ma told me it was a load of old cobblers. According to her, Dad and some mates had been playing snooker in a club when the shell arrived. He suffered injuries to his leg, but everything else he told me was something they saw in a film a few years after the end of the war, so I *guess I'll never get to know the truth.*

Anyway, after Cliff's recovery and subsequent return to the UK, they met when they were stationed in Lidlington, Bedfordshire, where she was a cook and Cliff was a Batman.

Oh for pity's sake! No, not that Batman! Gimme a break will you!

Batman drives officers around and he's required to meet newly arriving personnel at the railway station. Cliff's world changes forever on one particular chauffeuring trip, when he picks-up a few members of the ATS, Vera being one of them. Just after the train pulls in, he spots Vera and her mates walking along the platform. He decides she's worth impressing, so he scuttles along the platform, grabs her belongings, and heads back to the truck with Vera right behind him. He loads the baggage, and I don't mean Vera, onto the back of the truck and helps her climb into the passenger seat then bellows to her mates to tell them to sling their own luggage onto the truck and climb aboard.

Very impressive, Pa. Very impressive. Yuk! I can only assume they unloaded everything when they arrived at camp.

So, that's my world and you're welcome to it, but before we move on, there's one story I'd like to brag about, which comes to light during a visit to Mum's around the time her vascular dementia is beginning to rear its ugly head.

As I arrive, Mum is sitting in her favourite armchair watching the telly, so I head into the kitchen to make us a brew. I hear her call out 'teacake,' so I ask if she wants a toasted teacake. She shakes her head and points toward the TV. I check behind the TV but there's no sign of a teacake, but I notice there's a news item about our late Queen Elizabeth on the telly. Mum tells me that's who she's talking about, as during the War she knew the Queen as 'Teacake'. My first thought is that the dementia is taking hold faster then we'd anticipated, so I sit down before very calmly asking her what the hell she's going on about.

Mum goes on to explain that during the time she was doing the cooking in Lidlington, Princess Elizabeth, was an officer in the same camp. When her chauffeur driven car arrived each morning, the Princess would climb out and march through the cookhouse and up the three steps leading to her office. The moment she caught Vera's eye, she would wave and call out 'Teacake. Vera always obliged, and within five minutes she would be plonking a tray complete with toasted teacake, butter, jam and pot of tea would land onto the desk.

Apparently, the Princess was quite happy with the entire cookhouse brigade affectionately referring to her as 'Teacake', but what really impressed them was that whenever an army truck, with plumes of smoke billowing out from under the bonnet and a grumbling noise emanating from the engine came to a halt outside the cookhouse door, the Princess would stride out with tool bag in hand. Then, once she'd sorted out the problem, and the vehicle had been returned to good health, the greased-up Princess would head back to her office as the truck disappeared.

I find all this hard to believe I can't imagine our late Queen looking like a grease-monkey, and I always thought that during the war you remained on camp 24-7, so she wouldn't arrive each morning as she'd still be there from last night. As usual, I haven't done the homework, so of course, I've got it wrong!

Not long after the conversation, I'm watching a film about the Queen, and much of the story is about the aftermath of the death of Princess Diana, which occurs when the Queen and the Duke of Edinburgh are in Scotland. They're under pressure from both the media and Prime Minister Tony Blair to return to London, so Her Majesty decides to drive one of the royal vehicles out into the glen so she can have a bit of quiet time. The guy responsible for looking after the transport asks her not to take one vehicle in particular, as it has a mechanical fault which may result in a breakdown. The Queen reminds him that she was a mechanic during the war, and if the vehicle packs up for some reason, she'll fix it.

So that's one up for Mum!

Not long afterwards, I watch a TV documentary celebrating the Queen's reign, and it mentions that during the Second World War, no matter where she and her sister Margaret were during the day, they returned to Buckingham Palace every evening. So, that means she would arrive on camp each morning, unlike everyone else who actually lived there. So she really did know the Queen and even more incredible, she actually knew her as 'Teacake' and HRH didn't have a problem with it.

Hey, hang on a minute. I just had a thought. What if Princess Elizabeth had been on that train when it arrived in Bedfordshire? What if it had been her who caught Cliff's eye as she waltzed along the platform with her belongings in tow? What if she'd have been the one he helped into the cab? What if Cliff had cosied up to her rather than Vera on the way back to camp? What if? What if? What if?

Unfortunately, we'll never know now, so perhaps when you've stopped shaking your head in disbelief, we can move on.

Chapter Two

The Early Years

Unfortunately, as Dad never got the chance to overwhelm Princess Elizabeth, I doubt I'll not be living in that rather large house, standing at the far end of Pall Mall and going by the name of Buckingham Palace, so I'll just have to make the best of our pokey little one-up and one-down hovel in Pitsmoor. Unfortunately, life ain't easy in post-war Sheffield though, especially if you reside in what can only be described as one of the less affluent areas of the city.

1 Court 5 Oborne Street stands magnificently opposite the 'gennel,' leading from the street. It's one of eight homes around the perimeter of the yard, four of which are back-to-back houses, in which a different family occupies the half of the house that faces the street. It's an absolute dump, probably described in estate agent terms as 'nestling snugly amongst several similar and much sought after bombed-out, derelict and cockroach-infested properties with extensive and exclusive panoramic views of eight outside bogs and a huge stone wall, which separates the bottom of the street from Bridgehouses railway sidings and the main railway line between Sheffield Victoria Station and Manchester Piccadilly'.

We don't have the any extras such as a garden, bathroom, running hot water or central heating. Even Izal loo-roll is considered as an unnecessary and expensive luxury so roughly torn up newspapers, often with pictures of unpopular politicians facing outward, are hung on hooks whilst waiting to be put to good use. If you're lucky, there'll be a paraffin heater parked somewhere inside the loo to prevent the water in the cistern from freezing up in winter. If there's enough paraffin inside, it might also help prevent icicles forming on your dingly-dangly bits whilst you sit reading next week's toilet paper, with the help of the light from a solitary candle.

We still don't have a TV and neither do we have a car at our disposal, so according to the old photos I've seen, Ma has been chauffeuring me around the neighbourhood in a huge grey-coloured pram. Now I'm about to trade-in the pram for a pushchair although the new transport will make me more visible, so people are bound to notice that I'm a bit partial to pale-blue knitted bonnets, beautifully decorated crocheted matinee jackets and matching fluffy mittens.

Thanks Ma! Thanks a bunch!

Meanwhile, Dad clearly enjoys life as a porter-cum-lamp-man at Sheffield's Victoria Station, as he never stops his inane whistling from dawn to dusk.

He assists passengers with their luggage, and although I don't think it's actually in his job description, once they've handed over some kind of ransom for the return their luggage, he goes through the carriages and collects discarded newspapers and left-behind half-empty packets of cigarettes, pens, wallets and anything else of nominal value. I suppose he has a good reason to do it, especially from an income opportunity perspective, although I doubt he's given much consideration to it looking a bit odd, when this paid-a-pittance railway porter sets off for home on his bike, with a dozen newspapers secured under his arm and pockets bulging with packets of fags and an array of leather wallets and handbags full of cash and goodness knows what else.

Back on Oborne Street, parlours are transformed into makeshift bathrooms on Sunday evening, when the man-of-the-house brings in the tin-bath that hangs on the outside wall of the house during the rest of the week. The size of the bath indicates your position on the local rich-list, insomuch as the bigger the bath, the richer you're deemed to be. We have a very small tin bath, so I doubt we're even on the rich-list, although it could be due to the fact that Ma and Pa each stand no more than five feet tall in their stockinged-feet.

Anyway, water for the bath is heated-up in the 'copper', which comprises of a large cylindrical metal tank with four supporting legs and a hinged lid. Once you've filled the tank with water, it's heated up via a gas ring on the underside of the tank, which has a six-foot length of rubber hose attached to it, stretching all the way to the main gas supply tap in the fireplace. Whoever is designated to ignite the gas ring, has to carry out the procedure very quickly and carefully, and in most households it's the missus who stands by the fireplace holding a tolled-up sheet of newspaper in her hand, whilst hubby lays on the floor and levers himself forward until his head is directly underneath the tank and almost resting on the gas ring.

Once he's in position, the wife shoves one end of the newspaper into the coal fire to set it alight before handing it to hubby and reaching into the hearth to turn on the gas tap, just as her old man rams the burning paper against the gas ring. A slight 'pop' indicates the incoming jet of gas has ignited, and the water is now being heated up. It's pretty simple once you get the hang of it and you both work in unison throughout the process, although you wouldn't have a prayer of passing a Health & Safety inspection, as you're both messing around swapping rolls of burning paper with each other, whilst one of you is jammed underneath a gas ring that's about to burst into flame at any moment right above your left eyebrow.

Unfortunately, Pa doesn't know how to do a risk assessment, which makes one particular bath-night very entertaining. For some reason he decides to do the job on his own, so he takes a deep breath and positions himself prostrate on the floor, with a match between the fingers of his right hand and matchbox in the other, whilst wedging his head underneath the copper. His face is only a couple of millimetres from the gas ring, as he stretches out his left leg towards the gas tap in the hearth and turns on the supply with his big toe. The instant the gas is released into the rubber hose, he strikes the match on the matchbox before slamming it against the burner ring, but due to the contact being a tad too forceful, the match snaps in two before the incoming gas ignites. Then rather unwisely, instead of turning off the gas and restarting the process, he takes out another match, strikes it and plonks that one against the gas ring. This time in his haste, he fails to notice that once again the match fails to ignite, and it takes another few precious seconds for him to realise what's happened.

Even more disastrous is that his third attempt actually does the trick, but Pa hasn't taken into account that due to the length of time it's been shooting through the hose and into the burner ring since the first attempt, there's now an inevitable build-up of gas beneath the copper, I think they found him dangling somewhat precariously from somebody's roof guttering three streets away.

Exaggerating? Never! Well perhaps just a teeny weeny little bit

Right now, the damage from the explosion means we no longer have anything to heat-up the bathwater in, so Pa comes to an agreement with Bob Clack, one of the neighbours on the opposite side of the yard, for me to have my weekly bath in their kitchen. As it turns out, I'd much rather have been thrown into the kitchen sink with all the mucky pots and pans left over from one of Mum's roast pork dinners.

No offence to Ma, but years later I found out that what she called roast pork bore a striking resemblance to the stuff you'll find crammed inside a tin of Spam.

So Bob fills the copper and then he and Ma Clack carry out the heating-up procedure. Once the water boils, Ma Clack decants eight bucketfuls into the bath resting by the fireplace, and then tops it up with a couple of buckets of cold water. Bob climbs in and gives himself a good scrub, he decants four buckets of slightly grey and frothy bathwater down the outside drain, before topping-up the bath with three buckets of fresh boiling water and one of cold.

Now it's Ma Clack's turn to jump into the bath, and it then takes over an hour for the rest of Clack family to get themselves cleaned-up. Eventually, Bob pops across the yard to let Mum know I've reached the front of the queue, but by now the colour of the bathwater is a very dubious shade of grey, and the surface closely resembles the top couple of inches two of a freshly pulled pint of Guinness.

Can you think of any reason whatsoever why I might feel privileged to be taking a bath in the Clacks' imaginary bathroom? No, neither can I, so let's move on.

One afternoon, Pa arrives home from work to find Mum parked on the doorstep watching me tootling around the backyard on my tricycle. As he appears from the gennel and strolls towards the house with bike by his side, he notices several grazes on my knees. Ma tells him I fell off the tricycle whilst she was doing something in the kitchen earlier in the day, and Pa is absolutely furious.

"It's your job to look after him when I'm at work, so bugger the housework and from now on, you can bloody well watch him every minute when he's playing outside, and make damn sure he doesn't hurt himself again," yells Pa as he lifts the bike over Ma's head before slamming it against the kitchen wall. The bike that is, not Ma's bonce.

Finally, he reaches into the oven and grabs the plate of sausages, egg and chips Ma's prepared for his tea. The pair of them remain silent, not just for now, but for the rest of the evening.

The next day, Pa trudges up the gennel to find Mum sitting on the doorstep once again, this time with cup of tea and fag in hand whilst closely watching me race around the backyard. Without a single word being exchanged, he shoves his way past her and explodes back outside a few seconds later.

"Where the hell's me dinner? There's now't in t'oven. I've just done an eight-hour shift and there's sod-all to eat when I get home." He's clearly not a happy-chappie right now, especially as Mum responds with a smirk and more than a hint of spiteful sarcasm, as she takes a sip of lukewarm tea and takes a huge drag on the Park Drive Tipped.

"You told me to sit here and watch him all day and so that's what I've done. "Now you can take over so I can start cooking your dinner," Ma smirks as she takes another drag on the fag and calmly blows the smoke straight across Pa's mush.

No doubt it'll be very quiet in our house tonight!

"If you want something now, there's a loaf, some margarine and a tin of Spam in the pantry, otherwise sit there for an hour until the sausages and mash are ready."

Nice one, Ma! I can't help wondering if he'd have come home to all this nonsense if he was residing in Buckingham Palace?

On Saturdays, I accompany Mum whenever she does a bit of shopping in Sheffield's Rag and Tag Market. Then if he's on an afternoon shift, we head down towards the Wicker arches and take the lift up to Victoria Station to visit Pa.

When it's relatively quiet, he'll take me for a ride on a flat-back luggage trailer along a couple of platforms. Occasionally, once he's removed the lamps from the rear end of an incoming train, topped them up with paraffin and adjusted the wicks, he lets me climb up onto the buffer to stick the lamps back into position ready for the train to depart. I'm not sure it's legal, but who cares?

When Pa takes on the station announcer's role, a responsibility that comes complete with microphone and desk, he puts on his posh voice when a train pulls into the station.

"This is Sheffield. This is Sheffield. The train now arriving at Platform 4 is the 10.35 from London St Pancras. Passengers for Manchester and Doncaster change here. This is Sheffield. This is Sheffield."

Departing trains are seen off with, "The train now leaving Platform 6 is the 11.55 to Cleethorpes, calling at Darnall, Woodhouse, Kiveton Bridge, Kiveton Park, Shireoaks, Worksop, Retford, and so on all the way to Grimsby Town, Grimsby Docks and Cleethorpes."

When all the announcing is over, unbeknown to me he switches off the microphone before assuring me that one of Father Christmas's fairies is on the other end, and I can order whatever sweets I would like them to deliver and leave on the kitchen table for when I come downstairs in the morning. I usually request a bar of Fry's Five Boys chocolate, a tube of Smarties, a Lucky Bag and a packet of Spangles.

Yes, I know what you're thinking, but I couldn't care less?

As Dad ia about to clock-off one Saturday morning at the end of his night shift, his supervisor tells him that Billy Smart's Circus is due to arrive late that evening, so during his next shift Pa will be assisting in unloading the animals, and whatever might be hanging around in the wagons whilst they're parked up in Bridgehouses Sidings. That means he gets to spend a couple of hours going teeth-to-teeth with a pair of lions, eye-to-eye with a dozen chimpanzees, and nose-to-trunk with a quartet of African elephants.

I guess that's a first for a member of the Boocock clan.

In the meantime, Dad's colleague Harry has an allotment somewhere off Rock Street, and when he hears what Pa's going to be doing, he asks him to try and get hold of some elephant manure, although I doubt he uses that term exactly. Anyway, the animal keeper gladly explains to Pa that, as the train has been on-the-go for almost twenty four hours, there's at least a couple of tons of the stuff rolling around in a few of the wagons at the other end of the train, so he can nick as much as he can carry.

The animals are unloaded just before midnight, so Pa fills an empty coal sack with assorted animal-whoopsies, and his supervisor gives him permission to take it to his mate's place during his snap-break. By 2.40 in the morning, Pa has the bulging sack secured over his shoulder and is heading along Nursery Street. As he turns into Chatham Street, he passes the Tardis-style police box at the bottom of the hill, and moments later PC Plod steps out to enquire as to what he's doing.

"Excuse me, Sir. I would be most grateful if you would mind turning around and come back down the hill, to explain exactly what it is you're carrying in that rather heavy-looking sack, at a quarter to three on a Sunday morning."

No doubt you'll have your own thoughts as to the exact words the policeman used.

Pa turns toward the nice policeman and politely replies.

"It's a consignment of farmyard-type organic compound, for an acquaintance of mine to use in his horticultural activities."

Yes, your interpretation is still fine by me.

"Very funny," sneers our boy in blue. "Now get back here and empty it out, and for the second and final time, what's in the sack?'

"It's still full of shit," barks Dad with more than a hint of indignation, "and I can't empty it out as I don't have a shovel to get it back into the sack".

"It's not the sack that's full of shit it's you, you thieving sod," retorts Plod, "so get back here and empty it out and if it's full of shit I'll shovel it back up myself."

The sack is duly up-ended, allowing the contents to spill out and roll onto the policeman's shiny shoes, before continuing their journey to the inside of Tardis. Pa is back on duty ten minutes later, but it seems the allotment will have to do without the assistance of the elephants on this occasion. Meanwhile, Plod is wondering where he can buy a sweeping brush and shovel, a sack of sawdust and a gallon or two of air freshener at three o'clock on a Sunday morning. He's also regretting not standing a little further away when the open end of the sack was heading for the deck, and he's extremely annoyed with himself for not bringing a tin of Cherry Blossom boot polish and a shoe-brush with him when he started his shift.

Oh dear! How sad! Never mind!

Mrs Day's shop is on Railway Street. She's a lovely lady, but the shop interior is a complete mess, as she stocks just about everything from hat pins to helicopters, but she has very little storage space. Dry goods such as flour, tea, sugar and biscuits are stored at floor-level in large rectangular tubs with see-through lids. They're stacked all over the place in no particular order, so when you ask for half a pound of anything it usually takes Mrs Day at least five minutes to find the tub it's stored in, and another five to force the lid off and weigh-out the contents. An assortment of buns and cakes are usually piled up on top of the counter, but no doubt they'll be well past their use-by-date and more than likely by at least two years.

Anything else that might be described as having a 'long life', could have been hiding away in the shop since before Ma and Pa were born. Worse still, the low ceiling is covered with rolls of sticky fly-paper, probably left-over from the war, and most of them dangle down over the bun-counter. They're covered in dead flies, so whenever deceased insects become unstuck, they drop onto the display of cakes and pastries. Occasionally, Mum will buy a plain sponge cake, but when she arrives home and unwraps it, she finds it's somehow turned into a huge currant bun.

Shopping at Mrs Day's is not recommended, but nevertheless on his way home from Victoria on Bonfire Night, Pa decides to call in to buy me a two shillings and sixpence box fireworks, and of course things don't go according to plan.

Shortly after tea, Pa drags me out into the backyard before sticking a Moon Rocket into a milk bottle and lighting the taper. After a bit of a hiss, the rocket keels over and hits the deck, so Pa simply leaves it to die on the tarmac. Then he pins a Catherine Wheel to a strip of wood which is already propped-up against the outer wall of Boocock Towers, but after a stuttering spin and bit of a splutter, the firework falls off the wood to land on the ground, dead as a dodo. Pa shakes his head in disbelief before grabbing a Volcano, which is supposed to spit out columns of coloured flames and smoke, but of course it doesn't. Pa has clearly spent a huge part of his wages on a batch of duff fireworks, so he's seething as he drags me back up to the shop with the now half empty box jammed firmly under his arm.

The shop is now closed, so he starts hammering on the door until Mrs Day staggers out from the rear of the shop. He shoots past her and into the shop, before ripping the box open and chucking the fireworks all over the top of the counter.

"Look at this pile of crap. They must have been hanging around the shop since before Guy Fawkes was even born," Pa spits whilst grabbing the remaining fireworks from the box and piling them up into a pyramid on top of the counter.

Knowing the fireworks are completely kaput, he pulls out a couple of Roman Candles and the last Volcano from the pyramid and puts a match to the touch papers. As always, Pa hasn't weighed-up all the possibilities, and his lack of understanding in Health and Safety matters comes to the fore once again. Three of the fireworks aren't as kaput as he thought, so it only takes a few seconds for the shop interior to explode into life, as ribbons of red, blue and yellow flames shoot up to the ceiling and bounce off in all directions.

The shop soon becomes a raging inferno, but worse is to come when a moon rocket, lying prostrate on top of the counter, suddenly takes off towards the window and ignites the rest of the pyramid as it shoots past. Now we have multiple explosions and cascades of flames surrounding us as a fleet of rockets and balls of fire bounce off the ceiling, walls and windows. Mrs Day must think we're back in the Sheffield Blitz of World War 2, but the good news is that for the first time in living memory, the reels of fly paper hanging from the ceiling are now free of dead flies.

So Bonfire Night turns out to be very entertaining after all.

I suppose life gets even better when I decide to quit smoking at the age of seven.

In these days you don't need to prove you're old enough to buy a packet of fags from the corner shop, so kids of my age are regularly sent out to replenish Mum and Dad's stocks of Woodbines, Player's Weights and stuff like that, and following one of many such trips to Millie's shop further up Oborne Street, I ask Ma if I can have a fag. To my utter amazement she agrees and lights-up a Park Drive Tipped, before wedging it firmly between my lips and instructing me to suck on it as much as I can, swallow the smoke, and then blow it out in one long, steady puff. So I take a massive drag, until I find myself looking down at little more than a dog-end and feeling as though I'm probably releasing a trail of smoke from each ear-hole. The smoke goes down in one great gulp, but when I attempt to blow it out, 'Houston, we have a problem'.

No matter how hard I try, I just can't bring the smoke back up, but just as my eyeballs are about to explode, I finally manage it. Up it comes, but unfortunately so does most of this morning's porridge and a substantial part of last night's supper of fried egg, chips and baked beans. Due to me unexpectedly pebble-dashing most of the kitchen wall, I expect Ma to go ape, but not a bit of it as she calmly picks-up the soggy dog-end from the floor and looks me in the eye.

"I think that'll be the last fag you ever smoke."

It was indeed, and in my opinion I should now have an entry in the Guinness Book of World Records for the shortest length of time a human being has been a smoker. Thirty six seconds precisely!

It's around this time that some devastating news turns my world completely upside-down. Mum is pregnant, which is a huge surprise to us all, as she and Pa are supposed to be saving up to buy a car. What really troubles me though, is that I could soon be relegated to number two on their list of favourites, but I don't suppose there's not much I can do about it, but it's a shame about the car. Anyway, as we approach mid-February, I'm shipped back to Creswell for the duration of the school half-term break. I'm not particularly interested in what Ma's going through back in Pitsmoor, as I'm more concerned about the rash I've developed all over my body. It turns out to be chicken pox, so that means I'll be locked up at Reg and Winnie's until the huge spotty-rash finally clears up.

Early one afternoon whilst scratching my belly like crazy, the pit siren screeches into life, telling the world that Reg's morning shift is over, so Grannie leaps into action, and as Reg arrives home, she's checking the oven to make sure his lunch is almost ready. Then, with jacket, boots and snap-tin discarded, Reg gives his hands a good scrub before sitting down to a very welcome plate of Yorkshire puddings smothered in thick gravy, whilst Winnie slides a second batch into the oven. Grandpa barely has the time to clear his plate before another two land on it, followed by several slices of roast beef, half a dozen roast potatoes and a heap of mash, a small mountain of assorted vegetables and a jug of gravy.

I kid you not. You could feed a small African nation for a month on what Reg gets through after a shift down the pit. Oh, I forgot the dessert.

As Reg mops up the last few drops of gravy, it's no surprise to him when the final pair of Yorkies land on the plate, and this time they're smothered in a huge dollop of warm home-made strawberry jam. You might think he'd need Lake Windermere to wash down a meal like this, but a quart of stout suffices. Winnie finally hands him a mug of tea and a copy of the daily newspaper to read before Reg heads up the stairs to rest his weary head until tea time.

When he returns from the land of nod, he comes face-to-face with his afternoon tea, which includes a small range of sandwiches, a bowl of sherry trifle and a brace of buttered fruit scones topped with jam and cream, all freshly prepared by the love of his life. Half an hour later, and following a quick wash and shave at the kitchen sink, Reg heads off to one of the local hostelries, known as Dirty Dick's, where he devours another pint or six of stout before swaying his way home to be met by a supper of cold roast beef and a pile of bubble and squeak followed by apple crumble and custard, and the obligatory quart of stout, and then the land of nod beckons once again.

When Grandpa arrives home the following afternoon, he complains about something irritating him on his back, so Winnie carries out a quick medical inspection and discovers a massive oozing boil, nay carbuncle, somewhere around the bottom of his shoulder blade. She's obviously dealt with this kind of thing before, so just a few seconds later she slams a saucepan of milk onto the open-fire before cutting-up half a loaf of bread into thick chunks and chucking them into the pan with the milk.

It doesn't take long for the mixture to come to the boil and start rendering down into a steaming semi-solid gunge, at which point Reg is instructed to drop his braces over his waist, remove his shirt and vest and then wrap his arms tightly around the kitchen sink taps. Then, the moment he settles into position, Winnie lifts the pan of boiling goo from the fire, and using a pair of large wooden tongs, she lifts up and slams a great pile of boiling bread poultice straight into the festering mass on Reg's back.

Up to this point, I'd been wondering why he was told to tightly embrace the kitchen sink taps, and now I know!

As the poultice smashes onto the scarlet volcano erupting out from beneath his skin, Reg levitates at least six inches above the floor, as the indescribable pain shoots through his body, rendering his entire face and head a much brighter shade of scarlet than the carbuncle ever was.

With eyes squeezed tightly shut, he almost wrenches the taps from the sink, but I doubt he's too concerned about that, as he's now shaking like a jelly in a tornado. Then, as the pain starts to subside, he gently lowers his feet back down to earth and carefully peels his arms away from the taps, before reaching towards the bottle and glass standing on the kitchen table, and pouring himself a pint of stout and devouring the lot in less than three seconds. Finally, after releasing a somewhat large and socially-unfriendly burp, Reg scrubs his hands and heads to the table as the first batch of Yorkies arrive.

These are the days when men are men!

The very next day, due to Reg and Winnie not owning a telephone and the world not yet being introduced to mobile phones, social media and stuff like that, Ma and Pa unexpectedly appear at the door with a little pink bundle of love going by the name of Rita.

It soon becomes clear that the one-up-and-one-down one-bedroom mansion in Pitsmoor is far too small for the extended family, so three months after Ar Reet's arrival, I depart from Pye Bank School as we're relocating a few miles to 109 Wallace Road in Parkwood Springs. Luckily, Dad has a mate who drives a truck for the railway, and he's allowed to use it to assist colleagues when they move house. Well, at least that's what he claims should anybody ask.

I guess I've got used to living in the Pitsmoor hovel, but my first thought about moving to Parkwood Springs and into a new home which has four levels, is that it'll be like living in Buckingham Palace, and as you'll recall, I only just missed out on that when Pa was doing his Batman stuff. On the other hand, I guess my expectations could be a bit over the top.

You can bet your bottom dollar they are! I know it might sound like a plush area of down-town Los Angeles, but trust me, it most certainly ain't!

Chapter Three

Springing Into Life

Parkwood Springs began life as a deer park and hunting-ground owned by the Duke of Norfolk's estate, and then in the mid-1800s, loads of houses were built in to accommodate railway workers.

I don't think much has changed since then, apart from the result of a bit of collateral damage during the Second World War, as that nasty little Hitler chappie did his utmost to wipe the industrial areas of the city clean-off the map during the Sheffield Blitz in December 1940. Apparently, his prime targets for the bombing raids were the steelworks and foundries, but as many Parkwood residents lived close by, anything other than a perfect bull's eye could easily result in having a couple of tons of high-explosives being dispatched straight down the 'chimley.' Unfortunately, 'Jerry' didn't have a very good aim from 20,000 feet, so Wallace Road was directly on the receiving end.

Turning off Douglas Road into Wallace Road, you notice a couple of huge gaps as you stroll up the hill and past the houses. The gaps used to be occupied by a number of family homes which disappeared one night a few years ago, thanks to a few passing bombers, but they're now filled with craters full of rubble, rotting bed mattresses and even the odd one or two Ford Popular and Morris Minor 'skellingtons'. Our house is about halfway up the street, just past the local Methodist Chapel on the opposite side of the road. Looking out from the cellar-kitchen window across the backyard and beyond the block of outside toilets, we have a magnificent panoramic view of the main Sheffield to Manchester railway line and a pair of gasometers.

A stone staircase leads from the kitchen up to the street-level landing, where we have a front room to the left and a bedroom to the right. Another staircase then leads from the front room and up to another couple of bedrooms, and a third staircase takes you to the summit of the house which houses the attic. It's undoubtedly a significantly larger residence than the 'Wendy House' we left behind in Pitsmoor, although there's still no sign of a bathroom, running hot water or central heating. On the other hand, the Victorian gas lamp parked right outside the front door is an absolute godsend, as it lights-up the pavement from dusk until dawn, so we have no trouble avoiding any piles of doggy-poo whilst playing on the street after tea.

Sadly, not long after we've settled into the new abode, Dad takes up a new job as Chargehand Carriage Cleaner at the Nunnery railway sidings, just off the city-end of what is now the Sheffield Parkway, and as he no longer has access to the station announcer's microphone, I've lost contact with Santa's fairies. Anyway, I'm eight years old now, so I'm mature enough to know it's Pa who delivers the goodies, as Santa and Co only call round on Christmas Eve.

The best thing about moving to the Springs is that on the very day I join the Foreign Legion, I bump into a guy named Cliff Shaw, and we become best friends for the rest of our schooldays. It's not the real Foreign Legion, by the way, it's just that some dopey builder has deposited a huge pile of sand on the pavement just outside the chapel, and as I stroll by I notice Cliff is up to his neck in it. I decide to join him and then we take up positions as a pair of snipers, firing invisible bazookas at passing German army tanks, which look very similar to Ford Zephyrs and Triumph Heralds. We blow the tanks into oblivion of course, but to our dismay we're given medical discharges the very next day, as we're unable to fight-on due to being covered from head to toe in rashes caused by the extended contact with builders sand. It doesn't matter anyway, as some thieving git appears to have shovelled-up the desert and chucked it onto the back of a truck during the night.

Leave it! Leave it!

Meanwhile, the menfolk often turn the backyard into Wembley Stadium, by moving a few dustbins out of the way and taking down the washing lines that criss-cross the yard. Some kind soul has already painted a set of goalposts onto the gable-end of 99, which backs onto our yard, and another set recently appeared on the huge stone wall at the opposite end of the yard outside Mrs Slater's pad at 113.

Unfortunately, cup finals never flow smoothly, as every few minutes some clown manages to hammer the ball over the backyard wall, and I'm usually the idiot who gets to climb over and slide down the embankment to traverse four sets of railway lines in order to retrieve it. It never crosses my mind that hopping around on the main line between Sheffield and Manchester is more than a bit risky, as every few minutes a train travelling almost at the speed of light, hurtles past within touching distance. I guess it's just down to the grace of God that I manage to avoid being shredded to pieces on cup final days.

No, I don't want to know what you think about it.

I do have the occasional mishap however, but that's down to the Plumb family at 111 having a nasty habit of emptying the chip-pan over it. If they don't chuck it over with some force, the cold fat just clings to the top of the wall and dribbles down the other side, so if you're not careful when leaping over, you're likely to grab hold of a slimy patch of lard, which results in your hand and arm shooting out at an acute angle before your head smashes out of control against the greasy bricks as you hurtle down the other side and go bum-over-elbow to land face down in a puddle of stinking goo garnished with crispy bits of over-cooked spuds.

The good news is we're usually left to it as far as the footie's concerned, although there could be a problem or two if the cup final is on a Monday, as that's washday around here. That makes it difficult for the finalists, as there's always rows of bedsheets, pillow cases, shirts and an assortment of ladies' unmentionables flapping around from the washing lines.

One Monday afternoon, Ma Slater gives me a blasting, just because I miraculously deflect a goal-bound shot onto her kitchen window, via a row of newly washed underwear and bed linen. Then, whilst she's still bawling at me from inside the house, she notices a huge crack across the window pane, which she reckons is down to my incredible goalkeeping skills. In my view, the damage could have been done during a particularly heavy bombing raid during the Blitz, remaining unnoticed for the last two decades. On the other hand, the crack could be due to a slightly-pickled pigeon misjudging its landing on the window ledge and swooping beak-first into the glass.

Well, anything's possible isn't it? No, I thought not.

Whichever day it is, the womenfolk clearly have absolutely no interest in footie, so they tend to get a bit stroppy about the noise we make whenever a goal is scored. We all know that after working a night shift, hubbies remain in bed until teatime, but getting some well-earned shut-eye when a cup final is taking place below your bedroom window is nigh-on impossible. As it happens, Mr Lax at 105 is on nights this week, and upon hearing the verbal onslaught outside the back door following a brilliant headed goal by yours truly, his other half heads into the fray. It's no fault of ours that he suffers from an unfortunate medical condition, which renders him unable to sleep for more than a few minutes at a time, and it's no more than pure coincidence that he always seems to wake-up during our numerous goal-scoring celebrations, but his missus clearly needs to blame somebody, and it's always us.

It's a disgraceful accusation, and there's no justification whatsoever for the rollocking we get, so in some kind of warped retaliation, Cliff and I decide to invoke the Mucky Pup prank.

On Saturday morning we catch the bus into town, to purchase a very life-like lump of plastic doggy poo from the joke shop in Castle Market, and then just before the next cup final kicks-off, Cliff delicately positions the doggy poo on Ma Slater's doorstep. It's not long before she steps out of the house clutching a bowl of potato peelings and heads across the yard to the dustbin. Once she's disposed of the rubbish, she struts back towards the house without so much as a glance in our direction, and just as she's about to head back inside, she almost steps on the poo. When she realises what she's just avoided, she drops the empty bowl into the goal area and shoots down the right wing towards the Lax residence to smash a tightly clenched fist on the backdoor.

Seconds later Mrs Lax steps out and straight into World War Three. Ma Slater is furious that the Lax's family pooch has pooped on her doorstep, so the pair of them march back to 113 to carry out a forensic examination, whilst continuing their rather unneighbourly verbal exchange. Mrs Lax is adamant the offending article bears no resemblance to that which normally exits her dog's rear-end, so she has absolutely no intention of doing anything about it. Ma Slater is now close to boiling point and the cup final comes to an abrupt halt, due to both teams being in fits of laughter. Seconds later an eerie silence descends over Wembley, as Booey casually strolls across the yard, and as he squeezes past the pair of fuming gobs, he spits into the palms of his hands before rubbing them briskly together and carefully scooping the doggy mess up with his fingers. The ladies immediately agree a ceasefire, and are now muttering a few words of utter disgust to each other.

"What the chuffin' hell do you think you're doing, you dirty, filthy little sod?" screams Mrs Lax in total disbelief.

I simply turn and shrug my shoulders whilst squeezing past them once again, and upon reaching the dustbin I raise the lid with my elbow and release the poo into the darkness. Then, with perhaps the most horrific display the ladies have ever witnessed, I give my hands and fingers a thorough licking before wiping them dry on my shorts. You just won't believe the reaction to that little stunt.

Well, I can't play footie with dirty hands, can I?

Ma Slater goes all faint and bursts into tears, as Mrs Lax hurtles towards me and lands a massive well-aimed 'thwack' round the back of my head, before grabbing me by the ear and dragging me into 105. She shoves me toward the kitchen sink, and then forces my head into a bowl of hot soapy water she'd prepared for doing some washing up just before war broke out. Just before I drown, she yanks my head out then rams my hands into the water to give them a very painful going-over with the aid of steely-bristled scrubbing brush she keeps under the sink.

Some people just can't take a joke, can they?

Eventually, play resumes, and when the cup final is over and done with, me and Cliff decide to take things a step further later in the evening, once I've got the feeling back in my hands.

We know everybody in our yard watches the TV upstairs in the front room, so it's a safe bet there'll be nobody around in the cellar kitchen after 7pm. We quietly attach one end of Ma Slater's washing line to her back door-knob, and then, whilst making sure the line remains taut, we stretch it across the backyard and fasten the other end around her dustbin handle. Then we do the same outside the Lax's, before I position myself outside the back door of 113, whilst Cliff does the same outside 105. We silently count down from 10 to zero, at which point we simultaneously hammer on the door each of us is facing, before shooting part-way up the gennel between our house and the Wakelin's. We know what's coming, so it's almost impossible to control the giggling.

Right on cue, a few seconds later the doors are wrenched open almost simultaneously, further tightening the washing lines, which results in the bins being yanked forward from their concrete plinths. As luck would have it, today is the day prior to the weekly bin collection, so both receptacles are almost full to the brim. When they hit the deck, the lids become detached and shoot forward, spewing the entire contents of the bin across the backyard towards the two houses.

Unfortunately, our lovely neighbours hear the howls of laughter emanating from inside the gennel, so as Ma Slater and Mrs Lax approach rather menacingly we race up to the street and up the hill out of harm's way. We don't stop until we arrive at the top of the street outside Mrs Vickers' house. She's one of Wallace Road's oldest residents and unlike one or two of our neighbours, she's a very friendly lady.

It's only just after seven in the evening, so it hasn't crossed our stupid little minds that she might already be in bed, and wouldn't be too pleased about all the giggling going on beneath the bedroom window. Due to the ongoing Mucky Pup celebrations, we fail to notice that some ten feet above us a large one-handled porcelain pot, known locally as a 'guzzunder' appears from inside the bedroom window and starts to release its contents in our direction.

I won't go into great detail, but these receptacles are used during the night in homes yet to be equipped with indoor toilet facilities, and if you don't switch on the bedroom light before sliding the pot from underneath the bed, you won't know it's full until the thumb holding the handle suddenly becomes warm and wet.

When the contents land straight on top of our thick heads there's no doubt that if it wasn't game over five minutes ago, it most certainly is now, although it could have been much worse. Mrs Vickers could have been relieving herself from the rear-exit rather than the front, but perhaps it might be best not to dwell on that thought.

I still have another year to do in the juniors at Hillfoot County School. Whilst I know I'll never be in the same league as Albert Einstein, every Friday morning when class teacher Mr Turner reels off a load of mental arithmetic calculations, it's always my hand that shoots up into the air the moment Mr T takes a breath. I've absolutely no idea how I do it, but apparently it annoys him off so much, he decides to bar me from answering until it becomes clear that nobody else has a clue. Then he heaves a huge sigh of dismay as he instructs the 'Brain of Britain' to reveal the answer to the rest of his classmates.

Perhaps it's for this reason Pa decides to teach me how to play Cribbage and do the scoring. It only takes a couple of sessions for me to figure everything out, so now he decides that from now on the first to win three games wins the set, and then the first to win three sets wins the match. He warns me that he won't let me win just because I'm a kid, so whenever I beat him it'll be due to me being the better player. He also promises that sessions will never end in a draw, so one of us will always be the champion until the next session.

I still look back to the countless Cribbage sessions we enjoyed over the years, knowing that more than anything, they led to me and Dad always being great pals.

Mum has always been a regular churchgoer and she keeps harping on at me to start attending Sunday Evensong.

I eventually cave in, and to my great surprise, I quickly develop a huge interest in all the religious stuff I'm hearing. Keeping out of trouble and helping others is quite appealing and satisfying, and I think that's the main reason I decide to join the Sheffield 159th Wolf Cub Pack, based at Woodside Lane School. I make loads of new friends and learn some skills I've never even considered until now, and I get a badge for every one. It's also good to hear that numerous older local residents now consider me to be a very nice young man, and I guess popping round to various houses and offering to do bits of shopping doesn't go amiss either.

Right now, I'm looking forward to Bob-a-Job Week, but it turns out that someone decides to use the opportunity to wreak revenge for my earlier misdeeds.

As the snow on the Wallace Road rooftops starts to melt, I think I must be doing the shopping for almost every household in the Springs, but no doubt things will soon slow down once this year's Bob-a-Job week is over and done with. Unfortunately, at the back-end of the week, and even though she's completely blanked me recently, Ma Slater stops me in the street and asks me to pop round to hers later as she needs a little job doing. It appears that due to the melting snow, water is dripping through her roof, finding its way into the electrical system and pouring from the light fitting on the kitchen ceiling. I explain that she'll have to pay me a shilling in line with the Bob-a-Job rules, but I don't have the faintest idea what to do, so she simply tells me to climb up the step-ladder and carry out her instructions.

On reaching the top step, I come face-to-face with a length of wire with icy cold water dribbling from the end, so she hands me a tea towel to wipe it dry, and then orders me to twist a light bulb into the fitting. Then she presses the light switch but nothing happens, so she switches it off and instructs me to stick my index finger into the fitting and wriggle it about, as that'll loosen anything that shouldn't be in there, but the old bat fails to warn me that she's secretly switched the power back on again. Seconds later, a huge bolt of electricity shoots straight up my arm and neck and crashes into what little brain I have.

Then, just as I re-enter earth's atmosphere, Ma Slater chucks a bowl of cold water over my head.

"That'll teach you not to stick plastic dog-crap on my doorstep. You're not the smart-ass little sod you think you are, so bugger off home."

The Mucky Pup and Dustbin pranks appear to have turned Ma Slater into a bitter and twisted old witch, but I guess revenge is sweet, especially when eaten cold.

Meanwhile, my mate Cliff lives in a big house at the bottom of Pickering Road, with ten huge stone steps leading up from the street to the front door. Mum and Dad think the world of him, so from now on he's always invited to join us on trips to Belle Vue Zoo, Skegness, Cleethorpes and on visits to Creswell. He's as tough as they come and it's great that we both have a similar barmy sense of humour.

When the weather is bad, me, Cliff and a few mates often play various games in either our downstairs kitchen or in Cliff's front room, but as we aren't actually allowed in there we can only sneak in when his mother is out playing Bingo, and that's most afternoons and evenings. Whoever is involved in the games has to bring something they can use as gambling stakes, such as toys, books, comics and anything else that might be of value or interest to other members of the gang.

One afternoon, Cliff decides to take over the front room for the games session, so the usual assortment of stakes are put on display as the fun starts, and as always, the only rule is that if you lose all your stakes, you clear off home. My best mate has a bad day on this occasion, losing everything he puts up as a stake, and as I'm on a winning streak, most of his losses become my winnings. Having now become toy, book and comic bankrupt, he reaches over to the windowsill and picks up a metal tray, on top of which sits half a dozen beautiful gold-rimmed whisky glasses. They obviously belong to his mother, but he decides to take ownership and puts them up as a stake in the next game. Then when I head home for tea and hand them over to Mum, she's thrilled when I tell her I've been saving up my pocket money to buy her a present for Mother's Day.

What a kind and thoughtful boy I am, don't you think?

Cliff's mother's pride and joy is a piano that takes up half the wall in the front room, and when he's on yet another losing streak a couple of days later, he decides to put the piano up as a stake. Unfortunately for him, I'm on yet another winning streak, and it's not long before the piano has a new owner. I jokingly tell Cliff I need to figure out how to get the piano out of the front door and down the concrete steps, so I'll be able to manhandle it down to the bottom of the hill and up Wallace Road to 109. He begs me not to take it, and swears it doesn't matter about the whisky glasses as his Mum hardly ever uses them, but when she arrives home she's bound to notice the piano has gone AWOL.

You can bet your life she'd notice!

I keep up the pretence and shove the piano out of the front room towards the front door. I've no idea how I manage it, but it isn't long before the piano is hanging precariously over the top step leading down to the street below, and I'm only able to prevent it from going any further by clamping my arm over the keyboard cover. Cliff continues to plead with me, and in a blind panic he grabs the arm holding the piano in position and I start to lose my grip.

The piano starts to roll towards the top of the steps. If I let it go, there's no doubt it'll end up hurtling down the hill, past the chapel and onto Wallace Road. Then, rather than turning right at the junction and heading up to 109, it'll bear left and pick up even more speed as heads downhill and past the Hallamshire Steelworks towards the junction with Douglas Road where. Finally, without God's intervention it'll shoot straight across the road before smashing through the entrance and into the bar of the Parkwood Inn.

Fortunately, the Lord does intervene on this occasion, and I somehow manage to grab one of the foot-pedals sticking out from the base of the piano, and that provides a few valuable seconds for the rest of the gang to squeeze past and jump down half a dozen steps, to land at the front end so they can lift it up and shove it back up the steps and back into the house. Cliff's Mum arrives home just a few minutes later, to find her precious front room untouched and the gang sitting calmly around the kitchen table playing Rummy.

"Hello boys. I don't suppose you've been gambling again?" she asks as she looks around. "I hope you haven't lost again, Clifford!" Silence.

Me and the gang enjoy plenty of fun-time in our cellar-kitchen, and when we have a good mix of girls and boys we regularly play a game called Postman's Knock. The game gets underway when one of the boys steps into the unlit pantry and closes the door behind him. Whilst he's locked away, each of the girls is allocated a number, and then when the boy calls out a number, the girl issued with that particular number heads into the pantry, to spend the next two minutes snogging the face off the lucky boy. Eventually, the boy wipes his gob fry before vacating the pantry, whilst the girl remains in situ. The boys are now allocated numbers and when the girl in the pantry calls out her chosen number, the fun starts all over again. The game continues until hopefully, everyone has paid a visit to the inside of the pantry.

Yes, I'm sure there are one or two adult versions of the game kicking around, but perhaps you know more than I do.

The game sometimes gets a bit noisy as nobody in our neck of the woods has a refrigerator, so the bottles of Lemonade, Grapefruit Crush and Ginger Beer, that Ma buys from the local Co-op, are kept cool inside the copper which is parked just inside the pantry awaiting bath-night. Everyone has to be careful whilst enjoying a few sloppy minutes in the pantry, as anything more physical than a snog is likely to start the pop bottles rocking, rolling and crashing around inside the copper.

Cliff isn't keen to join in the Postman's Knock sessions, especially as Elaine always winds him up by pretending she has the hots for him and he's terrified she'll do something to embarrass him,. One Friday evening the rest of us agree that when it's his turn to call out a number from inside the pantry no numbers will be allocated, and regardless of which number he calls out it'll be Elaine who joins him in the darkness. The plan works a treat, and she starts eating his face off before the door even closes behind her. Then the pop bottles start rattling as if they're re-entering the earth's atmosphere after a trip to the moon, and when Cliff finally manages to open the door she's still eating his head, and he's looking as though he's just gone 10 rounds with the World Heavyweight Boxing Champion.

One evening Elaine invites her sister Angela to join us for an evening of pantry debauchery, and it turns out to be quite a pleasant evening. Angela is drop-dead gorgeous and in a totally different league than the rest of us, especially me. Cliff has his usual brush with death with Elaine, and then it's my turn in the pantry, and I don't believe it's just a coincidence when moments after I call out my chosen number, Angela is already spreading herself all over me in the darkness, causing the Cherryade to go into overdrive. I've never been kissed like this before, but even more exciting is the feelings I get as she presses her body against mine. I think I might be experiencing the 'growing' pains I hear Ma going on about occasionally, but then again that could be something completely different. Whatever it is, by the time Angela's done with me I'm completely breathless, but I'm already hoping for a second helping very soon.

Then it dawns on me I'm the leader of the gang, and in that role I simply shouldn't be thinking about girls in this way, because if these feelings somehow end up in the public domain, my credibility will no doubt be shot to pieces. I decide to say nothing whatsoever and to steer clear of 'Hot Lips' in the future, even though I'm aching for a replay.

Obviously I'm still rubbish when it comes to planning and making decisions.

Just before 8.30 on Monday morning, Dad answers a knock at the back door and comes face-to-face with a beaming Angela, hoping I'll escort her to school. It's the longest and most uncomfortable twenty minutes I've ever spent, and I haven't a clue what she's been talking about on the way, although I can now tell you the distance from our front door to the school gates is 3,672 paces. I'm now in a bit of a quandary, because although I have what I think are some sort of grown up feelings for her, my reputation requires me to avoid Angela at all costs.

Fortunately, Pa appears to understand my predicament, and despite being told I could be missing out on something very special, we agree a plan of action. So, when on Tuesday morning, the moment we hear the sound of footsteps coming down the gennel, I shoot upstairs and head out of the front door to sprint up the street, leaving Dad to greet Angela and explain that she's just missed me.

That turned out to be a decent plan, but not long after this little episode, Angela, Elaine and their parents sadly move to the other side of Sheffield, so I never get the chance to put things right.

What a twazzack! We blokes never learn, do we?

On second thoughts, I do meet Angela again, but it's more than 30 years later during a Parkwood Springs residents reunion held at the Ski Village, which was built after I'd left the area and unfortunately no longer exists.

As I'm checking in, a lady approaches me and asks if I'm Eric Boocock, and when I reply in the affirmative, she tells me her name is Elaine. She asks if I remember her and her sister, as she points towards the fabulous Angela looking even more angelic as she sits in the glow of the coal fire. When she smiles and waves to me, and blows a kiss in my direction, I can't help thinking how utterly stupid I was to shut her out of my life, just to protect my reputation as leader of the gang.

What a waste of all those years. You idiot!

Chapter Four

Growing Pains

It does my ego the world of good when I pass my 11-plus exam, and Mum and Dad are somewhat overjoyed when they hear I've achieved such high educational standards. I'm pretty sure it's a first for both sides of the family, but kid sister Rita doesn't have much to say about it, although that might be down to her only being three years old, so I might be expecting a bit too much of her.

When Ma Plumb hears the news, she bursts into tears, which is something of a surprise as I didn't think she liked me, especially when I'm hammering a football around the backyard on washday. It turns out that whilst she has four adult daughters, she always wanted a son, and according to her I'm the closest she's ever got to having one. My ego goes into orbit, but at the same time I feel a degree of sadness for her, and it makes me realise that perhaps you don't always get what you want in this life. I think I'll start to have a bit more consideration and respect for other people from now on, but then I guess it'll depend on who it is I'm dealing with at the time.

Meanwhile, life doesn't get any better than this, but maybe it will as I head into my teenage years. We'll soon find out!

It's not long before I'll be heading-off to Marlcliffe Intermediate School, where Year 1 consists of three classes, 1A, 1B and 1C, and due to my birthday being in March, I'm being dumped in the C Class.

I turn out to be pretty good at Maths, English Language, Art and Religious Education, but the Sciences and English Literature just aren't my thing. I don't like History and Geography either, but that's mainly down to the teachers. The good news is that come the December exams, I somehow manage to get promotion to the A class, but I soon realise that my new classmates seem to think school is purely about learning, and there's no time for larking about. Worse still, the teachers clearly believe nothing is anywhere near as important as education and the reputation of the school itself. The A Class is definitely not for me.

Meanwhile, the PE teacher is quite observant, and it's not long before he spots my world-class footballing skills, so one morning, he pins up the team sheet for the school football match due to take place on Saturday, and according to him I'll be playing on the left wing.

I'm not in the habit of crossing swords with teachers, so I politely explain I won't be playing for the school, as I'll be be playing on the other side of town for the youth club. He blows a gasket and tells me that representing Marlcliffe is much more important than playing for anybody else, so I'd better be there otherwise I'll be in deep trouble when I arrive back at school on Monday. Then he awards me a Friday night detention for my insolence.

Pa goes completely up the wall when I tell him what's happened and why I'll be late home on Friday. He's not best pleased about the threat, but he's more concerned about me being late home, as Mum departs for work at 4.15, and after sleeping off the effects of his night shift, Dad doesn't haul himself out of bed until around 5.30. By then I'll have been child-minding Ar Reet for more than an hour, so if I'm not home on time he'll be losing some valuable sleeping time.

Next morning, Dad decides to join me on the cycle ride to school, and once the bikes are secured, he grabs my arm and marches me into the building, straight past the School Secretary's desk and into the adjacent office to confront a somewhat startled headmaster, Mr Darvill. Dad wades straight in with a verbal onslaught.

"Listen, Mush! On Saturday mornings this lad of mine plays football for his youth club, then in the afternoon he captains the local cycle speedway team. He goes ten-pin bowling on Sunday mornings and does an hour's swimming before dinner and he wraps the day up by attending Evensong at the local chapel. During the week, he goes to the Wolf Cubs on Tuesday, and he plays five-a-side football, table tennis and does some wight-lifting at the youth club on Monday, Wednesday and Friday, and on Thursdays he goes to Sheffield Speedway. So you can tell that clown of a PE teacher not to bother putting his name down for the school football team, as he won't be in it on Saturday or any other day, as he doesn't have the bloody time."

Mr Darvill appears to be completely gobsmacked as Pa erupts again.

"You can also tell the dopey sod he can shove the detention up his ass as well. The boy looks after his sister for a couple of hours every day when he gets home from this dump, so regardless of what you or anybody else thinks, he's not going to be hanging around after school finishes. Is that clear?"

I thought I'd seen Pa in a bad mood before, but this is completely different.

The Head nods in the affirmative, but looks somewhat shell shocked as Dad goes into orbit once more.

"And whilst we're at it, from now on he'll only be doing an hour's homework at night, and not the three hours you lot expect him to do. If you can't teach him what he needs to know during school hours, then you should all be looking for other jobs," Pa concludes as we head out of the office and down the corridor.

Nice one, Pa!

Later in the morning, one of my mates tells me that on his way to the 'boy's room' just after I took my seat in the History Class, he noticed the PE teacher frantically deleting my name from the team sheet. The incident only increases my loathing of the A Class, and there's no doubt I'd be much happier elsewhere. With that in mind, I decide to make sure I get relegated in the June exams, and I'm pretty chuffed with myself when the plan works out so well, thanks to the 'most unfortunate' results in History, Geography, Chemistry and Physics. Come September I'll be down in 2B.

Nice one Booey!

I'm glad to say I love life in 2B, and by the onset of winter I have a decent reputation for my schoolwork, and my sporting abilities are improving by the day. It's around this time that Grandma Winnie decides to keep her feet warm during winter nights by crocheting herself a pair of pink bedsocks, complete with pink ribbon ties, but according to her they're a bit too big, so as it's been pretty cold recently, Mum suggests I take ownership of the bedsocks and wear them underneath my school socks, to help ward off frost-bite whilst biking to school.

I'm lying through my teeth when I tell Ma that's a great idea, so from now on, no matter how cold and wet it is as I cycle my way to and from Marlcliffe, my little tootsies will be keeping very snug and warm inside their little pink sleeping bags. Luckily, they'll be permanently hidden under my school socks, so nobody will ever know about them.

No doubt that's another plan that'll soon bite the dust!

Meanwhile, our weekly swimming lessons take place at Hillsborough Baths, and I cycle to the venue whilst everyone else takes the bus.

On arrival, we gather in the main entrance before heading to the poolside, where we're paired off into tiny cabins positioned all the way along either side of the pool, with boys to the right and girls to the left. Swimming instructor Mr Siviour always wants us in the water as quickly as possible, but as we're now adolescents, there's not much space for two of us to strip off and get changed. Fortunately, my cabin colleague is quick off the mark and out by the poolside before I get down to the bedsocks, but in my haste I fail to notice the neatly tied pink ribbon secured around my left ankle is knotted.

As I give the ribbon a sharp tug, the knot gets even tighter. I give it another tug which results in the blood supply to my foot almost being cut off, but as I'm prone to biting my finger nails there's no way I can prise the knot open. The only way to get the bedsock off my foot is to snip through the ribbon with a pair of scissors, but just like the rest of the boys I don't keep a pair in my satchel. By now the rest of the class are lined up along the poolside, but the instructor notices a few giggles on the boys' side, and he asks one of the lads why he's laughing.

"I'm laughing at Boocock, Sir."

"Boocock! Put your hand up. Where are you?"

"He's still in the cabin, Sir", replies the class snitch.

"Boocock! Out now, wherever you are," he yells. "Get out here. Now!"

Silence.

"Boocock! I won't tell you again! Wherever you are, come out. Now!

"He's in cabin five, Sir," giggles the snitch.

"Out! Now, Boocock!" he screams as he approaches the cabin door. "Don't make me come in there and drag you out."

I've no option but to head out onto the poolside, wearing my sexy blue swimming trunks and a gorgeous little pink cotton bedsock tightly secured to my left foot.

Oh dear, oh dear!

Regardless of all the mickey-taking from my classmates since the swimming pool pantomime, I really don't want promotion back to the A Class, so once again I just need to make sure I get a few bad results in the December exams. Naturally the plan fails spectacularly, so I end up being relegated once again, and I'm now back in the C Class with a shedload of other dipsticks.

I know what you're thinking, but I'm bound to get something right sooner or later.

I hit my teens in March 1964, and shortly after my birthday Cliff Shaw accompanies me on a visit to Reg and Winnie's in Creswell. A family living in the next yard up have a corgi called Binky, and it's a vicious little sod. It's never on a lead, and since I was little more than a toddler, whenever I've gone out to play on the village green, the bloody thing chases after me and takes a chunk out of the back of my ankle. It's no surprise then, that I've developed a huge fear and dislike of dogs, especially this one.

We've only been out on the green for a couple of minutes when Binky comes hurtling towards me, barking and growling like a demon. I'm just about to run in the opposite direction, when Cliff points out I'm much bigger and stronger than the dog, and it's time I turned the tables. I never thought of that, but with my reputation now on the line, I spin round and eyeball the little swine as he approaches. Then, the moment he gets within touching distance, I take a deep breath before somehow managing to grab him by the throat and yanking him off his feet and hauling him into the air. Binky does his best to slam his fangs into my face, but I manage to hold on tightly until he finally realises there's a new boss in town. Then, as he starts to calm down, I lower him to the ground, and as he turns his gaze from me and starts whimpering pathetically, I hold onto him and glare into his face for another few seconds, before releasing my grip and allowing him to scuttle off, never to be seen again.

Without doubt, this is the day I start to stand up for myself, but of course, that doesn't mean I'll be any less stupid than I am now, does it?

Even more exercise heads my way when we transfer our footie games and cup finals from our backyard Wembley Stadium to the football pitch just above the playground at the top of Pickering Road. Behind the far goal post, a small slope leads up to the cycle speedway track, where we also spend a great deal of time racing around and practising for meetings against teams from across the city.

When we play footie on Sunday afternoons, the regulars from the Douglas Inn, which stands just around the corner from the cycle speedway track, stagger out at closing time and suggest we take them on. Most of the blokes can barely stand up, let alone control a ball down the right wing, so we duly oblige knowing we'll run rings around them.

One of them, known to us as Bazza is a real tough guy, and clearly enjoys his well-earned reputation for getting into trouble. It's a no-brainer that whenever he has the ball at his feet, nobody ever tries to tackle him. One afternoon he and most of his boozing pals are relatively sober and less boisterous than usual, so it turns out to be a proper game, and as luck would have it I find myself in close proximity to the dreaded Bazza for much of the game.

We're about forty minutes into the game, and for the first time ever the score remains at nil-nil. Then, just before half-time Bazza receives the ball and starts heading down the wing, homing in fast on our goalkeeper. I'm known to be quicker and considerably stronger than most of my team mates, so I decide to put in a tackle. I head towards him at full speed, and as I get within range, I automatically lunge forward and slam my right leg behind the ball, just as he's about smash it towards the goalie.

He hits the ball with huge force but with my leg firmly planted against the other side, it stays put so he shoots up into the air and then hits the deck a couple of seconds later. His face slams into the grass and gravel, and as his body hits the ground he slides face-down for several yards before coming to a shuddering halt. As I sit up with the ball still firmly secured under my calf, he lies motionless some fifteen feet in front of me. My first thought is one of delight at the quality of the tackle, but then I remember who it is I've just taken down. A few seconds pass before he begins to stir and detach his face from a patch of blood-red grass and gravel, as one of his mates heads my way.

"I don't know who the hell you are, but take my advice, get up off yer ass and run home as fast you can. Don't stop to look back, and when you're safely inside, bolt the door behind you."

"But he might be hurt," I reply

"He'll be fine but you won't be when he scrapes himself up off the floor," he explains, as Bazza's bloodied face peers out from between the palms of his hands.

"But he looks like he's in a mess".

"For God's sake, clear off and don't say you haven't been warned," the guy yells as Bazza wipes the blood from his mouth and plucks the bits of gravel out of his face.

His right eye is swollen and almost closed, and then he spits out a couple of teeth before struggling to his feet and staggering towards me, wildly shaking his head with each step he takes. It's been a good life until now, and I really don't want it to end, but as the man-mountain is now standing over me, I'm beginning to wish I'd taken his mate's advice.

Bazza's left eye is now peering at me. He's not a pretty sight at the best of times, but right now he looks as though he's melting, as most of the skin on his face has disappeared. Bum-squeaking time doesn't come anywhere close to what I'm going through right now, as he finally manages to prise his right eye open, before spitting out even more teeth. When he finally manages to clear the blood from his throat, he plonks his arm across my shoulders and starts growling into my ear.

"Listen, kid. I've watched you playing during the last few weeks, so I know you're a good player," he splutters.

"Thank you," comes the pathetic reply.

"Nobody in their right mind ever tries to take the ball off me, 'cos they know what'll happen, so believe me when I tell you that's the best tackle anybody ever made on me. You could easily have bust your leg, but you went and bust my face."

"Thank you," comes another woeful reply.

"So now you can tell your mates that every Sunday from now on, you'll be playing for the Douglas Inn team and not for the kids."

Bazza finally releases my shoulders and pats me on the head before limping off the pitch, whilst my new teammates look on in disbelief. Maybe they've finally realised just how tough and fearless I am, but for some reason I can't explain, I just can't stop shaking like a blancmange on a trampoline.

I might be fit and strong, but tough? I think I have a long way to go just yet!

I'm delighted to report that due to much better planning, I crack the June exams, so following the closure of Marlcliffe, come September I'll be at Chaucer Comprehensive in Class 3B, however all does not end well at Marlcliffe, when after cycling back to school after lunch, I head into the classroom. Form teacher Mr Briggs is the only person around, and he looks very surprised to see me.

"Why are you here, Boocock? Where've you been?" he enquires.

"I've just come back from lunch lunch, Sir".

"Did you go to the Hillsborough Park?" he snaps.

"Why, Sir?"

"You know damn well why. You're wanted in the Headmaster's office, so get a move on, and don't speak to anybody on your way".

"Sir, I've been home. Where is everybody?"

"You'll find out when you get to the Headmaster's office. Now get a move on and make sure you go straight there and don't stop on the way."

"Yes, Sir," I mumble as I get the feeling something is very wrong.

Completely bewildered, I find all the rest of boys from our class, standing in a line stretching more than half way around the perimeter of his office. Mr Darvill grabs me by the ear and almost throws me to the end of the line.

"What was your part in all of this?" he barks. "And don't lie to me."

"All what, Sir?"

"You know what. All this business in the park. Now what did you get up to?"

"I haven't been to the park, Sir. I go home for lunch every day. When my Dad came in to see you, he told you my Mum goes to work in the evenings and I look after my sister, so when I go home at lunchtime Mum gives me my instructions for when I arrive home after school."

"Oh yes. You're Boocock, aren't you? I remember your father coming to see me. You can go back to the classroom and don't speak to anybody on the way."

It's almost an hour before the girls arrive back. Most of the boys return a few minutes later, to be greeted by an eerie silence as all the girls peer down towards the floor. The boys have been given Friday detentions every week from now until the end of term. Eventually, the remaining six boys arrive back, and it's noticeable that most of them are having difficulty in picking up and holding onto their pens, and that's down to each of them receiving several painful thrashes from a cane to the palm and fingers of each hand.

The next morning Mr Darvill addresses the entire school, with the exception of one or two absent boys from 2C.

"At lunchtime yesterday, and with the exception of one boy who cycles home for lunch, the pupils from Class 2C paid a visit to Hillsborough Park. Then several boys made inappropriate and possibly illegal physical contact a number of girls, resulting in the receipt of a range complaints which clearly required me to report the matter to the police. The outcome of the subsequent investigation resulted in all the boys involved in the assaults, being subjected to corporal punishment and a total of six have been excluded from further attendance at this school."

It's been a hard lesson for everyone, so let's move on once more.

Me, Cliff and a couple of the lads have now decided to form a pop group, so the cellar kitchen becomes a nightclub when the gang are in residence for the evening.

My record-player is always on full blast as we stand on the kitchen chairs, miming to the early songs of the Beatles and the Hollies, whilst the girls dance around us. I do a fantastic solo spot, miming to Gene Pitney's '24 Hours from Tulsa' and 'That Girl Belongs to Yesterday'. The impersonation is so good that a number of the neighbours, who turn out to be Pitney fans, have decided to line up and watch the show from outside the kitchen window. It blows my mind every time I hear the cheers and applause heading my way when the performance is over.

I know that's nothing to do with the story, but I just thought I'd do a bit of showing off, although you never know. I might just end up being a singer in the future.

Meanwhile, I don't know if it's due to Chaucer Comp being just the right school for me, or whether it's down to an age thing, but as I hit fourteen I'm beginning to calm down and grow up a little, I think. As a regular at the local Methodist chapel evensong on Sundays, to my great surprise I've become very interested in the biblical messages delivered each week by various visiting Methodist lay preachers. It's all having a very positive impact on the way I'm beginning to think and act. However, to my eternal shame I do have the occasional lapse in common decency.

No surprise there then!

Meanwhile, Pond Street Bus Station is a bustling hub of activity close to the city centre, and it's where one or two famous locals, who might not be considered as 'normal,' tend to hang around. As we're still in the mid 1960's, the aforementioned locals are regarded as persons to be avoided at all costs, or to be mercilessly tormented by idiots like me and the gang.

The first, known as the Colonel, spends his days reliving the Second World War, marching up and down the bus station, whilst sporting one of those old-fashioned handlebar moustaches, which shoots up and down endlessly as he barks out instructions to an invisible platoon.

"Left right, left right, left right! Company halt! Attention! Company, about turn! By the left quick march! Left right, left right, left right!"

I'm not in the least bit proud of it, but as soon as we spot him, we always temporarily enlist and line up behind him, so when he instructs us to 'present arms', our left arms shoot straight up into the air as our right arms slam across the chest. He never takes a backward glance, so he doesn't realise he has an extra half a dozen soldiers under his command. Fortunately, passing commuters do notice, and that makes it all worth while.

The second is a lady known to the entire Sheffield population as Pond Street Nora. She's a different kettle of fish from the Colonel, and nobody messes her around. She's about six-feet-and-a-gas-lamp tall, with short black hair and dark eyes which seem to glare at you from somewhere near the back of her head. Now, I have a hooter you can't miss, but Nora's is completely off the scale. I kid you not, if we sat opposite each other on the top table of a wedding reception, our simultaneous nod toward each other would almost certainly result in the 3-tier wedding cake being sliced straight down the middle from top to bottom.

Her wardrobe consists of a headscarf knotted underneath her chin, an old fashioned gaberdine raincoat, a pair of once-white plimsolls that must be at least a size 20, and one single accessory which is a huge shopping bag draped over her left arm and wedged firmly against her body. If you look her in the eye, the glare she returns is absolutely frightening and your legs immediately start to turn to jelly. Whenever she gets angry, Nora starts nodding like crazy, and that happens quite often whenever we're around Pond Street.

Nora usually sits at the top of the steps leading down to the ladies public toilets, which makes things a tad uncomfortable for any female travellers who unfortunately 'get caught short'. Whenever we spot her, we give her a huge wave to make sure she sees us.

"Nora. Nora. We're over here. Na-na-nee-na-na. Come and get us".

The moment she spots us, she hurls herself forward with feet flapping and shopping bag almost going into orbit. Luckily, we aren't as stupid as some people think, so before she gets within touching distance we head out of the bus station towards Fitzalan Square and relative safety, but still manages to hunt us down occasionally. Then the nodding goes into overdrive as a huge forefinger points and shakes menacingly in our direction.

"I know ya. I know ya," yells Nora as she heads our way.

Commuters witnessing Nora's rage think she'll catch up with us one day, but we know that'll never happen in a million years as the getaway is always well planned.

And we all know just how good I am at planning, don't we?

Anyway, on safer ground the Corner Cafe stands at the far end of Pond Street, looking across the road towards Midland Station, and whenever we do a bit of train spotting or play football against teams residing on that side of town, we pop into the cafe for a bottle of pop and a Kit Kat on our way home. Today we have a match in Norfolk Park, so we decide to celebrate the win we expected, by paying a visit to the cafe. We race down Granville Road and head towards Pond Street, before bursting into the cafe and coming to a grinding halt at the counter. Moments later, the cafe door unexpectedly slams behind us, and as we turn our heads back to see what's happening, we suddenly come very close to a bout of severe incontinence.

We're now standing face-to-conk with Pond Street Nora, and she's already shaking like a half-set jelly in a tumble-dryer. Worse still, is that for some reason she's glaring directly into my eyes whilst stabbing her index finger into my shoulder.

"I know ya. I know ya. I know ya," she yells at me whilst pumping up the volume and threat-level with each breath she takes.

The moment the cafe owner arrives at the counter, I beg her to let us out of the back door, and as she clearly understands the gravity of the situation, she leans slightly backwards and points toward the door at the far side of the kitchen. I'm first over the counter-top followed by a bunch of squawking football heroes, with no time to apologise for sending the cakes and buns flying all over the place. We never look back as we race up to Fitzalan Square and through the Hole in the Road to relative safety at the bus-stop outside the ABC Cinema. That's my first near-death experience, so on the way home I decide to have my first serious chat with my Maker, to thank him for saving our lives. As I bid farewell to the gang, I decide to avoid Nora for the rest of my life and to never do anything that might result in my coming hooter-to-hooter with her again.

Well, that's the plan, but something's bound to go wrong, isn't it?

Back at school I work hard on any subject that appeals to me but as you already know, History is one of the subjects that leaves me cold, and that's down to teacher Miss Smith. She's a really boring old tart, always droning on about past monarchs, and in particular the dates they ascended the throne and when they snuffed it. We're all bored to death within minutes of the lesson kicking-off, so just before we head into today's session, we agree to ignore her and to start miming to each other, so it'll look as though we're chatting amongst ourselves whilst she drones on and on. Even then, it still takes her a whole fifteen minutes to realise something's up. Miss Smith continues to scribble loads of meaningless dates on the blackboard, whilst asking questions about faceless kings and queens. When she finally turns away from the blackboard, she notices that she's being completely ignored as we're all deep in conversation with each other. Then she suddenly realises she can't hear a word that's being spoken by any of us, although the classroom should be buzzing. She immediately thinks she's lost her hearing, and still doesn't realise we're messing her about, even though she must have heard her own voice whilst asking questions just a few seconds earlier. Eventually, as we continue with the miming performance, she storms out of the classroom, probably to go and have a lie down or to make an appointment with her GP.

Meanwhile, I'm also experiencing some problem with Maths lessons. It's clear to all concerned that my mental arithmetic skills, which caused Mr Turner a few concerns back at Hillfoot County, are much greater than those of current teacher, one Mr Parker. The lessons are quite enjoyable. I love it when he's demonstrating how to calculate something or other, and then ends up with the wrong answer. Of course, being the smart-ass I am, I always stick my hand up in the air ready to point out his mistakes, so inevitably he tires of being corrected and gets into the habit of writing down the answers on the blackboard.

Then, without looking towards me, he just shouts "Boocock, if there's a problem, we don't want to know about it, so keep your trap shut."

I really shouldn't go on about the teachers at Chaucer, as most of them were brilliant. In fact it's Mr Harrington, known to us as 'Snoz', who in no small way opens the door to my future career.

Chapter Five

Schoolboy To Working Man

Woodwork and Technical Drawing classes are a complete waste of time as far as I'm concerned. I'm useless when it comes to using screwdrivers and stuff like that, and I'm no better at drawing straight lines and measuring angles via a protractor. Worse still, I just don't have it in me to improve my ability, but the good news is that teacher Snoz Harrington is fully aware of and accepts my lack of skills and motivation. It takes me almost a whole term to make four legs for a coffee table, and two of them were nicked from Ian Dunbar. Technical Drawing is also about as simple as Bio-Medical Engineering, Neuroscience and Astrophysics to me, but good old Snoz always bears that in mind when he's dishing out the homework.

"For your homework this week, I want you all to prepare a cross-section drawing of a dovetail joint on a scale of 1 to 6, but not you, Boocock. I want you to prepare a drawing of a twelve inch ruler on a scale of 1 to 1."

Then the following week, when the homework is handed in, anyone who messes up the dovetail thingy gets slippered, but when I hand my homework in, he simply screws it up before chucking it in the bin without even looking at it. It's patently clear I haven't a prayer of ever making it as a joiner in my adult life, and there's even less chance of me becoming an architect. I'm not as thick as some people think, so I do know I'll have to make my mind up pretty soon, with regard to what I'm going to do with my life post-Chaucer.

Coronation flag seller sounds OK, but I don't think that'll keep me in full-time employment for the next fifty years. I fancy being an airline pilot, but I doubt I have the brains to get through the training, and that also applies to any thought of a career in teaching. International speedway rider is a non-starter, as Ma and Pa don't have the dosh to buy me a motorbike, and football superstar doesn't appeal to me, as sooner or later I'm bound to find myself up against somebody even bigger and scarier than Bazza. I just need to sort myself out and come up with a plan that'll get me out of Woodwork and Technical Drawing. I've no idea why, but for some reason I decide to tell the Careers Teacher I want to be a chef, in the hope that might just do the trick, and there's no doubt in my mind I'll have absolutely nothing technical to worry about as a chef, as Mum does it all the time and she's no Albert Einstein. So, with any luck I'll soon be waving goodbye to Woodwork and Tech Drawing, and taking up the easy life in Domestic Science.

I know you won't believe it, but miraculously the plan works a treat

Come July, I'm flabbergasted to be told I'll be doing Domestic Science during my final year at school. It gets even better when I attend my first lesson in September, to find the teacher is the stunningly gorgeous Miss Dale and not only that, I have a dozen girls as classmates. I suppose it's no great surprise to hear that three more boys have suddenly realised they also want to be chefs, but there are no more spare places in the Domestic Science Class.

Oh what a shame! Bad luck, boys!

A few weeks after the summer break, one of my former Woodwork classmates tells me that Snoz has only just noticed I've gone AWOL. Apparently, whilst he was rollocking somebody for being completely useless, Snoz suddenly realised I haven't been on his radar since July. He ceases the onslaught and turns towards the class to ask where Boocock is these days. When he's advised I'm planning to be a chef and I'm now doing Domestic Science, Snoz instructs the class to get down on their knees and pray to God that Boocock is better at cooking than he is at making coffee tables, otherwise the entire population of Sheffield and most of Yorkshire are likely to end up being poisoned.

That was nice of him, don't you think?

It soon occurs to me that the girls have been doing cookery for the last three years, but I haven't a clue, due to never having to cook anything, apart from warming up Dad's tea just before he climbs out of bed. I do my level best of course, but I might just as well be trying to knock up another batch of coffee tables, minus the assistance of Ian Dunbar. It comes as no great surprise then, that the GCE Domestic Science O Level exam goes pear-shaped, so I'm already wondering if I should be thinking about a different career, and if nothing else at least Snoz's prayers would be answered.

So, after what I think has been a magnificent effort over the past 11 years, it doesn't go unnoticed back home, that utter failure in the Domestic Science GCE exam is more than a little embarrassing for a bloke who's supposed to be planning to be a top chef.

Leave it! Leave it!

Anyway, today is my final day at school, so all the guys in our class decide to present our form teacher, Mr 'Call Me Geoff' Wright with something to remember us by. Right now he's well pleased with the box of choccies he's received, but I doubt he'll be quite so happy with our second parting gift. Just outside the classroom window, there's a wall about a foot high running all the way down to the school gates and segregating the school yard from the playing field, and Geoff parks his Morris Minor next to the wall. Then fifteen minutes before the end of term assembly kicks off, we're instructed to clear our desks and pack our bags which only takes a couple of minutes, so as the girls line up to plant a farewell peck on Geoff's cheek, the boys sneak outside. Then after a great deal of huffing, puffing and coordinated teamwork, we somehow manage to lift his car up off the ground and delicately balance it on top of the wall.

From ten yards away it looks like a giant green four-wheeled see-saw swaying precariously from front to back, or to be more precise, from bonnet to boot. So, with the parting-gift in position, we head back to the classroom to say our own farewells to Geoff and the girls whilst picking up our belongings. It doesn't go unnoticed that a couple of boys are quietly swapping spit and cuddling in the far corner of the classroom, but the rest of us just smile and shake our heads as we head outside. Then, as we stroll past the new see-saw, we wonder what will happen when Geoff finally packs his briefcase and steps outside, but sadly we never find out, as the bus departs before he gets round to picking up the car keys.

My education finally comes to an end. I still think I'm as thick as a plank, but things are bound to improve because now I'm a working man, although I don't actually have a job yet. That's about to change when I stroll into the Youth Employment Office on Division Street, where some kind lady has promised to do her very best to find me a job. I think it best not to reveal too many personal details during the interview, especially as the Boocock family history alone is likely to render me unemployed for life. I also think it might be a good idea not to mention the recent Domestic Science exam fracas either, not that it would necessarily leave me without a job, but it most certainly wouldn't be as a chef.

I'm delighted to report that after spending less than half an hour with the Youth Employment princess, I've been invited to attend an interview at Cole Brothers, a branch of the John Lewis Partnership and one of the city's top department stores, and from next week I'll be in full-time employment as a trainee chef.

I can't wait to get home and break the news to all and sundry. Mum and Dad are thrilled to hear the news and Pa is absolutely amazed to hear I'll be earning a massive twenty quid a week. I wasn't expecting Mrs Plumb from next door to burst into tears. I think Ar Reet will be pleased when she hears that Dad doesn't want me to be coughing up any of my earnings in return for board and lodgings, but it would be nice if I would give my kid sister a bit of pocket money every week and buy her the occasional present. No surprise there then!

My new boss is Head Chef Rob, and he welcomes me into his office-cum-storeroom with a cup of tea and a piece of home made cake. Slap bang in the middle of the office is what he describes as his favourite piece of kit, namely the wooden butcher's block. It stands about four feet in height and is the length of a coffin and width of a snooker table. Apparently this is where he puts a great deal of effort in when he's not overseeing the mayhem that kicks off in the kitchen around noon. Then he gives me what might be described as not only a welcoming speech, but also a load of advice I wasn't expecting.

I clearly am still a bit thick, because half of what he says doesn't appear to make much sense, but no doubt it will once I get started.

"I'm glad to see you're already smiling son, as most of the people around here walk around all day with a face like a blistered guzzunder," claims Rob. "So, before I let you loose in the kitchen, just bear in mind that nobody has a clue when they first start out, but if you're willing to watch, listen and learn, then I'll teach you everything I know. You'll also learn a lot from these idiots you'll be working with, so take everything on board and then figure out what works best for you. If you can do that you'll be a better chef than the rest of us." suggests Rob.

Well there's not much chance of that. I'm only here because I just needed to get out of woodwork.

"And don't let it get you down when you make a cock-up. Every chef makes mistakes but only the best ones know how to put things right, so just use it as a learning opportunity. Nobody knows everything about cooking and that includes me, and just remember that any chef who tells you he knows it all and never gets it wrong, is a liar and he'll also be a rubbish chef," says Rob as I head out of the office.

"Oh, I nearly forgot. On your way around the kitchen, don't get too close to June in the pan-wash."

So here we go. I'm now a working man, and as I stroll through the central cooking area, the first thing I notice on a small stove is a huge pan, which appears to be almost the size of our bath night copper. It's almost full to the brim with liquid, and floating on top is a thick layer of scum.

"That's the stock-pot," explains Sous Chef Eddie as he introduces himself. "At the beginning of the week we chuck in a load of bones, bits of meat and veg. Then we fill it up with cold water, bring it to the boil and keep it simmering for the rest of the week, and keep topping it up with water and other bits of grub. Then on Saturday, we skim off the scum and pour the liquid through a strainer and Hey Presto, we now have a beautiful clear stock that's full of flavour.

"We use it for making gravy, soup and sauces. It tastes lovely. Do you want to try a spoonful?" Eddie stupidly enquires.

"I'll pass on that if you don't mind," says I.

"Just one bit of advice, son," says Eddie. "Whenever you empty the stock-pot at the end of the week, just plonk it on the floor outside the pan-wash and slide it inside. Whatever you do, don't let June get within touching distance. Ever!"

I've only met two people and both of them have warned me about June. I wonder what the problem is?

Just after 11.30 the kitchen bursts into life, and it's absolute mayhem, but as it looks a bit quieter in the veg section, so I think I'll have a word veg cook Nellie. As I approach, she's clinging onto a tea towel, whilst attempting to extract a tray of something from the steaming oven. She tells me she's just cooked today's spring cabbage, but she fails to notice the tea towel isn't completely protecting her finger-ends from the hot tray. Moments later the tray spins up into the air and ejects the cabbage on its way back down, and now we appear to have a new green carpet on the kitchen floor, but as I'm known to be quite an astute observer, I've already noticed a sweeping brush and dustpan propped up in the corner, so within seconds the new carpet has been swept up and is on its way to the waste bin.

“No, no. You can’t throw that away. It costs money,” Nellie screams.

“I just swept it up off the floor,” I shout back.

“Give it here,” she snaps whilst sticking several burnt fingers into her gob.

Nellie snatches the overflowing dustpan, plops the contents into a colander and then throws it into the sink, before running cold water over it for a couple of minutes. According to her, this will cool the cabbage and wash out any crap that might have got into it whilst it was pretending to be a carpet. Finally, she drains the cabbage and slaps it into a clean tray, before sliding it back into the steamer. I say nothing, but I decide not to risk nibbling on any veg whenever Nellie’s kicking around the place.

“Before you go, can you take the colander into the pan-wash for me,” she asks. “No, wait! On second thoughts, I’ll take it myself. We wouldn’t want you getting into any kind of trouble in there, would we?”

Oh, hell! Not another one!

Marge is the Bakeress and she has a great job in making huge amounts of pastries and fresh cream cakes. She comes across as an easy going kind of person, and I get the feeling I might enjoy working in the bakery with her. I’m pleased to hear she’s happy to show me the ropes, although she clearly won’t stand for any messing around. Then, as I head to the other end of the bakery to meet Ada, Marge asks if I’ve come up against Joan during my tour of the kitchen.

“Not yet,” comes the reply.

“I thought not,” says Marge. “You still have a smile on your face and you don’t look as though you’re any kind of pain down below”.

Ada makes all the hot desserts, but before she gives me the low-down on exactly what that means, she wants me to accompany her to the central pot-wash area, where all the used crockery and cutlery from the restaurant is washed and dried. She tells me she plans to shove a twelve-portion date and walnut roll down the waste disposal unit, as the pudding has ben hanging around since last Saturday and is now far too dry for anyone to eat.

Arriving in the pot-wash area, Ada switches on the waste disposal unit before wedging her hands down between each end of the roll and the inside of the steaming-sleeve, but just before she lifts the pudding out, one of the pot-wash ladies by the name of Vera, snatches it from her hands and rams the entire roll straight into her mouth. It only takes a matter of seconds before she realises the roll is so tightly packed inside her mouth, she can't chew it, and neither can she swallow it. Even worse, she can't spit it out either, so as her cheeks start to swell up like a couple of balloons, her face starts to go from a delicate pink colour to bright red and finally to turquoise and blue, whilst she sinks slowly to her knees.

As Vera topples over, her colleague Edna instructs me to run and fetch Eddie as fast as I can. Seconds later, he's pushing the gathering crowd away from the stricken lady, and the moment a bit of space is created, he swings a tightly clenched fist up into the air, and with as much power as he can muster, he slams it back down, right between Vera's shoulder blades.

In an instant, the crumbly remains of a saliva-coated date and walnut roll explode from Vera's mouth, Ada's face suddenly ends-up being completely pebble-dashed, as she peers into the lady's eyes to check if she's OK. Then, just as the last few crumbs see daylight, a pair of false teeth is unexpectedly launched from Vera's gums, landing with great accuracy right in the middle of a neatly displayed afternoon tea, prepared by the ladies on the sandwich and beverage section. The gnashers completely destroy a wedge of Victoria sponge, but nobody seems particularly bothered about that because Vera now appears to be struggling with a severe bout of incontinence.

All I can think of right now, is that this is much for fun than woodwork and technical drawing could ever be.

I think I'll slip away from the carnage and meet Meg and Brenda on the cold section, but as I squeeze past a somewhat speckled Ada, she suggests I go the long way round so I won't have to run run the risk of going past the pan- wash area.

What a surprise?

Meg is a tall gorgeous blonde with a great sense of humour, whilst Brenda appears to be a little more reserved. They sort out all the salads and cold desserts such as sherry trifles and ice cream sundaes.

As we exchange the usual pleasantries, one of the waitresses plonks an order for a knickerbocker glory onto the counter, so Meg picks up an ice cream scoop and slides open the chest freezer, which houses umpteen large tins of various flavoured ice cream. She doesn't appear to have the ability to fasten the upper buttons of her unbelievably short overall, so as she reaches down into the chest freezer I can't help noticing the very desirable cleavage, which is barely covered by an eye-watering range of silky red underwear, the likes of which have never been seen on any Wallace Road washing lines. In fact, the view is so amazing I fail to notice when she releases a huge scoop of vanilla ice cream into her hand, and I only come back down to earth as an icy cold ball if vanilla ice cream rolls down the inside of my chef's jacket.

I'm still trying my best to shake the ice cream out, when Brenda creeps up behind me and rams a load of chocolate ice cream down the back of my trousers. She thinks it's hilarious, but all I can think of is revenge. I'm in no doubt this could be a fun area to work in, so having just about completed the grand tour, I decide to head back to the central area.

I'm still focussing on trying to scrape the chocolate slime of my backside, I fail to realise I'm strolling straight past the entrance to the pan wash area, but it's already too late to do a U-turn as June steps out to block my route back to safety.

"Hello Darlin'. You're Eric, aren't you? My name's June. I'm in me forties and I've never even been touched. I like young men and you look like a nice boy. Have you got a girlfriend?"

"Yeah, loads," I reply with perhaps a hint of panic and a huge amount of exaggeration, due to the umpteen warnings I've received already.

"All I do is stand here all day scrubbing pans with me tatty bit of green," she sadly states whilst holding up a very sad-looking scouring pad. Clearly Meg is within earshot, so she offers a reply.

"After all them years without ever being touched, no doubt she'll also have something else that'll be a bit green and tatty by now, so if you don't want to find out what it is, you'd better get out of there, fast.

"Oh shut up Meg. I'm only looking for a nice young man and a bit of love."

"Well don't bother. There aren't any nice young men around here," retorts Meg. "And even if there was, they wouldn't have the stamina to give you the bit of love you need, as you'd be wanting to catch up on the forty years you've already missed out on."

"You see what I've got to put up with?" Joan asks with fake sadness. "I'm just a simple girl with needs, and lots of them, and I just happen to like nice young men. Are you sure you've got a girlfriend?"

She's clearly not a full shilling, but she does seem to have a decent sense of humour, despite the shortage of whatever it is she's in desperate need of. Unfortunately, just as I'm about to make a speedy exit from the pan-wash area, I find out exactly what that is, when June asks me to reach over her shoulder and remove a saucepan from high-up on the shelf above the sink in front of her.

To my absolute horror, as I lean forward she reaches behind her back to tightly grab me by the you-know-whats, and that's not quite what I was expecting on my first day at work. Having said that, if it had been Meg or one of the waitresses, it might not be a problem, but apart from anything else June's caked up to the armpits in fat and grease from the mucky pans she's been washing.

I'm beginning to wonder if it's just a bloke kind of thing, or is it simply down to the fact that I don't appear to be willing or able to take in anybody's advice?

After quite a bit of tussling with June's fingers, I finally manage to escape her clutches, I'm doing my level best to massage some feeling back into my goolies when she fires a parting shot in my direction.

"Hey, you shouldn't be walking around the kitchen interfering with yourself. If you need anything sorting out down there, just let me know. I'll always help you out with anything like that."

"Thanks, but no thanks," I reply without turning to face her. "I'm just checking to make sure my tackle's still in one piece, or rather three pieces."

Clearly, Meg is still within earshot.

"It's when you find a set of teeth hanging onto your nik-naks you'll know you have a problem, especially if they're still attached to June's gums."

Still limping slightly, I notice Rob is back in his office, so I decide to seek sanctuary by his desk.

"How did it go, son? Have you seen everything? I hope you didn't lose your virginity in the pan wash."

"I saw more than I was expecting, especially when I got to the cold section, and I only just managed to hang on to my virginity when I met Joan."

"Nice one, son. I suppose that was a stroke of luck on both counts. So, now you've had a look around and met the crew, what do you think?"

"I think I might go and see if the Furniture Department needs anybody to make coffee tables."

As the day draws to a close Eddie invites me to join him and the other trainee chef Jim for a pint. Rob can't join us as he has something important to do that can't wait before he locks up and heads home. I decide to use the single shower we have in the changing room. It's the first time I've ever seen one, let alone been in one, but by the time I start towelling myself dry, I realise how refreshing it is after all the heat and sweat in the kitchen, and there's no doubt a couple of minutes in there each evening will be much better than ten minutes in the old tin bath once a week. It's a bit rowdy as we're all getting dressed, and it doesn't get any better when I notice Eddie posing in front of the full length mirror on the wall. He's wearing nothing more than his blue budgie smugglers briefs and a string vest, with a tightly fitting pressure stocking squeezing against his right leg.

He admires his body for a second or two and then takes a deep breath, before inviting Jim to thump him in the stomach with as much force as he can muster He's more than happy to oblige, but as his fist lands right on target, Eddie merely steps back a couple of paces, shakes his head, and shrug his shoulders before turning towards me.

"What about you, kid? Can you do any better than that?" he asks whilst staring somewhat sarcastically toward the ceiling.

"I dunno. I've never belted anybody. I've always been told to walk away from trouble," comes the reply.

"This isn't trouble, it's just a game we play every night. Come on, give us your best shot," Eddie begs as he takes a second intake of breath.

A second or two later, the incoming left-hander lands just above his navel, but it turns out he isn't expecting it to land in his gut with such force, and I'm not expecting him to keel over backwards against the wall mirror, before sliding down the wall and ending up flat on his back across the floor. I'm now in shock.

"Leave the idiot where he is," shouts Jim. "He's been asking for that since I arrived here, and it serves him right. From now on he might think twice about winding us up, especially you. Let's go. I'll get the beer in."

This is not only the first time I've ever been in a pub, it's also the first pint I've ever downed. I'm delighted to say I'm enjoying the experience so much that by the time Eddie staggers in a few minutes later, I'm already at the bar and getting in my first-ever round. He parks himself next to me, but the beer will have to wait for a few minutes, as I've just realised my wallet is still in my locker. I apologise and excuse myself before racing back through the staff entrance.

As I stroll past the night-watchman's office, I ask if Rob has locked up yet. Fortunately, the kitchen key-hook remains unoccupied, so he must still be doing whatever it is that can't wait until tomorrow morning. Then I race up the staircase and down the corridor leading from the Carpet Department, but before I go into the changing room, I think the head chef should be aware I'm around.

As I enter the kitchen and turn towards his office, I pop my head round the door and I notice Rob appears to be doing something with a huge lump of meat on top of the butcher's block. A second glance tells me it's not a carcass of beef he's leaning over, because farm animals don't usually wear matching items of very sexy undergarments. A second glance around the door then reveals a waitress uniform screwed up in a heap on the floor, a black high-heeled shoe on top and another parked on the head chef's desk. Fortunately for the three of us I remain unnoticed, so I decide to creep into the changing room, grab the wallet and head back to the pub. As I pass the watchman's office on my way out, he asks if Rob is still busy up there.

"Very busy," is the honest reply. "He looks like he's up to his neck in it."

"I can never understand why he's always the last one left in the building most nights, and that waitress who gives him a lift home must be absolutely sick of it. You other chefs ought to take it in turns to stay late and do whatever it is he has to do when everybody else has buggered-off."

"I doubt Rob would want us to do that, and I'm sure the waitress is OK with whatever he's doing. Goodnight."

Back in the pub, Eddie's already got the next round in, and boy do I need it. In fact I need it so much, I'm back at the bar within five minutes ready to get the next round in, and ten minutes later, Eddie's buying the final round in as a thank you for all the hard work we put in earlier. We eventually call it a day, but then something dreadful occurs as I attempt to leave my seat. I appear to have become attached to somebody else's legs and they simply refuse to head in the same direction as the rest of my body. I hadn't realised until now that Eddie and Jim each have an identical twin brother, and there are now five of us standing at the table, although the new arrivals look just a bit hazy for some reason.

I'm still wondering what the hell is happening, when the barmaid decides to go all foggy as well. Worse still, I can't understand why I've suddenly started laughing, because this is a really serious situation and very, very scary. By the time I manage to stagger out and into fresh air, I can hear Eddie shouting something about a driver waiting for me, but I haven't the faintest idea what he's going on about. My immediate priority right now is to make sure I stay on my feet long enough to find my way home, but that could be a problem because for some reason I can't remember whether I live in Creswell, Pitsmoor or Parkwood Springs. To this day I've absolutely no idea what happened next, but I do recall falling bum-over-elbow out of a taxi somewhere pretty close to our house at 109 Wallace Road, whilst still laughing hysterically. I must have managed to fumble around in my pockets to find enough cash to pay the driver, because as I start the search for the front door of 109, the taxi does a U-turn as the driver pips his horn and heads into the ever-thickening fog that now envelopes the entire street. Fortunately, I manage to haul myself along the front of somebody's house and hang onto the windowsill until I'm steady enough to wobble along to the next house. I'm not even sure I'm on the right street, let alone anywhere near 109, so I figure that if I just shout to let Ma and Pa know I'm here, then they'll come and get me as soon as they hear me.

No problem there then!

Every time I attempt to call out, I start giggling, and the harder I try not to, the more I laugh. Thankfully, a woman with two blurry heads, and living about ten houses beyond ours, comes out to see what's going on. She recognises me as that nice boy from down the street, so she decides to drag me back to our abode before hammering on the front door, but just before the door is wrenched open, I notice Mrs Plumb is now standing right behind me, and the moment Mum appears in the doorway, Mrs P shoves me inside with all the force she can muster.

Ma must have been having a bust-up with Dad, because she appears to be in a bit of a rage. It doesn't help that I can't stop laughing, and according to her I should be ashamed of myself, coming home from work in such a state. Before I have time to reply, I keel over and land on the settee, but unfortunately, Dad is sitting right in the middle of it. It seems to take forever to unravel myself from his upper body, and when I finally free myself, I notice he doesn't look best pleased either. I guess the bust-up they were having a few minutes ago must have been a big one.

Mum tells me she'll probably never be able to show her face at the Chapel Sisterhood or Mother's Union again, and that I should also stay well-away from the place for a while. Dad just glares and says nothing, whilst Ma goes through a load of reasons why I should be setting an example, and why I could have a very short career if this is what I'm going to be like every night. Most worryingly, is that she's only just changed my bed, so if I puke-up, pee myself or worse during the night, I'll have to sleep between the same sheets until next Monday when she does the washing.

It's a huge relief when she finally sits back in the chair and lights up a Park Drive Tipped, forgetting she already has one sticking out of the other side of her gob. Pa has no doubt heard enough by now, so he jumps out of his chair and heads across the landing and into the bedroom. He comes back a minute later, with work jacket buttoned-up with hands tightly gripping the handlebars of his bike. He glares silently at me, before bending down to turn-on the lamps at either end of the bike, and then storming out of the door to ride-off to work without uttering another word. I don't even get the chance to warn him about the fog out there, but I doubt he cares.

That really must have been one hell of a ding-dong they just had!

Chapter Six

A Bit of a Blip

Before we go any further, can I just say that as you've somehow managed to get this far with my glorious past, I'm assuming you've got to know me well enough to realise I'm one of life's good guys at heart, although I might have been a wee bit naughty at times during my childhood, but then again who wasn't? So with that in mind, I'm not sure I should be telling you anything about the 'bit of a blip' I'm about to go through, although I guess it'll be OK as long as you promise to keep everything to yourself. If you don't think you can do that, then it might be best to rip-up the next few pages without reading them and go straight into the rest of this nonsense, and then nobody will ever know I haven't always been the saint the world thinks I am. Thank you very much!

So where was I? Oh yes, the morning after the night before!

I appear to be suffering from a few atomic explosions going off in my head this morning, but by the time I report for duty, I'm beginning to come round. Eddie asks if I'm OK and fully recovered from last night, but I've absolutely no idea what he's going on about. He tells me that when I punched him in the stomach last night, it was by far the best shot he's taken since his army days, and he wonders if I'm aware of the strength and punching power I have. I wasn't even aware I'd walloped him and even more worrying, I can't think of any reason why I would, so I can only apologise and promise it won't happen again.

I'm even more surprised when he tells me I got pickled in the pub last night, and he reckons if I'm not careful I could end up inviting a whole load of unnecessary grief, especially if I start using my fists when overdoing the booze. He suggests I keep the alcohol intake to a minimum to make sure I stay in control, although there's no doubt that anybody crossing my path won't be coming back for a second helping. That's not what Ma and Pa have always drummed into me, as their view is you should do unto others as you'd have them do to you, but Eddie's philosophy appears to be that you should always do unto others before they do it to you. I think I'm with him on this occasion, although it doesn't really matter because I'll never go overboard when it comes to boozing, fighting or any other kind of bother. I'm just not that sort of person.

Please refer to the first paragraph at the top of the page!

Anyway, I've more important things to focus on right now, because Eddie's decided I'll be working in Rob's office this morning, although I don't think I'm quite ready for the head chef's job just yet.

"As Rob isn't in today you can use the butcher's block to work on, but just make sure you give the top a good scrub before you start. You never know what he might have been doing with it last night."

"Absolutely," I reply with a wry smile. "I guess we'll never know."

The day goes really well, and I'm delighted when Eddie tells me I've done a great job and he'd like me to join him and Jim in the pub after work. I notice whilst we're getting changed that he doesn't invite me to give him another thump in the gut, so I guess that's a relief to the pair of us. We're in the pub for quite some time, as each of us gets in a couple of rounds.

On the way home, I'm the only person sitting on the upper deck of the bus and I'm feeling very relaxed, so relaxed that for some unknown reason I start laughing to myself, and it's not just a bit of a giggle, I'm absolutely howling and I can't stop. I'm still in hysterics when I arrive home, and that could well be the reason why I don't give a damn when, once again I find myself on the receiving end of a shedload of criticism. When Ma finally shuts up and starts puffing on a Park Drive Tipped, I give her a piece of my mind for the first time ever. She now knows I don't give a stuff what she thinks of me, as I'm no longer a schoolboy and I can do as I please, so if she doesn't like it then she can shove it.

So now I'm public enemy number one, and she decides to blank me for the rest of the week, but at least it'll be a peaceful few days then.

She's obviously brings Pa up to speed, so whilst Ma's taking her turn on bath-night, he asks me what's wrong. I've never had a real in-depth conversation with Pa, apart from when he was teaching me how to play cribbage, so I'm relieved to find he shows great patience and understanding. No doubt he's also been given the silent treatment a few times over the years, but better still he tells me not to worry, as there's a name for what's wrong with me. It's called growing up.

Oh give me a break, Pa!

Apparently, it's exactly what he and thousands of others went through when they joined the forces during the war, and it's also what Grandpa Reg went through twenty-odd years before that. They went from boy to man overnight, when they had to leave their home, relatives and friends behind, not knowing if they would ever see them again, whereas I know I'll be coming home every day.

Finally, he reassures me everything will turn out just fine, especially as I'm actually a really nice kid at heart. I'm more than happy with all that, so I agree to take on board everything he's told me. I genuinely care about what people think of me, especially as I've never been aggressive in any way, although I must admit to getting very close to it with that bloody corgi back in Creswell.

It makes it even more worrying that for several years now, I've been attending Sunday Evensong at our local Methodist Chapel, and until recently my Christian beliefs have always been paramount to my general behaviour and my respect for other people. I even take the annual Sheffield Christian Education Council Scripture Examination, and I'm considering enrolling at Cliff College with the aim of becoming a Methodist Lay Preacher at some point in the future. There's no way I can do that if I'm going to continue acting like a thug and a complete fool, so I have to change my ways right now or my life will become worthless and I just can't let that happen.

Anyway, Pa suggests I sleep on it and I'm glad to say I feel much better when I wake up on Monday morning. I'm in a very positive mood and ready to face the world once again, so I decide to take a bike-ride just to get a bit of fresh air and to finally clear my head of all the negative thoughts. Then I'll be able to get on with enjoying my life.

As I cycle past Neepsend Post Office and onto the bridge over the River Don, I'm as happy as Larry for the first time in ages. Then a mail delivery van overtakes me and then immediately screeches to a halt, almost within touching distance of the handlebars. I simply can't stop the volcanic eruption inside, so I just sling the bike onto the pavement and hurtle to the driver's door. I wrench the door open and jump into the cab to land a right-hander straight into the driver's face, and then I slam his head against the steering wheel. I grab the keys from the ignition as I leap out, and with the driver now safely locked inside, I throw the keys over the bridge and into the water some twenty or thirty feet below.

By the time I've calmed down and arrived home, Ma and Pa are back on speaking terms. No doubt she's aware of the chat I had with Pa, and he'll have told her to give me a bit of breathing space. Then just after Ma heads off to do her evening shift, Dad asks if I had a good day out on the bike.

"Yeah, I had a nice relaxing ride and I'm feeling pretty good," I lie.

So, it's all smiles as we settle into our weekly best of five sets of Cribbage. Unfortunately, I don't seem to be able to concentrate for some reason, and Pa thrashes me three sets to nil. I'm already beginning to think I'll never be able to sort myself out, and it doesn't help when things go downhill yet again a couple of nights later.

As I'm strolling up Douglas Road and under the railway bridge on my way home after another day's work and a couple of hours and several pints in the pub, I notice a guy known to me and my mates as Pig Face, one half of a pair of local bullies, the other half being Porky. They enjoy a dubious reputation for bullying younger kids, but due to Ma and Pa's instructions I've always avoided them. Unfortunately for Pig Face however, I'm now an adult, and as I explained to Ma just a short time ago, I can please myself what I do, and right now it's payback time for this particular slime ball.

He gets within touching distance, and he certainly isn't expecting the fist that lands in his eye to send him flying backwards and face down onto the pavement. I lean over his body and let him know why he's been thumped. I expect him to go berserk and I'm looking forward to it, but he simply raises his head to wipe the blood from his face, and just mumbles something about calling it quits and not telling anyone what just happened. I neither see nor hear from him ever again.

That little altercation unexpectedly puts me on a high for a couple of days, but it doesn't last of course. On my home after another hard day's work and a session in the boozer with Eddie and Jim, I can't believe my eyes as I weave my way under the railway bridge and notice it's now Porky who's strolling down the hill towards me. He's bound to have been tipped off by his well-battered sidekick, so no doubt he'll be looking to exact some kind of sick revenge on behalf of his mate. I think it best not to wait to find out what he's thinking, so with as Ernie's philosophy suddenly springs to mind, I do it to him before he does anything to me.

Before Porky has time to block my path, I leap forward to unleash a size nine left-foot straight into his groin, and as he doubles-up in agony, the right foot says hello to the side of his face full on, sending him bum-over-elbow to land face-down on the Douglas Road tarmac. I decide to just leave him to rot where he is, but just as I step away from him I hear a roaring sound coming from underneath the bridge behind me. As I glance over my shoulder, I realise to my absolute horror that the sound is coming from the engine of a fully loaded Hallamshire Steelworks truck, which is heading up the hill, and a semi-conscious Porky is laying right in its path. I find myself rooted to the spot, knowing full well I'm responsible for what's about to happen, but I guess somebody 'up there' must be looking out for the pair of us. I've no idea how he does it, but the truck driver somehow manages to swerve across to the other side of the road and avoid Porky by a matter of inches.

For crying out loud, Booey get yourself sorted out, and quick!

During our lunch break on Tuesday, I open up to Jim about my troubled mind and what it's doing to me. To say I'm more than a little surprised to hear he feels like that most of the time, is something of an understatement, so we decide to figure out a solution that works for both of us. We've got on really well since I started work, and it's beginning to look as though we could end up being the best of buddies, so we decide to invite a couple of waitresses to join us for Sunday lunch at the Marquis of Granby in Bamford, just to help us get started on a new approach to life. Judy agrees to accompany Jim whilst I'll have Pat by my side, and as this will be my very first grown-up date, I'll need to be on my best behaviour.

We all meet up in the bus station, and I can't help feeling just a little relieved to find that Sunday appears to be Pond Street Nora's day off. Me and Jim are feeling pretty cool in our smart casuals, and the girls look absolutely stunning in mini-skirts and high heels. I've only ever seen them wearing the boring pale-green waitress uniforms, so in the nicest possible way, I barely recognise them with their clothes on. Anyway, me and Jim have our arms tightly wrapped around our respective partner's waist, as we stroll through the Marquis car park entrance, doing our level best to avoid the numerous puddles of rainwater left behind by last night's heavy downpour. Unbelievably and without warning, a Ford Escort Cabriolet with the top down, comes speeding through the car park entrance and smashes straight into a couple of overflowing potholes.

The murky water shoots up and drenches all four of us, but what really pees me off is that the two guys in the front seats, start laughing when they realise the state they've left us in. I somehow manage to hold myself together, although I can't take my eyes off the pair of idiots still giggling at the bar whilst we're doing our best to enjoy the Sunday roast. Then, just as we're about to depart, I notice one of the clowns heading into the gents toilet, so I decide to follow him.

It's beginning to look like payback time again!

He's already taking a pee by the time I walk in, so I just give him a quick, hard shove in the back as I stroll past. I hadn't noticed he's wearing light brown trousers, and he doesn't look quite as pleased with himself as he did just a couple of minutes ago, when he realises the crotch area suddenly appears to be quite damp and much darker than it was when he strolled in. It's a shame they haven't heard of hot air hand-dryers just yet, so he's likely to be in here for quite a while until his trousers dry out.

I can't help having a look of great satisfaction on my face as I head towards the exit door, but just as I'm about to grab the handle, in walks his mate. Luckily, he hasn't got far enough inside to realise what's happened, and he obviously doesn't realise I'm one of the guys the pair of them drenched about an hour ago.

Here we go again!

Quite unexpectedly, he acts like a gentleman and holds the door open to allow me to exit. Unfortunately for him, I haven't been a gentleman for quite a while now, so I thank him by grabbing hold of the other side of the door and slamming it against his body, before treating him to an elbow in the face to send him sprawling across the floor towards his soggy-trousered mate. As I walk out and head back to Jim and the girls, I can't help thinking that's by far the best pudding I've ever had.

I think it best not to mention the incident to Jim and the girls, but I already realise I'm still behaving very badly and losing my cool much too often and far too quickly. I know for certain that if I keep letting myself down like this, sooner or later I'll end up venting my anger on somebody who's built like a brick-outhouse, or something of that ilk, so with that in mind I think it might be a good idea to get clued up a bit on self defence, just in case I really am that stupid.

I'm pleased to hear Jim is happy to give it a shot as well, and as luck would have it, the police run a weekly Judo class up on the 11th floor of West Bar Police Station, so we decide to give it a go. With a bit of luck, it might also help me get back a degree of self-control and subsequently, to keep the promise I made to Ma and Pa. Having said that, I may have deliberately forgotten to mention it to them for the time being, as they'll probably see things from a very different perspective.

We arrive at the police headquarters just before seven on Thursday evening, and the first thing I notice is the number of young kids already kitted-out in judo togs. They're giving a few coppers a bit of a scrap. In spite of their age and stature, a number of them are clearly able to handle themselves already, so I can't wait to get into the white pyjama top and baggy trousers the instructor just handed to me. Then, whilst I'm fastening the ribbon around my waist, he asks why we're here. I tell him about my issues, but his response takes me completely by surprise.

"Before I teach you how to throw people around, you need to know what to do when somebody decides to do the same to you, so you'll be spending quite some time literally flying around the place tonight. By the time we're done, you'll feel like you've been hit by a train. Then, if you've managed to get the feeling back into your limbs by next week, I'll teach you what you really want to know."

Perhaps this is not such a good idea after all!

"In the meantime, there's no doubt in my mind that the pair of you are still in the process of growing up, and that many of your problems relate to the need for you to establish yourself in the adult world. Trust me, there are plenty of ways gain people's respect without looking for trouble, and that's what you should be focusing on. How does that sound?"

"Sounds good to me," I reply, as Jim silently nods in agreement.

"It's also clear from what you've told me, that you simply can't handle all the booze you appear to be getting through lately. We all like to think we can, but most of us can't. I guess your parents aren't drinkers, and if that's the case then you won't have been brought up with it so you need to stop drinking and I mean STOP. Then it'll be an absolute doddle for you to get your head sorted out and get back in control so you can start enjoying your life again."

Wow! Having heard all that I think I'm already halfway there!

The instructor then lays a couple of rectangular coconut-mats in front of us, and tells us to sit on the floor with our backs towards the mats. Once we're in position, he explains that when a wrestler is slammed to the canvas, the explosive 'thwack' you hear isn't caused by the contact his back makes with the canvas, it's actually the sound of his forearms slapping onto the canvas to break the fall. With that in mind, he then instructs us to fall backwards twenty times onto the mat whilst breaking each fall by slamming our arms down onto the mat.

That's easy for him to say, but my soon-to-be black and blue forearms suggest it's probably much less painful to slam your arms onto a soft, flexible canvas rather than a thin bit of coconut matting laid out on top of a rock-hard wooden floor.

What makes it worse is that each time I fall backwards, regardless of my arms supposedly breaking the fall, my head still keeps smashing onto the mat, which unfortunately isn't much thicker than a couple of squares of cheap Izal loo paper. By the time I've completed my eighth backward fall, my head is thumping just as much as it does the morning after spending a night in the pub with Jim and Eddie.

I think there's even more torture heading our way.

Once we're back on our feet, the instructor stands in front of me and grabs my pyjama top, before warning me he's about to throw me over his shoulder and onto the mat. He tells me that if he slings me over his left shoulder, I need to tuck my head in and adjust the angle of my body to make sure I land on my right shoulder whilst simultaneously breaking the fall with my forearms. Conversely, if he throws me over his right shoulder, I need to land on my left shoulder.

No problem there then!

A couple of seconds later the instructor yells 'right shoulder,' and before I realise what's happening, the ceiling flashes past my eyes as my thirteen stone body slams down onto the mat. The gym lights go out for a moment as the instructor drags me back onto my feet, and I think I'm already losing all the feelings in my body, once again, just like I do after an evening in the pub.

The instructor advises me to be on my guard in situations like this, because an assailant isn't going to warn me of the pending slam to the floor, and he most certainly won't be telling me which shoulder I'm about to be hurled over. With that bit of worthless advice in mind, we get back into launch mode once again and the ceiling flashes by for a second time. I still don't have the time to figure out which side of the instructor's head I'm zipping past, so I crash down onto the mat yet again whilst forgetting to tuck-in the pounding head.

When the lights finally come back on again, I simply can't understand why Jim finds it so funny, but the smile disappears when the instructor heads his way and grabs his pyjama top, before sending him into orbit for a change.

After a few more short flights, Jim is instructed to stand close to the near-end of my mat and to bend forward to take hold of his ankles. This time, I have to run toward him as fast as I can and then leap into the air to fly head-first over his crouching body. Then, whilst I'm in orbit I need to tuck my head and chin in towards my chest, and go into a forward roll as I land on the mat at the other side of my mate. I'm clearly no acrobat, so as you can imagine, the pain is almost unbearable when I hit the mat, and after three goes apiece, we both appear to have a heavy-metal rock band playing at full blast inside our stupid heads. We also seem to have something akin to a coat hook poking out from the base of our necks where a bone used to be.

Jim is now told to take up the leap-frog position again, and once he's done that, the instructor does the same, but he's about six feet away from my mate at the opposite end of the mat. I can't believe my ears when the instructor looks up and tells me to step back about ten yard from my mate, and then run as fast as I can toward him. I have to make sure I have sufficient momentum to hurl myself up into the air, fly head-first over my mate, the mat and the instructor, and then tuck my head in and land shoulders first on the mat, not forgetting of course, to break the fall with my forearms.

As Jim gets into position, I can see he's beginning to shake a little, and as I glance down underneath his body, it's pretty clear he's silently laughing his head off.

"What do you think about this next little stunt?" I ask as I bend down to look Jim straight in the eye.

"I'll tell you what I think," comes the reply. "I don't give a sod what you do, but when he tells me it's my turn, I'll keep stepping back until I reach the exit door."

"Thank God for that. I'll see you outside."

The next morning I wake up with aches and pains on top of my aches and pains, but this time I'm relieved to know yet another plan has gone pear-shaped. I guess it could be down to the trauma my body went through last night, which resulted in it being impossible to sleep. However, I managed to spend about eight hours just thinking my way through all the rubbish that's been hounding me recently, and I now realise I've really had enough of all the nonsense I've been putting myself and everybody else through, so from now on there'll be absolutely no more getting blathered, and I really will get my self-control back into shape.

So with my new head on, the first thing I do is apologise to Ma for all the grief I've caused her lately. It's a huge relief to find we're finally back on speaking terms, and according to her it's about time we had a proper mother-and-son chat. I've never had one of those before, so I don't know exactly what she means. She tells me how proud she is of me and that she, like most of the neighbours thinks I'm a really nice young man, although most of them aren't aware of my recent problems. Apparently I have a bright future ahead of me, so I just need to just make sure I look after myself, learn as much as I can, and don't make things difficult through drinking too much and getting into bother. She also tells me that nice girls tend to like nice boys, and if I end up getting a bad reputation I'll probably end up with a girlfriend who has likewise, and that'll mean I won't be happy in the long run. Finally, she promises that she and Pa are on my side, but I mustn't lose sight of where I want to be with my life in a few years time.

That's all good news, but a bit of bad news heads my way, when Eddie tells the kitchen brigade that Head Chef Rob handed in his notice a couple of weeks ago. He'll be leaving us at the end of the week to take up a new job somewhere in the Derbyshire Peak District, and our new head chef is an ex-navy bloke called Ray. Rumours start circulating that Rob's departure is probably down to his inappropriate and rather unhygienic use of the butcher's block. Then, as me and Jim are discussing it with a few waitresses during our coffee break, I notice my girlfriend Pat appears to be just a wee bit too concerned about which waitresses might be implicated. The look on her face suggests she could well be one of them, so I decide to put an end to the relationship even though it's barely started.

As it turns out, the sudden loss of Pat doesn't really matter, because after work a couple of days later I find myself sitting in the pub next to Val, yet another gorgeous waitress. During our brief conversation, she mentions that whenever she goes out for the evening, her Dad insists on her being back home by 9pm, so there's no doubt in my mind she'll be a very nice girl, and spot on for me. I must have impressed her as well, because the very next evening we're enjoying a Wimpy cheeseburger and I offer to accompany her on the bus journey home, just to make sure she arrives safe and sound before nine o'clock.

She leads me up to the back seat of the upper deck, and to my surprise as we sit holding hands, she offers me a taste of the lipstick she's wearing before the bus has even reached the Wicker arches less than a mile away. Then, after a very nice brief tasting session, she asks a very intriguing question.

"Do you know what a giggle-band is?"

"I haven't a clue. What is it?" I reply somewhat baffled, as Val slowly rolls up her mini-skirt almost to the waist, to reveal the darker shade of stocking-top.

"It's one of these," she smiles whilst placing a fingertip on the stocking top.

"So why is it called a giggle-band?"

Yes, yes, I'm sure you already know, but don't forget right now I'm only sixteen.

"Because when a bloke gets this far, he's laughing, and lucky for you my Dad's out tonight, so when we get home do you fancy coming upstairs with me, just to find out if it's true?" Val smiles as she goes on to reveal the giggle-band at the top of her other stocking and a glimpse of her extremely brief panties. I can't believe I turn down her very kind offer but as it turns out, I did the right thing for once.

The very next morning, Eddie tells me to head off to the staff canteen for a coffee before the lunchtime mayhem kicks off, so a few minutes later, I'm slouching in one of the canteen armchairs whilst quietly sipping a mug of coffee. I must be out of sight of incoming colleagues, as I'm sprawled out low down in the chair with my back towards the entrance of the sitting area. A few minutes go by before several waitresses stroll in with their own hot drinks, as they approach I can hear Val going on about something I don't think she'd want me to hear.

Apparently, she had a great time in a night club with her boyfriend last night, and she goes on to explain in great detail that as her parents were away for the night, the guy was allowed to go way beyond the giggle band when they arrived back at her house at three o'clock this morning. I most certainly don't recall taking her to a night club last night, and I know for a fact I was in the land of nod back on Wallace Road just after ten thirty. Furthermore, if it was me she's going on about, I would undoubtedly remember anything I did with regard to the promised land that lies beyond the giggle band.

So another one bites the dust, but it doesn't bother me on this occasion, because during yet another sleepless night, I suddenly realise I haven't asked The Man Upstairs for his help and guidance. After all those hours spent in Parkwood Springs Methodist Chapel during recent years, I simply can't believe I hadn't thought of it sooner. So after opening my heart to Him, I'm back on track by daybreak, so my life won't become worthless, and neither will I be letting Ma, Pa and My Maker down from now on.

So the bit of a blip is over and done with, and the real me is back up and running. Yabadabadoo!

Chapter Seven

Back On Track

I don't have a chance to tell Jim about my chat with Him Above, because the only thing he's bothered about right now is that I owe him ten quid. According to him, the News of the World newspaper has been advertising mushroom growing kits at twenty quid a time, and he's in no doubt that if we invest in a box of the stuff, we can earn ourselves a small fortune by selling mushrooms to residents and pub customers around the High Green area. He also reckons that once we become known for selling high quality produce, we could also end up supplying local farm shops and greengrocers. I think that might be a bit on the optimistic side, but I go along with it as it sounds like easy money, although I could be wrong as usual.

Anyway, the kit is made up of nothing more than a plastic bag of mushroom spore and a bag of fertiliser, Fortunately there's also a book of instructions and a shedload of leaflets, which highlight the success of numerous mushroom growers, none of whom I hasten to add, come from anywhere near the Sheffield area. The book goes into great detail about the process we'll need to go through before we make our fortune, so instead of wasting time right now, we decide to take everything just one step at a time and get the ball rolling at the weekend, back at Jim's house at the top end of High Green.

With hindsight, perhaps we should have read the entire instruction book before we got started, and then we might have thrown everything straight into the bin and said farewell to a tenner apiece. Unfortunately we didn't, so now you're going to hear all about it. Sorry about that!

So, according the instruction book we need to acquire a bale of straw, and as it happens Jim is a bit of a horse rider and knows exactly where such luxuries can be found, so he drives off in his Morris Marina to return twenty minutes later with the boot duly loaded. A second glance at the instructions tells us we now have to cut the straw into millions of one-inch pieces, so Jim gets back into the car to sneak down to his Dad's house to pinch the new hover-mower he's recently purchased. Ten minutes later, the mower is parked in the middle of the back garden, and he runs the lead back into the kitchen to ram the plug into an electric socket. Back outside, he presses the start button but in less than five seconds Jim's new pride and joy is completely jammed-up with bits of straw, and there's a nasty stench of electrical burning.

Jim is now in panic mode, so we quickly remove every bit of straw from inside the mower before plonking it back into its delivery box. Then finally, we heave the box back into the car boot ready for him to race back to his Dad's to place the mower carefully back into its original position on the floor of the garden shed. Our only option now is to cut up the straw manually, so we pop round to the local ironmonger's to invest even more dosh in a couple of pairs of large, sturdy kitchen scissors. We start snipping away early in the afternoon, but we don't seem to have got very far by the time it starts to go dark. When we finally call it a day I notice several throbbing blisters on my fingertips, which prove to be even more painful when I attempt to slide the scissors back over them.

I just hope nobody notices the blisters on my fingers, as I could end up being on the receiving end of numerous derogatory remarks about my sexual activities.

It takes us another painful day to get the straw chopped up, and that's mainly due to Jim purloining a pair of blunt garden shears from his Pa's garden shed. Meanwhile, not being a farmer, and not being one of the three little pigs who built a house for the big bad wolf to blow down, I've never even seen a bale of straw close up, let alone one that's been sliced up and spread over the back garden. Now I can tell with great certainty, that if you were to unravel a couple of bales of the stuff, it would probably cover the entire football pitch of Wembley Stadium, and I don't mean the one on which we play our cup finals back in Parkwood Springs.

Now, according to the instructions we have to stack the straw in an enclosed or sheltered area, saturate it with water and then keep it wet for about a week. Luckily, standing at the bottom of Jim's garden is the shell of an empty, and no longer used outside toilet, which just about fits the bill. He attaches a hose pipe to the kitchen sink cold water tap, before running the hose down the outer edge of the sink unit, along the floor and up the back of the kitchen door, through the letter box, down the other side, along the garden path, and up the wall overlooking the loo. Then I climb the wall to wedge the hose between the roof gutter and the gap at the top of the door, ensuring that the hose is aiming down onto the mountain of straw below. It's seems to have taken forever to get this far, but now we're just about ready to start growing the mushrooms, so Jim turns on the cold water tap, and we breathe a huge sigh of relief as the water begins to shoot out from the hose and onto the straw. It takes almost an hour to make sure that the it's absolutely soaking wet, so all we have to do now is leave it until next week. We decide to call it a day for now, so Jim invites me back to his place for a pint.

Bearing in mind I've just turned over a new leaf, that's a pint of Coca Cola, not Stones Best Bitter, and no, I couldn't care less whether you believe me or not!

During the alcohol-free boozing session, I tell him about the little chat I had with My Maker, so we both decide to make sure we enjoy every day from now on. I think we particularly need to bring some fun back into our lives, and when I tell him about the Mucky Pup trick we played on the neighbours back in the Springs, we agree to try it out on Meg and Brenda in the cold section at work. They always enjoy winding us up and it's time we returned the favour, so after a quick visit to Castle Market, we're fully armed and ready to go with the plastic poo.

It sure feels good to get back to enjoying life!

As it happens, me and Jim are working together in the bakehouse this week, and apart from the cleaning team, there's only the two of us around between six and eight o'clock in the mornings, so we have plenty of time set up the prank before getting stuck into churning out the daily batch of scones and sausage rolls.

We creep into the cold section and slide open the lid of the chest freezer. There are about twenty large tins of ice cream sitting in the bowels of the freezer, so we lift one out before Jim carefully removes the seal and scoops out the top few inches of vanilla ice cream. I position the doggy-poo on top of the remaining contents, then he firmly presses the decanted ice cream back into place before I smooth the surface with a palette knife and seal the lid back on. Finally, I throw the tin back into the freezer and just like we're doing with the mushroom growing back at Jim's place, all we have to do now is wait for something to happen.

Meanwhile, the mushroom growing instruction book comes out again at the weekend, and all we have to do today is open the bag of dried fertiliser, sprinkle it over the pile of straw and compress it. Unfortunately there's a strong wind today, and each time we release a handful of fertiliser, most of it does a U-turn back into our faces. Eventually, the job is done, so Jim lays a couple of horse blankets over the straw and then I plonk a load of house bricks on top to keep it compacted.

The book promises that within 7 to 10 days, the interior of the pile of straw will have heated up and started steaming, but the book lied of course, and the straw isn't even lukewarm when we check it a fortnight later. Luckily there's no rush, so it's back to reality and it's good to know our new Head Chef Ray, doesn't mind a bit of fun now and then, provided the job gets done properly.

We also have a third chef with us now, and Mark is already demonstrating great capability in avoiding work of any kind. It might be down to his excess weight, but even if he were to sit down all day with a mug of tea clasped in his hands, he'd still be sweating like a pig from the moment he arrives until he clocks out eight hours later.

He's a very messy worker and will do anything to avoid having to clean up his section after lunchtime service. As the lunchtime service ends each day, Ray and Eddie depart for a bite to eat, so Mark instructs either me or my pal to clean up the mess he's left, whilst he heads into the changing room to spend the next half hour parked on the toilet seat reading a couple of newspapers. So today, just before Ray and Eddie take their lunch break, I quietly disappear into the changing room to secretly smear a handful of liquid soap all over the white plastic toilet seat. The soap is now virtually invisible to both the naked eye and naked bum, especially the huge hairy one Mark owns.

The moment Ray and Eddie depart Mark bellows out the usual instructions, telling Jim to get cracking on cleaning up his mess whilst he heads into the changing room. On this occasion, he storms out in less than two minutes, and for some reason his face has turned bright red in shock and anger. Mark doesn't realise how ridiculous he looks, as he shuffles his 20-odd stone frame back into the kitchen, with chef's trousers tightly wrapped around his ankles. It doesn't help that he's gripping his whatsits in his left hand to avoid flashing to half the kitchen brigade. Worse still, he's completely unaware there's about half a mile of noticeably soiled Izal loo roll trailing behind him, firmly held in place by his buttocks. A warning shot is now heading my way.

I won't repeat exactly what he says, so as usual you just need to use your imagination, but it goes something like this.

"Eric. I wonder if you would mind telling me if it was you who smeared the toilet seat with liquid soap".

No comment.

"I would rather not have to enquire again. Was it you, you silly boy?"

"Whatever it is you're going on about, it wasn't me," comes the delayed reply.

“Whatever it is you’re going on about, it wasn’t me,” comes the delayed reply.

“Rubbish! You know bloody well what I’m going on about,” screams Mark. “I’d been sitting on the bog for about five seconds when I felt something wet sticking to my backside, then when I stood up, I noticed a bloody great ring of soapy bubbles all over my ass. I tried to wipe them off with the bog roll I had in my hand, but it turns out my arms aren’t long enough to reach all the way round my butt. Now I’ve got to spend the rest of the soddin’ day with a bubbling bum,” he explains with not the slightest hint of humour.

Oh dear. How sad. Never mind. One up for the trainees!

A whole month drags by before the straw in Jim’s outside loo finally starts steaming, so now we have to turn it inside out and leave it until it starts festering again. The instruction book tells us we’re going to need something to grow the mushrooms in, and somewhere dark and cool for the them to grow. Fortunately, back at work, the bread is delivered in large rectangular wooden stacking-trays, so we nick a couple of dozen over the next few days and take them back to Jim’s, as he’s more than happy to grow them down in the cellar. We also need a load of top soil to lay into the trays, but I leave that to my mate to sort out.

Another month comes and goes before the interior of the loo starts spewing steam out of every orifice, but that means we’re finally ready for the final leg of the project. We half-fill twenty four stolen bread trays with the similarly acquired top soil, before sprinkling the mushroom spore on top and carting the trays through the kitchen and down into the cellar. No doubt it won’t happen, but according to the instruction book, the trays will be covered in beautiful pure white mushrooms within five days. Not only that, if we pick the mushrooms early in the morning, another batch will be ready and waiting for us the next day.

Oh really? Who the hell wrote these instructions?

Five days come and go, then another five and another. In fact it’s another month before Jim tells me there were three mushrooms waiting for him when he checked the cellar this morning. That means the mushrooms work out at almost seven quid apiece so far, and that’s not taking into account the cost of the scissors, but fortunately the bale of straw and the top soil didn’t cost anything as I recall.

Even so, I'm not very pleased that my friend gobbled down all three mushrooms for his breakfast, but as they were very tasty, I guess that makes it OK then.

The greedy git!

That's not just the first batch of mushrooms we grow in this business venture, it also turns out to be the last. The problem is that me and Jim have lives to live, and we can't keep waiting week after week, and month after month for a handful of mushrooms to pop up whenever they feel like it. We've gone from early spring to mid-summer, and we've only seen a total of seven mushrooms, although I didn't actually see them, as my pal scoffed the lot moments after they were brought out of his cellar and up into daylight, so we decide to have a board meeting, although in my view it turns out to be more like a 'bored' meeting, and after a very brief discussion we agree to close the mushroom growing business down.

As I arrive outside Jim's back door door on Sunday morning, I can't help noticing the house stinks something awful. I don't mean there's a bit of an odour, I mean the stench is absolutely gut-wrenching and there's no doubt it's coming up from the cellar, so we head down into the darkness and by now the smell is so bad you could probably slice through it. As we reach the bottom step, Jim switches on the light to reveal what can only be described as a dense fog lingering above the stacks of filthy bread trays. As I peer at the swirling mist it seems to be heading in my direction, but then I realise it isn't fog and I'm actually staring at a swarm of what must be at least a million tiny insects.

Too late! They're already landing all over my face, my hair, mouth and ears, and up my hooter, and the remaining half a million are drifting over the cellar steps and up towards the kitchen. It's pretty obvious this mushroom growing nonsense just isn't for us, so we decide that now is the time to take the bread trays and their stinking contents to the local tip, just down the road.

Unfortunately, the Marina will only take four trays at a time so we'll have to do six trips to the tip, but according to Jim, that'll make it less obvious to the tip supervisor what we're up to, especially as the tip is for domestic waste only and twenty four bread trays of rubbish will look as though this is a business operation. He also thinks it might be a good idea to throw the trays randomly around the perimeter of the tip, as that'll make it even less obvious what we're doing.

Bear in mind local tips weren't as well organised as they are now. In the early 1970's, they were nothing more than a spare plot of land where you can throw anything onto the mountains of rubbish already lined up around the perimeter.

Two hours later the last tray and its steaming contents are duly deposited and that's the mushroom growing business over and done with. So on the short drive home, Jim decides to replace his sink units and repaint the kitchen walls, with the aim of freshening up the place and getting rid of the smell as soon as possible. I'm not into DIY and stuff like that, but after all we've been through it's only right I should give him a hand. He tells me he has a couple of spare tins of paint lying around in the shed, but when he picks them up he decides to leave the walls as they are. I think it's probably due to the paint turning out to be Dulux Mushroom, and for some reason or other he appears to have suddenly gone off that particular shade.

Nevertheless, with the help of Jim's dad, it only takes us a few evenings to get the kitchen done up, so by the next weekend we're ready to load up the car once again, but this time with obsolete kitchen fixtures and fittings. As we approach the entrance to the tip, Dougie suddenly hits the brake so hard, I almost shoot straight through the windscreen.

"Tell me it's been snowing," he screams.

"What are you on about," says I. "It's the back end of July."

Jim points toward the mountains of waste stacked up around the perimeter of the tip, and I can't believe my eyes when I realise the place is completely covered in huge, beautiful pure white mushrooms, and millions of the little buggers are stretching out as far as the eye can see. People are clambering all over the place, just picking them up and stuffing them into their pockets, shopping bags and whatever else they can use to carry them home. We've spent months trying in vain to grow the things down in the cellar, but the moment we pack it in and dump everything, tons of them suddenly decide to spring up.

Then after sitting in the front seats of the car, open-mouthed and utterly speechless for at least five minutes, there's a knock on the driver's door window at the side of my mate's head. He glances sideways to come face to face with a bloke who looks as though he might be a gipsy.

"You buy mushrooms? "Lovely, fresh, home-grown mushrooms. Very tasty."

His very kind offer is turned down.

The truth is that Jim suggests in no uncertain terms that the gipsy should simply go away, but as he uses a phrase often used by Dee Dahs, I think it might be best if I just leave you once again to figure it out for yourself. End of!

As I'm now back to being the nice young man I was just a short while ago, I decide to get involved with the Cole Brothers' Retirement Committee, which is chaired by the store General Manager, Ken Stenton. Members of the committee regularly visit the homes of retired employees to provide them with a bit of company, and whilst we're there we make a mental note of anything the store might be able to help with, such as replacement curtains, carpets or items of furniture. Then we report back to Mr S, and he arranges for replacements to be delivered.

Surely you'll agree it's really nice of me to give up so much of my time? Oh please yourself then!

I'm the only teenager on the committee, so Mr Stenton is delighted when a few weeks later, he becomes aware of just how many evenings this particular teenager has given up, and how many retirees have enjoyed his company during the last couple of months. In fact he's so pleased, he tells me that from now on I can address him as Ken, and that has a huge impact on the old ego. You can imagine how pleased Ma and Pa are, when they hear I'm already a pal of the store's General Manager, although I might have slightly exaggerated the story.

Meanwhile, Mark has informed veg cook Nellie that she'll be cleaning up after him when me and Jim go to college on Tuesday afternoon, and that makes him something of a hated man around here. Something needs to be done about it, so whilst we're getting changed before heading off to Pond Street College of Technology, I grab an old pair of chef's shoes that have been lying around on top of the lockers for quite a while. As you might expect they're covered in all sorts of stuff such as flour, grease and gravy stains. I fasten the laces into neat bows before placing them side by side on the floor of the toilet cubicle, just in front of the pedestal, and then I drop a rolled-up pair of chef's trousers across the shoes as I step backwards through the toilet door and back into the changing area. Finally, I stick my left foot underneath the door and lever it towards me and as the door closes, I lock it from the outside by sticking a sixpence piece into the centre of the latch bolt and giving it a twist until the 'engaged' sign comes into view.

The idea is that when Mark enters the changing room for his half hour sit down, he'll realise the toilet cubicle door is locked, and a quick glance under the door will suggest somebody is already sitting on the toilet with their trousers draped over their shoes. He'll have no choice other than to return to the kitchen and do his own cleaning up until the cubicle is vacated, and even then he'll have to give it the proverbial 'five minutes' before he goes back in.

Now that's not a bad plan, is it?

As I stroll towards the staff entrance the next morning, it looks as though the night watchman might have had a heart attack or something. Parked right outside the entrance are a couple of police cars, an ambulance and a fire engine. When I reach the top of the stairs leading up to the watchman's office, I almost jump out of my skin when a hand unexpectedly shoots out from the doorway of the office and grabs me by the throat. Restaurant Manager Mr Hill is on the other end of the arm and he's clearly not a happy bunny, especially as he's been called in at such an unearthly hour by Mr Stenton, who apparently is also on his way.

"You bloody idiot! You stupid boy! Have you any idea what you've done?" yells Mr Hill. "I can't believe how stupid you are! I know you're always larking about, but this time you're in real trouble," he continues whilst pinning me firmly against the wall.

"Why? What's happened?" I ask rather meekly.

Whatever it is, it can't be down to me, as I haven't been around for nearly a day! Well at least that'll be my excuse.

"Don't tell me you don't know, because whenever anything stupid happens around here, you're always suspect number one," he retorts. "You've obviously been up to one of your stupid pranks again, but this time you're in deep trouble, you stupid little clown."

Apparently, our little plan was spot on.

Shortly after we'd headed off to college, Mark went into the changing room, but as the toilet cubicle was 'engaged', he returned to the kitchen and forgot all about it. It was a busy afternoon, and as that resulted in Mark, Ray and Eddie being a bit late finishing work, they were in a bit of a rush to get changed and go home.

We're all aware that Ray usually waits until everyone else has departed before he gets into the shower, as he doesn't want anyone to see him without his toupee. Last night however, he gave the shower a miss, so he got changed and left with his colleagues. As luck would have it, not a single one of them noticed the locked cubicle door or the chef's shoes and trousers on the floor behind it, and would you believe none of them thought to turn off the changing room light as they left.

So, around five thirty this morning, the three cleaners head along the corridor, and as Daphne is about to enter the changing room with mop and bucket at the ready, she notices from under the door that the light is on. Knowing they're the first to arrive every morning, she taps on the door and calls out to ask if anyone is inside. Nobody replies, so she pops her head round the door and to her horror, she notices the shoes and trousers piled up on the toilet cubicle floor, and that the door is locked and displaying the engaged sign. She has no doubt that Ray's corpse has been sitting on the loo since last night, and the sudden realisation results in her fainting and falling backwards into the arms of one of her colleagues.

Ethel gently lowers her to the floor whilst the third cleaner, Emily peeps into the changing room to check what's wrong, and she immediately comes to the same conclusion as Daphne. She races back up the corridor and down the stairs to tell the night watchman, so he grabs the telephone and dials 999.

Apparently, the police cars are first on the scene, followed seconds later by the ambulance and a fire engine. A couple of policemen then accompany the night watchman up to the changing room, followed by four burly firemen with axes at the ready, and a pair of ambulancemen carrying a stretcher and a little tank of oxygen. Then one of the firemen smashes down the toilet cubicle door with his axe, and as he steps inside he looks down to discover you know what.

Oops!

Just as Mr Hill is just about to erupt once again, Mr Stenton arrives still wearing his pyjamas underneath his coat.

"Morning Brian. What's going on?"

Mr Hill does his best but just can't get the words out, so Mr S turns to me.

"Hello Eric. What are you doing here?"

“Morning, Ken. I think I’m in a bit of trouble,” I reply as Mr Hill goes into orbit.

“How dare you!” he spits. “It’s Mister Stenton to you, not Ken!”

“It’s fine, Brian. Eric knows me as Ken. “So what’s happened?”

I explain everything, and to everyone’s utter amazement, Ken bursts out into howls of laughter.

“That’s absolutely brilliant. What a prank. It sounds like the kind of stuff we used to get up to in my younger days. I love it. Well done Eric. Well done.”

The look on Mr Hill’s face suggests he isn’t quite so pleased with my performance.

“Let it go Brian,” suggests my friend. “There’s no harm done and it’s nice to have a bit of a chuckle now and then. Even our friends from the wonderful emergency services are finding it funny, aren’t you?” he laughingly enquires as he turns toward several other smiling faces, which also comes as a bit of relief, especially as I’m already expecting to be carted away in the back of a police car.

Jim thinks it’s hilarious when he arrives a few minutes later, and so does Eddie when he hears about the stunt during our coffee break, but Mark apparently has nothing to say about the incident. I’m not sure about Ray’s view, although a little incident that occurs during lunchtime service helps him make up his mind.

We’ve all been making the usual heroic attempt to control the mayhem during the last couple of hours, when an almighty scream comes from the cold section. The lunchtime service comes to an immediate halt as the entire kitchen brigade hurtle towards the area to see what the hell has happened, and moments later the door adjacent to the cold section, which leads directly into the restaurant, swings wide open as all the waitresses pile in as well, followed by a blustering Mr Hill.

Brenda is sprawled out flat on her back at the side of the cold section chest freezer. She’s clinging on to an ice cream scoop with her right hand. There’s no sign of any ice cream, but there is a pile of doggy poo on the floor just beneath her wrist, and that’s what the index finger of her left hand is pointing at. The kitchen is now not only at a standstill, it’s also deathly quiet as everyone begins to realise why it is that Brenda isn’t quite her usual bouncy self at the moment.

Then Mr Hill shoves his way through the gathering crowd to assist the stricken lady back onto her feet. He holds on to her for a few moments until he's sure she's OK, then as he slowly removes his hands from her shoulders, he decides I must have been involved somewhere along the line.

"Eric, I'd like a quiet word in my office, and the rest of you can get back to whatever you were doing five minutes ago."

Trust me when I tell you Brian was lying. It was nothing like a quiet word.

The rest of the team find it hilarious and one or two of them tell me I'm a genius when it comes to setting up pranks, so regardless of the huge rollocking I get from the boss, I'm so pleased with the way it all turned out, that I decide to treat Jim and a couple of waitresses to a Saturday night out at the Top Rank Suite. As it happens, the Saturday night chef hasn't turned up, and we're told he won't be coming back for some reason. The barman then overhears one of my guests jokingly suggest I should go into the kitchen and sort out the food. They must be desperate, as a few seconds later the Catering Manager appears out of thin air to offer me the Saturday night job. I'm sure it's only due to my ever-growing ego, but for no other reason I can think of, I accept.

To be honest, it's not something I really want to do, but if nothing else, it'll give me some experience in another kitchen, and it'll also bring in some extra cash. Nice!

A couple of Saturdays later, I'm chatting to one of the older female members of the Top Rank bar staff and she asks why I decided to be a chef. Apparently, she hates cooking for herself and her hubby, and she just can't understand why anyone in their right mind would want to do it for a living. She never bats an eyelid when I explain that even though Snoz Harrington was a good teacher and a really nice bloke, I just wanted to get out of woodwork and technical drawing, so telling the careers teacher I wanted to be a chef seemed to be the best way of doing it.

The following week you could knock me down with a pastry brush, when the lady tells me that Snoz sends his regards and best wishes for the future. It turns out she's married to Mr Harrington, and she holds up a wedding photo of the pair of them, just to prove it. Apparently, when she told him I was cheffing at the Top Rank, he said that in all his years as a teacher, he'd never come across anyone who'd conjured up such a plan, and that earned me his respect.

He also told her that whilst it was common knowledge around the staffroom that Boocock was the worst performer in woodwork and technical drawing lessons he'd ever come across, he did appreciate that I never gave him a problem whereas most boys in a similar position would have been quite troublesome and disruptive.

What a wonderful guy Snoz turned out to be.

It's not long before I decide to pack in the part-time job, and tonight will be my final shift. One of the barmaids tells me that when the club closes at two o'clock in the morning they're all heading to a party at the DJ's house, and I'm more than welcome to join them. She tells me it'll be much more fun than usual, because the bouncers' boss won't be attending due to him recently having a nasty fall down the club staircase recently. I decide not to let on that he didn't actually fall down the stairs, because as it's right outside the kitchen door I'd overheard several members of his team flexing their muscles and using their feet to assist him down the steps.

It soon becomes clear that the pop bottle rattling sessions we used to have back home were a long way short of this kind of caper, and if I'd known every sofa and armchair was going to be in use all night, I would have booked one for myself. There's even one of the bouncers and a barmaid snuggled up in the bath but fortunately, they're much too busy to notice me sneaking in to take a pee. Then as I exit the bathroom, I'm dragged into the kitchen by one of the barmaids to witness something quite unexpected but most entertaining, as a completely naked bouncer climbs onto the kitchen table and he obviously finding it quite exciting up there. He picks up the pint of ale he has between his feet and gulps it straight down in a matter of seconds. When he puts the glass back down it lands on top of a small pile of baking powder, although on second thoughts it could be something very different judging by the amount of powder stuck to the end of his nose.

At this point I realise this simply isn't my kind of party, so make my exit and I don't think I'll be missed. So apart from the goings on behind the scenes at the Top Rank, the world already seems to be a much better place than it did just a short while ago. I can't help thinking it's mainly down to Him Upstairs having a bit of sympathy for me, even though I left it far too late before asking for His help. All I need to do now is keep myself on track and to make sure I get back to enjoying life, no matter what gets thrown my way from time to time. I guess I can only give it my best shot, and then we'll see how things turn out.

Fingers crossed on that one then!

Chapter Eight

Onwards and Upwards

I must be doing something right in my proper job, because whilst Marge the bakeress is on holiday, Ray wants me to give some bakery training to a student by the name of Janet. He tells me not to get up to any of my usual tricks, so that means I have to be on my best behaviour for an entire week, something that hasn't happened for quite some time by all accounts.

I somehow manage not to put a foot wrong all week, and Janet has been shown how to prepare most of our bakery items and dishes. She's only on duty until noon on Saturday, and the last bit of training on the agenda is for her to learn how to make College Pudding, which comes out something like Christmas Pudding and is one of the best sellers in the restaurant. Throughout the week, any unused cakes and pastries are thrown into an old-fashioned metal dustbin which stands in the corner of the bakehouse. Any fresh cream cakes and gateaux returned from the restaurant at the end of each day, are kept in the bakery fridge overnight, then during the following morning we dump them into the bin with all the other stuff, once we've discarded the fresh cream.

Don't worry! Somebody has painted the letters 'CP' on the dustbin lid to signify it's to be used only for storing the left overs for College Pudding, so nothing else goes into the bin. We're not that stupid around here!

So, once we've sent all the fresh cream goodies out into the restaurant on Saturday morning, I tell Janet that she can make the College Pudding by following my instructions throughout the process. First, she weighs out the butter and sugar before dropping it into the huge 3-speed electric mixing bowl and beating the hell out of it, and then she adds the mixed spices, golden syrup, sultans, raisins and eggs. Once that's all done, I take the lid off the CP dustbin and tip the contents into the mixing bowl with everything else, and now we just have to steam the pudding mixture for a couple of hours.

Janet brushes melted butter around the inside edges of a couple of dozen bowls, and as she starts pouring the mixture into them ready for steaming, I explain that the pudding is a best seller, though due to the amount of leftover ingredients used, it's by far the least expensive dessert on the menu. I invite her to have a taste before she puts the bowls into the steamer.

"There's no way I'm ever going to put that anywhere near my lips," she replies.

"Why not?" I ask somewhat surprised. "It's delicious."

"You must be joking," says Janet. "Because it's full of rubbish."

"How do you mean?" I enquire.

"Every day this week, when you've gone home at three o'clock, I've cleaned-down all the preparation tables and swept the floor. Nobody told me the dustbin was only used for storing leftover bits of cake and pastries for college pudding, so I just put all the rubbish from the tables into the bin. Then when I swept the floor, I emptied the dustpan into it as well. I just thought some of the paint on the lid had worn off and that it originally said CRAP, as I wasn't aware of it being an abbreviation for College Pudding, so that's why I'm not going to taste it either before or after it's been steamed."

I'm sure you already know I'm about to make yet another bad decision.

"Well in that case, just keep your mouth well and truly shut, otherwise there'll be no pudding for the customers next week".

Luckily she does as she's told, and later in the afternoon it's a huge relief to hear we've had some excellent customer comments about the College Pudding.

Perhaps it wasn't such a bad decision after all, so that's one up for me, and maybe you don't know as much think you know about this industry, so there!

Anyway, you'll be pleased to know that having achieved my City & Guilds 147 Basic Cookery qualification in late spring 1967, I've now achieved the 151 Advanced Cookery qualification, so perhaps you wouldn't mind referring to me 'Chef' from now on, regardless of my somewhat dubious bakery standards.

My apprenticeship is finally coming to an end, but as John Lewis is such a wonderful employer, there's little chance of any career development opportunities heading my way any time soon, and that could be a problem. Then out of the blue one morning, Mr Hill tells me he's arranged for the organisation to provide me with a six-month tour of its London and southern branches in the role of Trainee Catering Manager, and in the unlikely event I somehow manage to impress everyone on my travels, a full time job will be waiting for me next year.

Yep, I know what you're thinking, and I can assure you I also doubt it!

During my last couple of weeks at Cole Brothers, I almost miss out on the opportunity when Ray entrusts me with training another student called Sally. Unfortunately my stupidity gets the better of me for one final time when I decide to demonstrate my juggling skills, which turn out to be virtually non-existent.

When a teaspoonful of Eggello powder is dissolved in boiling water, it turns the solution into a bright yellow colour. We use it when making pastry so the dough looks as though it's been made with butter, rather than the cheap lard we actually use. We keep the colouring in a vinegar bottle, and as it only takes a few drops of the stuff to turn four pints of cold water into banana-yellow, the only thing I have to worry about is to make sure it doesn't get onto the front of my pristine-white chef's jacket. If it does, then there's no way the stain can be removed, so I'll end up waltzing around the kitchen looking like an overgrown canary.

Yes thank you! I know this hooter of mine doesn't help either, so can we please leave it at that and move on.

It's late night opening on Wednesday, so I've agreed to help out in the kitchen when I finish in the bakehouse this afternoon. Then, shortly before Sally finishes her shift at five o'clock, I pick up the bottle of Eggello solution and a couple of sultana scones, before repeatedly throwing them all up into the air one after the other and then catching them on the way back down. Unfortunately, I'm not as good as I thought, and as I attempt to snatch the bottle out of mid-air on it's way down from the ceiling strip-light, it slips straight out of my hand to crash onto the light-grey floor tiles below. The colouring seeps from the shattered bottle and onto the tiles. I don't really need Ray to spot the mess on the floor, so I tell Sally to pack up and head home right now, and not to speak to anyone on her way out.

I can't believe how stupid I can be at times, but it's not Ray I'm bothered about, it's Mr Hill. If he saw the state of the floor right now he'd go absolutely ape. The only thing I can do is to mop it up pronto, especially as the boss is bound to keep coming through to the bakehouse every few minutes to collect a tray or two of fresh cream cakes for topping-up the display in the restaurant. Unfortunately, not being a housewife, I've never slammed a mop-head into a quickly-expanding lake, so I have no idea that the more I mop, the further the colouring spreads across the bakehouse floor, so now the floor tiles have gone from a classy light-grey colour into what I can only describe as Bird's custard-yellow.

I'm still trying to figure out what to do, when I glance over the bakehouse wall and see Mr Hill heading my way. Fortunately, he's in such a rush he somehow fails to notice the floor tiles, so he opens the fridge door and grabs a tray of cakes, before lifting it up onto his shoulder and then racing back towards the restaurant. I heave a huge sigh of relief, but I'm almost gobsmacked when he reappears just a couple of seconds later, but this time he's walking backwards with the tray still across his shoulder. He also looks a tad puzzled as he speaks.

"It looks very bright in here, Eric. What have you been doing?"

"Oh, nothing much," I lie. "I just got all the cakes, gateaux and pastries prepared sooner than I expected, so I decided to give the place a good clean."

"What?" Are you telling me you cleaned the place up without being told to?"

"Yes. I just thought it needed doing."

"Well, I never expected that! Well done Chef. I have to tell you I'm delighted with your newly acquired professionalism. Good for you, son. Good for you!

He heads back towards the restaurant, but once again he puts himself into reverse gear and arrives back in the bakehouse just a few seconds later.

"Aren't Sheffield Wednesday playing at home tonight?" he enquires.

"Yes they are, but as I'll be here until eight o'clock I won't be going," I reply with a very clear display of mock sadness.

"Well you can forget about work for the rest of the day, so go and get showered right now and buzz off to Hillsborough. You'll just about make it for the kick-off if you get your skates on. With your performance today you deserve a treat, so get a move on and I'll let Ray know I've kicked you out. I'll see you tomorrow," he beams as the chocolate eclairs, apple turnovers and strawberry gateaux finally head for the restaurant display counter.

I can't believe my luck so I don't hang around, especially as I've just noticed the bright yellow footprints Mr H is lining up all the way past June's pan-wash. Heaven knows what the restaurant carpet will look like in less than two minutes.

Just before I head south I receive some very sad news. Grandma Winnie has lost her long battle with dementia and that hits me really hard, especially as it's the first time I've experienced the loss of such a close relative. I know for sure I'll completely fall apart if I attend the funeral, so to my eternal shame and regret I apologise to the rest of the family and head to London as planned.

I'm staying at the Hyelm Hostel in the Swiss Cottage area, but within a couple of weeks I move into a nice little first floor flat in a terraced house in Holloway. I'm working at the John Lewis store on Oxford Street, but as I've never used the London Underground until now, it takes me an eternity to figure out how to get to from Holloway Road to the centre of London. When I finally get my head around all the maps, routes, and the colour coded system for identifying which line I'm supposed to be travelling on, I make my way to the Holloway Road tube station accompanied by what appears to be the rest of the local population. At first glance the platform appears to be choc-a-bloc with commuters, but then I notice a gap in the crowd a few yards ahead of me. I can't believe these London idiots are all squashed-up together in a tiny section of the platform, whilst leaving an empty space between them and the next group of clowns, so I push my way through the first pack of commuters and park myself between them and the next group further along. You wouldn't believe the looks I get, but if they can't see just how stupid they are then why should I care. Unfortunately as the incoming train comes to a stop, I realise why I should care. I'm the only one of about two hundred commuters who isn't standing directly in front of one of the train's doors.

The next morning I decide to join everybody else, and standing immediately in front of me on the edge of the platform, exactly where the door of the train will be when it grinds to a halt, is an extremely tall man. He's impeccably dressed in a black jacket and pristine white shirt complete with gold cufflinks, grey waistcoat with matching bow tie, pinstriped trousers and sparkling black shoes. If that's not classy enough, then the bowler hat finally does the trick. He also has a copy of the Times neatly tucked under his arm whilst he clings onto a leather briefcase.

The incoming train eventually judders to a halt and the doors slide open. Nobody steps out onto the platform, and nobody gets onto the train either, probably because the inside of the carriage resembles a tightly packed can of sardines. Absolutely nothing happens for the next sixty seconds, and then the guard's voice bellows along the platform.

"Mind the doors."

Still nothing happens as the doors begin to close, but then with only a matter of inches to go before the door in front of him completely closes, Mr Westminster hurls himself head-first into the carriage, as if he's been fired out of a circus entertainer's cannon. With bowler hat, Times and briefcase still in position, he lands directly on top of several very surprised commuters, and remains motionless where he landed as the train pulls away from the platform. There's no doubt he'll still be sprawled-out in exactly the same position when the train arrives at the next station, so heaven knows what will happen when the doors slide open once again,

Jeremy, the manager of the Oxford Street branch staff restaurant isn't a very nice person, especially as he possesses a noticeable dislike of all non-white members of his team. His attitude towards them is disgraceful and I simply can't understand why that should be. Back in Parkwood Springs, loads of our neighbours are proud to be of various ethnic backgrounds and religious persuasion, but it's been an absolute pleasure to have known and become close friends with every single one of them.

Unfortunately, most of the ladies who work in the pot wash area are of West Indian origin, and even though their sense of humour makes them an absolute delight to work with, Jeremy does nothing but scowl at them every time he passes their work area. It's true to say that just like a number of other employees, several of them aren't very good when it comes to timekeeping, but they most certainly make up for it with the sheer effort they put into their work. I'm really annoyed one afternoon, when I find myself on the receiving end of a blasting from Jeremy for helping the ladies out for half an hour, as due to illness they're a team member short. I have no choice other than to stand and listen to the rubbish he's churning out, as he's the boss and therefore has the upper hand over a mere trainee manager.

Anyway, the next morning, three of the pot wash team arrive together, but unfortunately the shift started fifteen minutes ago. It doesn't really matter as there's nothing much for them to do, but Jeremy doesn't see it that way, and he's far from happy. He has absolutely no time for one of the ladies called Pearl, a larger-than-life character who perhaps could be described as the team's spokesperson, so the Boss instructs me to go and tell her she's fired.

I'm sorry, but as a trainee manager I don't have the authority to fire anyone but if I did, then I'd start with Jeremy.

I actually like Pearl and I know she likes me, especially as the pair of us enjoy a similar sense of humour, so as I stroll towards the gathering ensemble, I just can't believe the position Jeremy has put me in. The look on her face as I approach, suggests she already has a good idea what's heading her way, and just as I take a deep breath, Pearl takes the opportunity to get in first.

"Don't worry, my friend. I know exactly what that coward has told you to do, so just go back and tell him you've done it, but you can also tell him that if I don't have my job back by this time tomorrow, my husband will catch up with him and he'll be eaten alive somewhere between Oxford Street and his home in Highgate."

I have no idea what happened after that, but the next morning Pearl is back on duty ten minutes late as usual, but as she passes by she hands me a very expensive looking gold-plated pen followed by a peck on the cheek, a wink and a huge smile.

"You're a lovely, caring young man, and it's nice to know not every honky is a racist," she beams. "You'll do well as a boss, and I'd be happy to work for you."

"That'd be great, as long as I can find a shift for you that starts an hour later than everybody else's," I promise with a huge smile and a return peck on the cheek.

Next on my travels is the Peter Jones store in Sloane Square, and I feel like I'm working with a load of zombies for the next few weeks, as nobody ever speaks. A few of the company's senior directors are booked in for a three-course lunch today. I wasn't aware that they've been told about the northerner in the kitchen, so I'm stunned when the company Chairman pops his head round the kitchen door and invites me to join them, just so they can get to know a bit about me. Apparently, I'm the company's first ever nomadic trainee catering manager and head chef Jamie has already cooked an extra steak just for me. Just before I head back to the kitchen, the Chairman asks if the meal was to my satisfaction, so I tell him it was OK we Sheffielders would prefer a plate of corned beef, egg and chips with a few Heinz baked beans drizzled on top. Apparently, I'll go a long way with a sense of humour like that, and he hopes it'll be with the John Lewis Partnership. That's nice of him, but I don't really enjoy working in this neck of the woods and it doesn't help being a Dee Dah. So when the offer of full time employment as a relief catering manager for John Lewis in the London and south eastcomes my way, I gratefully decline and head back to God's Garden.

That'll be Sheffield then!

I'm glad I've kept in touch with my mate Jim during the last few months. I've only been out of work since five o'clock yesterday, and after a good night's kip back home in Sheffield, I wake up to the sound of him hammering on the door. He's now an assistant catering manager and running the catering services at King Edward V11 Orthopaedic Hospital, and he tells me his boss, District Catering Manager Bill Beatson has an Assistant Head Chef job waiting for me at Lodge Moor Hospital, and he wants to meet me at ten o'clock this morning.

The first thing I notice is the extraordinarily long corridor, which goes all the way from the hospital's main entrance all the way to the far end of the building, passing numerous smaller corridors which lead to the wards. This might not necessarily be the healthiest hospital to be in though, as every few seconds somebody appears from out of nowhere and hurtles along the main corridor on something resembling a kid's scooter, although this one is much bigger and fitted with a car battery on the back. It turns out the scooters are the chosen mode of transport for nursing staff to commute between wards.

I must have impressed Mr B because I'll be working here from next Monday, but right now I need to get the Vauxhall Viva tested, and that means I'll be asking Mick, another good friend of mine from the High Green area to sort it out for me. He doesn't actually work in the car industry, but anything he doesn't know about cars, isn't worth knowing in the first place.

Mick's wife Anne is lovely, and even before I get through the front door, she has a mug of tea waiting for me on the dining room table, where her hubby has all the necessary tools ready and waiting. I park myself at the end of the table before handing-over the expiring MOT Certificate for processing.

You have to bear in mind this is in the days before MOT Test Certificates are issued electronically, so when the Ministry of Transport approved testing station has made sure your car is fit for purpose, the start and end dates of the certificate's period of validity are hand-written onto the certificate and whoever is responsible at the centre then adds his signature.

Anyway, as the driveway at the side of Mick's house is not an approved testing station, it's much quicker and cheaper to let him sort it out, and I'm just about to find out why that should be, as Mick spreads out a copy of yesterday's newspaper over the table top and fills an egg cup with turpentine.

He folds several squares of Izal loo paper and plants them one on top of the other over the certificate's hand-written dates of validity. Then he picks up the kiddie's paint brush from the table, dips it into the egg cup and then carefully brushes the turpentine over the top sheet of bog roll. He repeats the process a few times, and by now the ink on the certificate has disappeared, so all that's left for him to do now is to write in the new validity dates. Hey Presto, the certificate is now valid for another year, although it doesn't mean the car is actually roadworthy of course, but as it's only cost me a couple of quid and as Mick will be doing all the routine servicing and repairs during the year, I don't give a stuff.

I'm sure you'll be thinking something's bound to go wrong, but I assure you it won't, as Mick is brilliant at what he does.

Unfortunately, about six weeks later, and due to no fault on my part, I'm involved in a little accident with a Triumph Herald, when a driving instructor fails to stop a learner driver coming out of a side street and straight across Penistone Road outside Hillsborough Park whilst I'm waiting for an elderly lady to head along the pedestrian crossing. The Triumph slams into the driver's door, but luckily it doesn't do me any harm, although I think I might be about to have a heart attack as I glance through the side window as the vehicle slams into the door. The instructor accepts full responsibility, and tells me I'll be required to take my driving licence, insurance details and MOT Test Certificate to the local cop shop. The desk sergeant turns out to be a local bloke, and after examining the certificate he asks what appear to be a couple of routine questions.

"Can you confirm exactly when and where your vehicle was last tested?"

"I think it was just over a month ago at Bob Jackson's testing station in High Green," says I without the slightest concern.

"Me and Bob were neighbours when we were kids and we went to school together, but when I last saw him about about six months ago, he wasn't very well. Was he OK when he signed the certificate?" asks plod.

"Yes, he was very chatty and looked absolutely fine to me," I lie.

"That's good news," says the policeman as he screws-up the test certificate and dumps it into the waste paper basket underneath his desk. He continues.

"The problem is that when I last saw Bob, he was in hospital after suffering a very severe stroke. He died two days later, and I helped carry his coffin into the church at his funeral, so I wasn't expecting him to be testing cars and being so chatty five months later."

Oops!

All I'll say is that the MOT Test ended up costing me a lot more than a quid! So let's move on and leave it at that, shall we?

Chapter Nine

The National Hell Service

It doesn't take long for me to realise that, apart from Kitchen Superintendent Maurice, who just like Ray back at Cole Brothers is an ex-navy chef, virtually none of the other chefs or cooks possesses a single cookery qualification between them. My new colleagues include an ex-Australian sheep farmer, a bankrupt haulage contractor and a hippie-cum-druggie, so even though this is my very first full time job without the word 'trainee' in its title, according to Bill Beatson I soon become a most valued member of the crew. It's also good to know that, in spite of their somewhat dodgy backgrounds, the rest of the gang appear to have a barmy sense of humour, so that makes Lodge Moor a great place to work as far as I'm concerned.

No doubt something's bound to happen to upset the apple cart sooner or later, and that's exactly what happens after just two weeks into my new role.

Just as I'm about to clock out on Friday evening, after completing five afternoon shifts in a row, Dining Room Supervisor Marion strolls in with some bad news. The landlord of the Shiny Sheff pub up the road, has called to say that night cook Dennis has had too much to drink, yet again. He's currently laying underneath a table in the snug and hasn't a prayer of making it to work, so that means after doing my own nine hour shift, I now have to do another ten before I go home tomorrow morning.

I'm aware that if the night cook doesn't turn up, the on-duty assistant head chef has to stay all night to feed the night nurses, and then get all the preparation work done for the early morning shift. What I didn't know, is there's a good chance I won't actually be alone during the night, but I'm just about to find out when Marian invites me to join her for a quick cuppa before she and the rest of the crew head home.

The entrance to the rear of the dining room service counter stands opposite the entrance to the kitchen, half way down the short corridor leading from the 'scooter racing' track and down to Bill's office. As you enter the dining room you find yourself standing behind the long 'L' shaped counter where food and beverages are served to incoming diners. Once they've plonked a plate of food onto a tray, they slide it along a rail toward the beverage section to pick up their drinks and then hand over the payment at the cash register, which is positioned right at the end of the counter.

Disposable plastic cups for tea, coffee and cold drinks are stacked in a long dispenser, which is screwed onto the wall at the rear of the counter, but no matter how carefully you try to ease the bottom cup out from the bottom of the dispenser, you always end up pulling out at least half a dozen. It doesn't get any better if you simply give the bottom cup a quick hard tug, as you'll then end up with at least ten cups in the palm of your hand.

Anyway, Marion reminds me that the first diners arrive just after midnight, but she strongly advises me not to start loading food onto the counter until I hear the sound of incoming voices. I ask why, but then I wish I hadn't when she explains that the dining room is haunted, and that lots of scary things happen regularly around the beverage section. Apparently, Marion and other members of the team often neatly lay out rows of chocolate bars inside the display cabinet, but when they return a few minutes later, the goodies have been piles up into a heap in the corner of the cabinet. If that's not scary enough, on numerous occasions when one of the staff has poured out a cup of tea from the huge teapot, before she's even had time to put the teapot down, the cup decides to lift itself up and empty the tea back out and all over the counter.

And there's more to come.

Marion tells me that sometimes, when a customer complains about the gravy or soup being cold, a quick check reveals that the hot section of the counter has been switched off by unseen hands. Then, on at least a couple of occasions almost every week, usually when the dining room staff are sitting around the table closest to the counter, the cash register inexplicably pings open. The cash tray inside shoots forward, and then as it comes to a sudden halt, it chucks most of the coins up into the air and down onto the dining room floor, and once the coins have been ejected, the tray somehow shoots back into the cash register.

What a load of old cobblers! She's just trying to scare me, but it won't work.

So, once the team has departed, I know I'll be the only person hanging around the place until the night staff start arriving around midnight, and then when they've been fed, the only person I'll be seeing is the night porter when he pops in to check that I'm OK. That doesn't bother me, because I'm already aware that when the porter heads my way, I'll hear his footsteps as he marches up the main corridor, and then he'll start whistling as he approaches the kitchen entrance, so I won't get the fright of my life when I suddenly come face-to-face with him.

Just before midnight I hear voices approaching, so I stroll across the corridor with a tray of freshly cooked chips. For no reason whatsoever, I glance to towards the beverage section and I come very close to being incontinent. About a dozen disposable cups suddenly eject from the dispenser one at a time, before landing and rolling off in different directions on the floor, and I'm still trying to catch my breath when my first diner arrives.

"Hi, it's nice to see you," says Sister Nicholson. "Are you OK? You look like you've just seen a ghost."

"Yeah, I'm fine. It's just been a long day and I wasn't expecting to be working a nineteen hour shift," I reply as she drags her supper along the tray slide towards the beverage section, where she spots the new carpet of disposable cups.

"Oh dear. I see you're not on your own either, but there's no need to worry, as she's one of our night sisters who left us a few years ago. She's lovely and she won't do you any harm. I'll see you later," she smiles before looking up to the ceiling and spitting out a totally unexpected parting shot.

"Martha! For crying out loud! Can't you find something else to do up there? You've got an eternity to sort yourself out, so why on earth do you keep coming back down here every night and start buggering about while we're having our supper. Just clear off and find somebody else to annoy."

So, with everybody fed and watered, I know I won't be seeing anyone else until my colleagues start arriving in the morning, so I decide to take a bit of a break before starting on the twelve gallons of porridge my friends will need for shipping out to the wards for breakfast.

In the far corner of the kitchen, we have a line of four boiling pans, each resembling a giant egg cup with a lid on top. They're used for cooking things like potatoes, vegetables, soups and gravy, and each pan is connected to a steam pipe which runs between the boiler house and the kitchen. I use one of them for making the porridge, and once it's ready, I decant it into several huge saucepans and position them side by side on top of the gas stove to keep the porridge warm until the morning shift arrive at 7am, when they transfer it into food trolleys ready for the hospital porters to collect for delivery to the wards.

I refill the giant egg cup with water before adding a load of washing up liquid and heating it up ready to be cleaned. It's a somewhat difficult process, because the pan is so big that four people could comfortably stand together inside it. This means I have to lean over the edge of the pan and stretch down as far as possible in order to scrape the porridge from the bottom and then give the pan a good clean. If I'm not careful, I could easily end up falling head first into the pan, so as it has a capacity of about forty gallons, I'm glad I'm a decent swimmer.

I don't suppose you've ever given a thought to the immense dangers a top chef has to face every day of his working life, have you?

I've only just managed to position myself very precariously over the edge of the boiling pan, with my head almost touching the water below, when I suddenly get the feeling that somebody or something is silently approaching from behind. I almost jump out of my skin when, before I even have the chance to lift my head to take a sideways glance, an outstretched arm grabs my shoulder. The bout of incontinence starts to rear it ugly head once more as a croaky voice calls out.

"Are you OK, Eric? I just thought I'd check if everyth............"

I missed the last bit, due to my shooting head first into the boiling pan. Luckily I'd cooled the water down only a couple of minutes ago, but as I sink towards the bottom, a pair of bony hands grab me by the ankles and start pulling me out. As I finally reach the surface and take a most welcome breath of fresh air, I come face to face with Colin, the night porter.

"What the flippin' heck were you thinking?" or words to that effect, I enquire. "I thought the porters were supposed to whistle when they get anywhere near the kitchen during the night."

"We are, but I haven't got me teeth in, so I can't whistle," comes the reply.

I notice he's also wearing what we call 'brothel creepers', namely shoes with such a soft sole, they never make a sound as you walk.

"For the love of God! I've just had one run-in tonight with a night sister who pegged out years ago, and then you decide to creep up on me."

"Oh, Martha's back again is she?"

What a place to be working in! I'm just glad tomorrow's my day off!

During the next year or so I work a few night shifts, but apart from the occasional dining room chair deciding to do the Cha Cha at three o'clock in the morning, and a couple of salt and pepper pots committing suicide by doing a bit of ski jumping over the edge of a table, there are no further incidents to report.

I get on really well with the night staff, and just before Christmas I'm pleased to hear the night sisters have offered to run the bar for us when we have a party that Bill Beatson has organised. Apparently, the Sheffield Health Authority's senior management team holds numerous routine meetings at Lodge Moor during the year. Bill purchases plenty of wine for the meetings, but after parking a couple of bottled on each table, he only replenishes them each time one emptied. The scam works a treat, as numerous bottles always remain unopened, so the boss simply stashes them away for the catering staff Christmas party. As we're still in the early 1970's, we don't worry too much about drink-driving. By now I'm residing in Penistone, so as I head to the hospital for this year's party, I decide to take a detour to visit Ma and Pa in their new home in Ecclesfield.

Since the bit of a blip I had a while ago, I haven't touched a single drop of alcohol, but as I've no wish to offend Ma, I gratefully accept the couple of cans of Newcastle Brown she pours out for me. I arrive at the party about an hour or so later, to be met by one of the volunteer barmaids who asks what I'd like to drink. I glance across the array of booze before suggesting that the bottles of red wine on the edge of the table look very nice. They turn out to be Sweet Martini, and as I manage to get down the first glass in one gulp, I suggest she pours the next one into a half pint beer glass. That does the trick, so I decide to stick with the Martini for the rest of the evening.

For some reason I have no recollection of the party, but according to Jim I got through two bottles of Martini before we headed off to Maurice's house with several other party goers. The house stands just outside the gates at the bottom of the hospital drive, and Jim tells me that as we strolled down the drive, I overheard somebody mention that an older members of the Royal Family enjoys the odd Gin and Dubonnet. As a non-drinker for some time now I've no idea what that is, let alone what it tastes like, but if it's good enough for them, it'll do for me, although I very much doubt I got through a couple of pints of the stuff as Jim suggests.

I'm fully aware that my mate sometimes exaggerates things, so I know everything he tells me is just a load of baloney. Nobody could get through that little lot in a single evening, could they?

I've no idea how I got home, and due to the unexpectedly loud drumbeat going off inside my head when I wake up I don't actually care, although there's a hand written note on the kitchen table telling me that Jim will be picking me up for work this morning, as my Vauxhall Viva is still in the hospital car park. I just hope he doesn't arrive too early. Then just after sunrise I decide now would be a good time to do a bit of pleading with 'Him Upstairs', because if he's ever thought about having me back up there anytime soon, now might be a good time and then I won't have to put up with this blinding headache any longer than necessary.

Whilst I'm having a word, it occurs to me that it might be a good idea to apologise for the bit of a relapse I seem to be going through. I'm not supposed to be getting blathered these days, but perhaps I could put most of the blame onto Ma and Pa on this occasion, due to the cans of Newcastle Brown they forced down my throat, and the rest of the blame onto the night sisters for unlimited amount of Sweet Martini they handed over earlier. I can't put any blame onto Maurice for all the Gin and Dubonnets I managed to get through, because I was smashed out of my stupid skull before I even got to his front door.

It comes a quite a surprise when completely out of the blue, the boss tells me I'll be the next Kitchen Superintendent when Maurice finally calls it a day. That's still some time away, so in the meantime Bill offers to show me everything he does in managing the catering services. I'm not expecting him to offer me the Head Chef job down the hill at King Edward's Hospital a few weeks later, but of course I'm more than happy to accept, especially as my mate Jim manages the catering services there. Unfortunately they're in a bit of a mess right now, due to the departing chef recently being caught out by suggesting something he shouldn't to a plain clothes copper in one of the Weston Park public toilets.

Apparently, when the rest of the staff heard the news, the other male chefs refused to use the same changing room as the offender, and that's probably why he's already departed without working his notice period. It's only a matter of days before I arrive to start supervising the preparation and cooking of meals for loads of patients suffering from severe orthopaedic problems, and it doesn't take long for me, Jim and the team to get the service back onto its feet.

As King Ted's is a relatively small hospital, I soon get to know most people who work here. It's not long before I become friends with one of the orthopaedic doctors, Romane Zgabronski, and he invites me to join him for a couple of games of tennis on the hospital's tennis court. He's a good player and as my only experience was the few games I played during my final term at school, he runs me into the ground every time we play. Fortunately, Romane is also a decent coach, so he gives me a great deal of advice, and it doesn't take long for me to improve my game. That results in us having many extremely competitive battles on the court.

As you'd expect by now, something just has to go wrong, and it most certainly does when I discover that my hands and fingers have become infected with about two dozen warts, each one complete with a black crusty head. Playing tennis immediately becomes almost impossible, as the pain is absolutely excruciating when I'm squeezing the racket handle, but I'm more concerned about my being a chef and what damage I could do to the patient's food if I'm not careful.

A visit to my GP suggests I could be out of action on both the tennis court and in the kitchen for quite some time, as he can't get me an appointment with the skin specialist at the Hallamshire Hospital for six weeks. Luckily my tennis partner is able to pull a few strings, so now I have an appointment for tomorrow afternoon.

Perhaps that might not be as lucky as I think it is!

As I head out of the lift several floors up at the Hallamshire Hospital, I notice a row of eight chairs lined up side by side along the corridor wall outside the consultation room, and the receptionist invites me to take the empty seat at the end of the line. Within three minutes of parking myself on the chair, I'm already wishing that the ninth patient, who is now standing by my left shoulder, had arrived just before I did, and then I could creep back out unnoticed. The seven patients to my right are sitting in total silence and staring blankly across the corridor towards the reception desk. A few moments pass before all eight of us almost jump out of our seats, when a gut-wrenching scream unexpectedly emits from the consultation room. We all remain silent, but with a somewhat worryingly puzzled look on each of our faces, but that changes when a young lady shoots straight out of the consultation room and past the reception desk towards the lift, where she immediately starts pressing her finger repeatedly on the button to summon the lift to this floor.

The patient sitting closest to the consultation room, looks somewhat puzzled for a moment, but then she grabs her handbag and almost sprints off to the lift. The rest of us take a quick glance at each other before shuffling one seat along, which eventually leaves the chair to my left vacant for the guy to my right. I'm not sure whether or not he'll take it, as right now he appears to be reconsidering the need for him to see the doctor.

A couple of minutes go by before the man who is now sitting closest to the consultation room door is called in, so he stands up and raises his eyebrows along the line of fellow patients to indicate his apprehension at the thought of going inside. He's a well-built bloke, probably in his early thirties, so no doubt whatever is about to happen in there, he'll be fine.

Oh really?

I think this guy must be from Switzerland, because shortly after he goes into the room we suddenly hear him yodelling at a pitch and a volume you simply couldn't imagine. Even the receptionist looks stunned, but I'm not really surprised especially when the guy sitting immediately to my right, turns to wish me good luck and tells me there's absolutely no way he's going into the torture chamber. By now the lift but be getting dizzy with all this constant button thumping.

A small exodus of patients takes place, and now there are only two ladies left before it's my turn to head into the torture chamber. The lady sitting next to me suggests she'd rather have a baby than go into the consultation room, so I jokingly suggest that she quickly removes her underwear and then lays flat on her back across the row of chairs, and hopefully I'll still have the time to fulfil her wishes. The look on her face suggests she's actually considering the offer, but just then the lady at the front of the queue is called in, so my new friend suggests maybe some other time as she makes an early exit.

I assume she's joking of course, but my ego suggests otherwise!

The lady now in the consultation room decides to depart only seconds after going in, but even after all that's been going on, I decide to hang around.

I've always known I'm a bit thick, but it's never crossed my mind I could be as stupid as this!

I take a deep breath as I head in to be greeted by a couple of nurses, one of whom instructs me to lay the palms of my hands flat onto the desk and spread my fingers out as much as possible. The majority of warts are stuck on the back of my hands and fingers, with only four on my palms. Apparently, one of the nurses will firmly press down on my wrists to hold my hands in position, whilst the other will be tasked with freezing the warts. I've no idea what this all means, so I just nod as I take a seat and plonk my hands onto the top of the desk.

The 'freezing' nurse suggests it will help if I scream whenever the pain becomes unbearable, so once we're all in position, she removes the top from a thermos flask, before dipping a cotton bud into what turns out to be a couple of pints of liquid nitrogen. Now I'm ordered to take another deep breath, just before the cotton bud is pressed firmly onto the head of the first wart.

Up to this point in time, I had no idea that liquid nitrogen is so cold that when it's forced onto your skin, the pain is indescribable as it shoots straight up your arm and into your brain.

I wouldn't have thought that'd be a problem for me, as I don't have a brain, and right now I wish that was actually the case.

My pride simply won't let me scream, so I just clench my teeth and count the number of times this sick nurse rams the cotton bud into the nitrogen and onto my skin. On the count of twenty four, I feel as though my eyes are about to pop out and my head is about to explode.

I can now understand why one of my fellow patients would have preferred to have a baby, rather than go through this degree of pain, and I think I would have also taken that option if it was offered.

Just as I think it's all over, I notice a couple of dozen huge blisters almost covering my hands and fingers, each one with a crusty black head on top. I'm told to soak my hands and fingers in warm water for at least thirty minutes each day, and when the black heads appear to have softened-up and the blisters are ready to burst, I need to gently rub the side of a matchbox over them until they finally pop. Then, I must carefully peel the skin away and gently apply warm salted water over the wound.

So my ordeal is finally over, but then as I lift myself up from the chair I notice the room is becoming very hazy and the stationery cupboard behind the desk appears to be moving around. Then without warning the lights go out.

I wake up to find myself back in the chair and being told that if I'd screamed out during my torture session, I probably wouldn't have passed out, so now I'm advised to take the lift down to the ground floor and have a calming mug of tea in the WRVS cafe before heading home. That sounds like good advice but unfortunately, I haven't taken into account how sore my fingers are going to be right now, so I get another very painful shock when I press the ground floor button inside the lift. I get another one a couple of minutes later, when I arrive at the service counter in the cafe and order a mug of tea and attempt to shove my hand into my pocket to retrieve some cash.

Try as I might, I simply can't force my fingers far enough inside my pocket, so now there appears to be only one way out of this. Rather embarrassingly, I show the service assistant my hands and fingers and ask if she'd mind sticking her hand down into my trouser pocket and grab hold of my loose change, and for an instant I think she's about to call the police. Fortunately, she changes her mind at the last moment, and whilst I'm somewhat relieved, I can't help feeling just a wee bit guilty in accepting a free mug of tea from a charity.

A month goes by before the tennis matches resume, and in the meantime I eventually get used to wearing surgical gloves when handling food. All of this makes the job somewhat less enjoyable for a while, and it gets even worse one Friday morning when the hospital matron pops her head round the kitchen door and asks me to step into the main corridor.

She points to a round plastic tub standing on the floor of the corridor which leads to the wards. She tells me that the guy who delivers the meat to the catering department has left a tub, with a joint of pork in it, so I need to transfer it into the kitchen refrigerator and then contact the supplier to let them know their driver made a careless mistake and to ask them to make sure it doesn't happen again. I assure her that we weren't expecting a meat delivery this morning, but she doesn't appear to be interested as she picks up the tub and leads me into her office so I can call the supplier. Then she carefully places the tub of meat onto the floor underneath her desk, before handing the phone to me.

The supplier appears to be as confused as I am, but whilst we're trying to figure out exactly what's happened, the operating theatre charge nurse appears. He tells matron that a kneecap removed from a patient's leg about twenty minutes ago, has somehow disappeared from the main corridor whilst waiting collection and transfer to another hospital to undergo a detailed examination. I decide not to hang around any longer, as the look in matron's eye suggests the charge nurse is about to receive the biggest rollocking he's ever had, but as I head back to the kitchen, I can't help thinking that if it had been left to matron, this coming Sunday's roast pork lunch might not have been exactly what the patients were expecting.

That was close, don't you think?

One morning Jim tells me that Bill Beatson urgently needs to talk to me, and will be arriving within the hour. This is a bit worrying, as the bloke who oversees the catering at several hospitals doesn't make a habit of driving anywhere unless he really needs to. I've hardly seen Bill since I left Lodge Moor, so I'm relieved when he greets me with a firm handshake and then slaps his arm across my shoulders as he leads me into Jim's office. He tells me they need a head chef at Nether Edge Hospital, so he wants to know if I'd like the job. He reminds me that he wants to see me moving up the ladder, and as Maurice still hasn't called it a day, the job at Nether Edge is mine if I want it, and it'll be the last one I have before moving into management. Meanwhile, the interviews are on Friday and I'll be starting next Monday, so right now I'm just a bit confused.

"Sorry Bill," I reply. "I'm interested, but on the one hand I have to be interviewed, whilst on the other you tell me the job's mine. Are there any other applicants?"

"Yes, of course there are," confirms Bill "There are two more applicants, but they're just a couple of ringers, and are only there to make up the numbers.

"How can you be so sure?" I enquire.

"That's easy. They both work for me in different hospitals, but neither of them has the necessary skills or experience. They know they won't get the job, but they're happy to attend to get the interview experience. So, on that basis, if you want the job, it's yours for the taking and the interview is no more than a formality. I can even tell you what you'll be asked during the interview, so you can get yourself prepared well in advance. Meanwhile, I'll see you on Friday.

Well that's that sorted then!

I have three assistant head chefs in my corner at Nether Edge Hospital, namely Fred, George and Tom, and it's Fred who gives me the rundown over a mug of coffee in my office.

Please note, that's not just any old office, it's My Office, but I promise not to let it go to my head.

Fred tells me he's been here for more years than he cares to remember, and he's just running down the clock to retirement. He says he'll do whatever I need him to do and he'll cover my back whenever necessary, so that sounds good to me.

According to him, George is a bit of a dodgy character, so I'll need to keep an eye on him. Everybody knows he's a 'tea leaf' but after perfecting his pilfering skills over the last twenty years or so, he's never been caught in the act, although he's been pretty close on several occasions. Apparently George is ferried around by his wife, and she drops him off at the hospital entrance every morning on her way to work, and that means he clocks in at 6am, a full hour before the start of his shift.

It's also a well known fact that when he arrives each morning, he has a habit of clocking in any and all colleagues rostered to start at the same time as him, so all the clock-cards suggest that the entire shift arrives together sixty minutes before they need to, although the catering manager doesn't appear to have noticed what's happening. The good news is that George is due to retire soon, but of course it could be even sooner if he gets caught out thieving or fiddling the clock cards in the meantime.

My third assistant head chef is Tom, who is in his mid-thirties and is obsessed with motorbikes, especially the BMW 950RS he owns. Apparently, he isn't a particularly good chef, and it doesn't help that he spends half his working day chatting-up any female members of staff who give him the slightest hint of being interested in listening.

Finally, there's a member of staff right at the very top of Fred's hit list, and that's Jerry the union shop steward. He's a slimy geezer who takes great pleasure in humiliating managers, supervisors and anyone else he considers to be fair game, so I need to make sure she's on my watch list as well.

I've only been at Nether Edge for a fortnight, when manageress Kath heads into the kitchen accompanied by the hospital security officer and two policemen. Apparently, one of the assistant cooks had asked if she could start an hour earlier than normal this morning, due to having doctor's appointment later in the day, and on entering the kitchen she spotted George heading into the changing room with a load of stuff such as butter, boiled ham, sausages and rashers of bacon. She reported it to Kate, who then notified the security officer and he called the cops.

The security officer asks if I'm aware of stuff going missing occasionally, so I tell him I was warned about such things on my first day here, but I haven't personally witnessed anything to date. One of the policemen then decides search through all the lockers in the changing room, so he'll need all the keys. It then crosses my mind that this could well be George's day of reckoning.

As we stride toward the changing room, I notice George isn't in the line-up, but then I see him stepping out of the boss's empty office. He gathers speed as he heads in our direction, and then he calls out to Kath.

"Oh there you are," he says with a hint of fake surprise. "I just popped into your office to let you know that all the men's lockers appear to have been broken into for some reason," he lies.

Sure enough, as we enter the changing room we can see that every single locker door has been forced open, and there are several small broken padlocks scattered across the floor. The policemen start to check the inside of each locker, and it's no great surprise when they find several items as described by the assistant cook, inside every single one, including George's. He'd clearly rumbled what was happening, so he's well and truly covered his tracks. The coppers have absolutely no doubt what's happened and exactly who the culprit is, but as the evidence is only circumstantial, that's the end of the matter.

Kath takes on a new job shortly after George's near miss, and my old pal Jim takes over. On his first morning in his new role, he gets everybody together to introduce himself, and he makes sure they all know about our working relationship during our apprenticeship at Cole Brothers, and more recently at King Edward VII Hospital. He's smiling contentedly when he tells us his main interests are horse riding and horse racing, but his smile becomes even wider when he glances in my direction and tells everyone his pet hate is mushrooms.

The management carousel gets back into action yet again when Bill Beatson announces his retirement, so now we also have a new District Catering Manager by the name of Tony Elms, who tells me he's already been advised by several members of the health authority to get me into a management as soon as possible. That's good to hear, so the old ego goes up a notch or two.

Our kitchen storekeeper Harry is another guy close to retirement. He's a regular churchgoer and a real gentleman, and we soon become good buddies. Late one Friday evening, He calls me at home to tell me he's been taken ill, and won't be able to work on Saturday. He had a heart attack a few years ago, so as he lives alone, I tell him I'll drive to his house and stay for the night to make sure he's OK. When I arrive, Harry is laying on the sofa, as he simply doesn't have the strength to climb the stairs to go to bed. I make sure he's comfortable and I assure him I'll be sleeping in the armchair next to the sofa, so I'll be there all night if he needs me. By now it's turned midnight, and I know Jim will have been in the land of nod for at least a couple of hours, but I think it best for me to phone him to let him know the situation, and he suggests I take the weekend off to look after my new friend.

By six thirty on Monday morning Harry is already in the kitchen making a cup of tea. He tells me he's feeling much better, but promises to take it easy for the rest of the day, so I decide to go to work on the proviso that he calls me if his condition worsens during the day. I call Jim at home to let him know I'll be making sure Harry has all he needs before I set off, so I'll be arriving at Nether Edge a couple of hours later than planned. When I stroll in just before ten, Jim calls me into his office, where I unexpectedly come face to face with Mr Elms and the Jerry shop steward. No doubt there's trouble ahead, but for some reason Jim and Mr Elms don't look too bothered about it. Mr Elms explains that he received a call from the union man at eight o'clock this morning, to report me for fiddling the clock machine, and that Jerry is now about to explain what happened. The look in his eyes suggests he's going to get a great deal of pleasure from this little stunt.

Jerry explains that, at the end of his shift on Sunday afternoon, and for reasons he doesn't go into, he decided to check my clock card. He noticed I'd clocked in at 7am and clocked out at 3.30pm on both Saturday and Sunday, but I didn't actually turn up for work on either day. He then presented the clock card to his close ally, cleaning supervisor Pam, and then she called several staff together for them to witness my wrongdoing. He clearly smells victory, as there's no doubt whatsoever I fiddled the clock machine in order to be paid time and a half on Saturday and double time on Sunday for work I didn't do, and that's a sackable offence.

The idiot even mentions that as me and Jim are known to be close friends, he wouldn't trust him to deal with the matter appropriately, so he decided to keep the clock card and call in Mr Elms. Finally, the steward removes the clock card from his wallet and slams it onto Jim's desk for all to see, before folding his huge fat arms across his chest and shuffling back contentedly in the chair. Jim looks across his desk towards me, with what I can only describe as a self-congratulatory smirk, as Mr Elms asks me to respond to this very serious allegation, which if correct could result in my downfall. I go into some detail regarding Harry's bout of ill health and my subsequent telephone conversation with Jim, which resulted in our agreeing that I wouldn't be attending for duty throughout the weekend.

Once my defence statement has been made, Jim goes on to explain that, as it's the first day of the week, his first task is to check all the clock cards from the previous week, and then to prepare the pay analysis report for the payroll manager. He pulls out a copy of the report from a file and lays it on the desk for all to see, before pointing out that in view of our telephone conversation on Friday evening, the pay analysis report clearly shows I was not on duty during the weekend as was previously planned, so no offence has been committed. For some reason, the union rep isn't looking quite as confident as he was just a couple of minutes ago, and he looks even less pleased when Mr Elms calls the payroll manager and asks him to pop over with his own copy of the pay analysis report, just so the steward is left in no doubt he just made one almighty cock-up.

Mr Elms receives a grovelling apology, but as Jerry crawls out of the office he's instructed to make a personal apology to me for bringing my honesty and integrity into question, and to Jim for doubting his professional integrity. Once that's done, Mr Elms calls the entire catering team together to explain what's happened and why the shop steward will have to tread very carefully in future, should he ever decide to slag us off again. Then when they've been brought up to speed Jerry is instructed to accompany George to the office, where he's about to be disciplined for clocking me in and out on Saturday and Sunday without my knowledge.

A few days later, George steps onto the carousel and heads into retirement. He doesn't seem to be particularly bothered about departing earlier than expected, and I feel somewhat humbled when he apologises to me for fiddling the clock machine, even though he's always known it's not something I would ever ask him to or anyone else to do.

I just happen to be accompanying him to the clock machine as he heads home after his final shift, and I'm quite taken aback when he offers to bring me up to speed on his light-fingered shenanigans.

He always dresses quite elegantly, and on this occasion he's well kitted out in a navy blue suit, white shirt and floral tie, all topped off with a smart trilby hat. His pilfering is legendary, so I ask him how he's managed to continue for so long without ever being caught. He simply smiles and shakes his head.

"Do you think I'm nicking anything right now?"

"Of course not," I reply. "I've always assumed that, as you clock everybody in an hour before they actually arrive, you go straight into the kitchen, pick up whatever stuff you're going to nick, and then head back outside to the wife's car and lob it all onto the back seat as she drives off."

He just smiles and shakes his head, before removing his trilby to reveal several slices of boiled ham, all wrapped in cling-film and sellotaped to the inside of the hat. Then he pulls out the posh handkerchief from the top pocket of his jacket, and opens it up to reveal four tightly wrapped, buttered cream crackers. A frozen cod fillet wrapped in tin foil then appears from each of his jacket pockets, and then four rashers of bacon and four pork sausages appear from his trouser pockets. Finally, when he opens the newspaper he's been holding under his arm, four slices of roast beef drop out from between pages 15 and 16.

"The wife meets me at the bottom-end of the road, and I unload everything into her shopping bag before we drive off home. You're the only one who knows how it's done, so don't tell anybody otherwise they'll all be at it."

I just can't believe what I just witnessed, as we shake hands for the last time, and it another couple of hours before I realise I should have taken the 'swag' from him, but he waltzed off with the lot.

Chapter Ten

Music To My Ears

I'm quite surprised to find I get on very well with my other assistant head chef at Nether Edge Hospital. I guess it helps that Tim enjoys a self-deprecating sense of humour similar to my own. During one of our conversations, I mention my childhood love of cycle speedway racing and going to Sheffield Speedway matches at the Owlerton Stadium. I'm absolutely overjoyed, when he invites me to join him on his trip to Wembley to see the World Speedway Final. I've never been on a BMW RS500 before, and it turns out to be one of the greatest thrills I've ever experienced.

Ove Fundin won the World Championship by the way, but there's no need to start Googling again.

A few months later, Tom and his wife are due to take a holiday in the South of France, but due to some problem or other on her side of the family, she decides not to go with him, and I just can't believe my luck when he invites to go with him instead. I think his wife is pleased with the arrangement, as she knows he'll keep out of trouble if I'm with him. He decides to rethink the holiday plans, so instead of heading to the South of France via Dover, Calais and the French Autoroute down to Mandelieu la Napoule near Nice, we'll now be heading to Marrakesh and Casablanca in Morocco, via Plymouth, Santander and Tangier. Then we'll head back to southern Spain and eventually into the South of France to Mandelieu La Napoule, not far from Nice. Brilliant!

I haven't been involved in drawing up the travel plan, so you can be sure nothing could possibly go wrong this time.

We haven't even reached the M1 turn-off for Nottingham when the motorbike gears start playing up, so we coast into the nearest service station so Tom can have yet another rethink. After giving the matter some consideration and having a close look at his Michelin Roadmap, he decides to take us on a slow ride to Taunton in Somerset for an overnight hotel stay, and then we'll catch the ferry from Plymouth tomorrow morning. He doesn't think it's a good idea to attempt the drive through Spain, and he doesn't want to risk breaking down in Morocco, so when the ferry docks in Santander, we'll be heading over the Pyrenees and then straight through France to Mandelieu. Then he'll try to find a garage where he can take the bike to be repaired.

I'm amazed the bike makes it to Mandelieu, but it does, so we have a couple of days of rest and relaxation before Tom starts to think about the repairs. He spends an entire morning in the blazing sun, examining all sorts of bits and pieces on the bike, and eventually figures out that it needs a new a new clutch-plate, whatever that is. The nearest BMW spare parts centre is in Cannes, so Tom decides that we should spend the rest of this week in Mandelieu, and then head to Cannes. Where he hopes to find somewhere he can buy a new clutch plate for him to replace the knackered one before we drive back to the Autoroute and head north towards Calais and home.

So, with a new plan firmly in place, we go for a walk along the sea front, pick up a couple of cans of beer and then perch on top of a wall on the coast road and have a drink, before strolling back to the campsite. We then have a three-hour sunbathing session on the beach, and after a very welcome and cooling shower, we get into our best casual togs and head to the campsite bar. It's now early evening and we've had the first relaxing day of our holiday, but when he orders the first couple of drinks, Tom realises he left his money belt on the wall where we perched early this afternoon. Not only that, his passport, return ferry ticket, traveller's cheques and cash were all secured inside the belt pockets, so now we have another problem to sort out. What a trip this is turning out to be. We'd have been better off just going to Mablethorpe for a long weekend!

With very little cash and few traveller's cheques, I'm not much help, so we hatch yet another plan. We're going to start the long journey home tomorrow, calling into Cannes to see if we can get hold of a clutch-plate, and then we'll find the British Embassy so we can get a replacement passport for Tom. It turns out to be very easy to locate the BMW dealer in Cannes, but Tom tells me I'll have to do all the talking, because even though he's been to this part of the world many times, he's never bothered to learn the language. I explain that I only did French at school and ended up with a CSE Grade 2, so that won't do much good, but he thinks I'll do just fine.

I wouldn't have a problem if I had to ask a French citizen what the time, and I could also ask them their name and tell them to open the window but ordering a clutch-plate for a BMW 950RS motor bike is on a completely different level.

So, let's just move on, and please read the rest of this bit without picking me up on the spelling. OK?

"Bonjour Monsieur. Je suis Anglaise et je ne parlez pas le Francais. Parlez vous l'Anglaise?"

OK so far?

"Non, mon ami," comes the expected reply.

"OK. Avez vous un plait de clutch pour un BMW motorcycle neuf, cinq, zero RS series?"

"Uh?"

"OK. Le BMW gears est knackered."

"Uh?"

It's no more than a fluke that as I look up to heaven for some kind of inspiration, I notice what looks like a motorcycle maintenance manual on the shelf behind the counter, so I point my index finger towards it and almost before it's placed onto the counter, Tom is flicking through the pages. I could have stood at the counter for the next thousand years, but I would never have figured out that I should be asking for 'un disque d'embrayage.

This all occurred over forty years ago, but you'll notice I can still remember what the bloody thing was called. Impressed or what?

Tom manages to get a replacement passport via the embassy, but he still has no cash, so once he manages to fit the clutch plate, we're soon get back onto the Autoroute and are heading home, albeit at the pace of a snail with a broken leg.

Yes, of course I know they don't have legs. I'm just doing my best to explain.

It takes us three days to drive up the Autoroute, and as we're completely skint by now we're in no position to pay for accommodation. Each night we park the motorbike in a rest area, roll out the tent onto the grass and sleep underneath it. Then as we finally close in on Paris, Tom takes another look at the Michelin map and spots somewhere by the name of Periferique, which looks as though it's located about halfway between Paris and Calais, so all we have to do now is watch out for the sign to take us there.

A few minutes later, we're still biking along what appears to be an endless dual carriageway. I can see the Eiffel Tower in the distance to my right, so it shouldn't be long now before we spot the sign to take us to Periferique. We continue for quite a few more miles, or rather kilometres as we're now in Paris, and I notice the Eiffel Tower is now in the distance behind me to the left. A few kilometres further and the tower appears once more to my right, so that suggests we're right back where we started almost an hour ago. Tom carries on regardless, but now I'm noticing buildings we've already passed once or twice before, so as we approach the forecourt of the English pub I already seem to know pretty well, I shout into his ear to tell him to pull in.

It's been a week since we had a wash or a shower, and we haven't changed our underwear in all that time either, so perhaps we shouldn't be surprised at the looks we get from the locals as we stroll up to the bar to be greeted by the lovely landlady, who apparently comes from Cornwall. I explain we've been on the carriageway for about three hours and have passed the Eiffel Tower at least twice, but we can't find a single signpost for Periferique, a place somewhere between Paris and Calais. Upon hearing of our problem, the landlady simply starts howling with laughter as Tom opens the map to show her.

"Typical Brits," she smirks. "It looks as though Michelin didn't have any space on the map to type in 'Periferique', other than between the words 'Paris' and 'Calais'. Periferique isn't a place, you daft buggers, it's the ring road that goes around Paris, and that's why you keep seeing the Eiffel Tower. That's the funniest thing I've heard around here for ages, so as you've cheered me up no end, you can have a pint on me before you hit the road again," she laughs.

We finally reach Calais and hop onto the ferry, and a few hours later we're closing in on London. Alas, the bike breathes its last in the Blackwall Tunnel somewhere in south London, but the AA turn up to take us back to Sheffield. I haven't given much thought as to just how tired I am by the time I arrive home, but having spent almost a week on the road and sleeping in the open air, I'm more concerned about the awful stink emanating from my flesh. In fact my entire body is so filthy, I have to take three consecutive showers before I feel clean enough to finally drag myself to bed and a most welcome twelve hours sleep.

And it's not quite over yet!

A few days after getting back to some kind of normality, I start itching and scratching, and I can also see tiny little blobs beneath my skin which appear to move up and down my arms and legs as I scratch. It turns out to be scabies, which comes as a surprise to the GP, because he would only expect someone who lives on the street or in very unhygienic conditions to suffer from it. When he tells me the condition is contagious, it gives me the opportunity to suggest I must have picked it up from somebody I recently came into contact with, so I'll need to be a bit more careful in the future. In the meantime, I think I may have forgotten to mention it to the Staff Health Sister at Nether Edge Hospital, so nobody gets to know about it.

Nevertheless, everything clears up within a month or so, and I'm delighted when my good friend Harry invites me to join him in the audience at a Barbershop Singing show at Sheffield University. I haven't the faintest idea what that is, although I very much doubt it'll have anything to do with rock and roll, the sounds of the sixties or the country and western songs I love so much. Nevertheless, I accept Harry's kind invitation, although I think I'll probably feel just a wee bit out of place, as I'm sure the singers will be about a hundred years old and singing songs from the last couple of world wars.

Just how wrong can you be?

When we arrive, the place is already buzzing with people of all ages, and it seems that with every couple of steps we take, we're being welcomed by someone dressed immaculately in their stage outfits. Most of the guys we meet are members of Sheffield's own Hallmark of Harmony Barbershop Chorus, and several appear to be around my age, whilst others look as though they could be Harry's grandpa.

We're also introduced to the headline act, a quartet from Boston USA, and that's not something you'd expect anywhere else. When the show starts I'm amazed at the perfect harmonies of the American quartet, each of whom is dressed as a character from the Wizard of Oz. I'll never forget the bass-singing lion, and I'm certain that if a pint of Guinness could sing, it would sound just like this guy.

The two dozen singers who make up the Hallmark of Harmony chorus belt out a number of popular songs such as Alexander's Ragtime Band and I'll Take You Home Kathleen, and I'm completely in awe for the next three hours.

Now another of my infamous decisions is about to be made.

On our way out at the end of the show, the members of the local Hallmark of Harmony chorus line-up to thank everyone in the audience for coming. When one of them asks what I thought of the show, I assure him I've never enjoyed an evening so much. I'm completely taken aback when he asks if I'd like to come along to the Tuesday evening rehearsal evening at the United Reform Church Hall in Gleadless, with a view to joining the chorus. The only singing I've done so far, was when me and Cliff used to stand on the chairs and table in the cellar kitchen at Parkwood Springs. As far as I know, my incredible skills in the miming of Gene Pitney songs, wouldn't suggest in any shape or form, that I'd be any good at Barbershop singing. Having said that, there's absolutely no way I can turn down the invitation.

I arrive at the church hall just as the entire chorus is beginning to line up on the 3-tier platform known as a riser. Then, once they're all in position, Musical Director John Grant instructs everyone to take a deep breath before belting out the first song. Even though there are only a couple of dozen guys in the chorus the sound is amazing, and I'm completely mesmerised by what I hear, and I find myself in another world for the next hour. Then during a short break in the rehearsal, John comes over to offer me a warm welcome. He recalls seeing me at the recent show, and asks my name and whether I would be interested in joining the chorus. I give him my name, but I have to tell him that I've never done any singing, and even if I had, there's just no way I could sing to the same standard as these guys. John appears to have a different opinion, and suggests I should give it a try in a private room to the rear of the hall.

Without thinking, I accept the invitation, so he asks his assistant director Tony to join us as we head into the room. John asks if I've ever heard of the song I'll Take You Home Kathleen, and his eyes light up when I tell him not only have I heard of the song, we also have a Slim Whitman recording of it. With that said, he suggests that he and Tony sing the first line of the song, and then I sing it once they've finished. I'm utterly stunned a minute later, when John smiles and shakes my hand and tells me I'll be in the lead section. In less than five minutes, I find myself being introduced to the rest of the chorus, who welcome me with a rendition of another song adopted by Barbershop singers, namely 'You're As Welcome As The Flowers In May'. Once I've dried the flood of tears from my cheeks, I head back to my seat for the remainder of the rehearsal.

What an evening that's turned out to be!

Looking back, I loved my childhood, especially growing up in Parkwood Springs, and I particularly enjoyed my time as an apprentice chef at Cole Brothers, but being a member of the Hallmark of Harmony Barbershop Chorus is on a completely different level. Not only are the rehearsals the highlight of my week, but the members are also unbelievably friendly and in possession of a sense of humour on a par with my own.

We regularly have what are known as 'sing-outs' in various locations, and I particularly enjoy it when we're doing a show for the residents in care homes, especially one evening when the entire audience is brought to its knees with laughter. By now the number of members in the chorus is more than thirty, and we're all lined up in the communal lounge, belting out popular songs from many years ago, and the audience is absolutely loving every minute. The compere of our shows Ernest, does a brief stand-up comedy routine after every two or three songs, and as he simply can't bring himself to swearing or saying anything that might be considered to be offensive to anyone, his act is similar to the one Max Miller was famous for back in the 1940's. Ernest is a really good stand-up comedian, and when he gets to the punch-line of one particular gag, an elderly lady sitting in a front row chair calls to one of the carers to let her know she's about to be incontinent. The carer takes the lady by the arm and attempts to lift her from the chair, but she refuses to be led to the toilet as she'll miss the rest of Ernest's act, and we just can't believe it when the carer looks towards him and asks him to stop for a moment whilst she runs to fetch a commode for the lady.

Total silence spreads across the entire room, and then the residents suddenly burst into applause when the carer crashes back through the door whilst pushing the commode along the front row of the audience. The very moment the lady's rear-end hits the seat of the commode, the residents quieten down and Ernest heads straight into the next and final joke, before the rest of the chorus gets back into action. The lady on the commode simply smiles adoringly throughout the remainder of our compere's routine.

During the next few months, we enjoy numerous sing-outs all across the country. We do shows at the Winter Gardens in Blackpool, the Assembly Rooms in Derby, one at the London Barbican Centre, and we even appear on ITV's Calendar News on Christmas Eve, but the stuff we do for care homes and hospitals is no less enjoyable, although a charity event at the Crucible theatre is one that will live in my memory forever.

We haven't a clue about the other performers, but as we're gathering in the darkness beneath the stage and getting ready for our performance, we can hear the ear-shattering sound of what we think is a heavy-rock group above our heads. Bertie, one of our older members is a heavy smoker, and he always has a cigarette in his mouth right up to the last moment before we head out onto the stage. Right now he only has the dog-end of the fag left between his lips, and as usual the smoke is drifting upwards straight into his eyes. Unfortunately for him, it turns out not be a rock band ending their act above, but just the pre-recorded background music for someone billed as an exotic dancer.

As the music starts to fade and the applause from the audience dies-down, we hear footsteps heading down the staircase leading to the under-stage waiting area where we're ready and waiting. To everyone's utter surprise and amazement, a stunningly beautiful, and almost completely naked lady suddenly trots past the entire chorus, and she's in such close proximity to each of us as she passes by, when she squeezes past the five-feet tall Bertie, her bazoomahs hit him straight in the face. We'll never know if I was the force of the boobs smashing into him, or whether it was simply the huge shock that resulted in him swallowing the burning fag, but nevertheless it took a couple of chorus members almost fifteen minutes to go through the Heimlich manoeuvre in an attempt to get the fag out of his stomach.

My working life takes a huge step in the right direction when I finally step up into management to become an assistant catering manager at Sheffield's Northern General Hospital. I might also say that my sporting life also moves on a little, when a new kitchen porter by the name of Jack hears I'm a decent squash player. I have no idea who told him, but that is correct as far as I'm concerned, and I agree to have an hour with him on a court at the Concord Sports Centre.

Some hospital porters earn a bit of a reputation as being, should we say, bone idle and very street-wise, and Jack's squash outfit makes him look as though he could well be one of them. We make our way to the curt, where I remove my tracksuit top to reveal my usual pristine white tee-shirt and shorts with snow-white sports socks and shoes. Jack is wearing a needs-to-be-washed string vest with matching tee-shirt underneath a tatty old greying sweatshirt, and he has a badly stained track-suit on top of everything else. Then he wraps a mucky towel around his neck, before stretching a black bobble hat over his head. He finally bends down to adjust the Lycra leggings he's wearing underneath a pair of sports socks, with a pair of football socks over them. The only thing he seems to be without is a pair of woolly gloves, but I say nothing.

If I was to play squash in that lot, I'd melt all over the court in less than ten minutes, but Jack reckons he needs to lose a bit of weight, so all the clobber he's wearing should help him sweat it off. That might well be the case, but running around a squash court in his outfit for an hour trying to lose a bit of weight, might end up being be the least of his worries. Anyway, I've no doubt this match will be an absolute doddle for me, but then again, you never know. No surprise then, when he absolutely annihilates me. He has me hurtling from one end of the court to the other, and I barely manage to hit the ball during the next sixty minutes. As we finally leave the court, I'm more than relieved when Jack tucks his arm under mine and assists me to the door. My entire body feels as though it's falling apart and I can feel the huge blisters bursting inside my shoes.

"Bloody hell, Jack. I thought I was good, but where did you learn to play like that?" I gasp as we head out into fresh air.

"Before I started at the hospital last week, I was a fitness instructor in the Army, and I just spent two years in Northern Ireland, doing nothing but play squash with the NCO's."

"You crafty swine. You might have warned me."

"Na, I was told you're a good player, so that would have spoiled the fun. I don't suppose you fancy playing regularly, once your blisters have healed up, do you?"

"You can bet your life on it. I want revenge."

"Brilliant," smiles Jack. "They could do with people like you in the army."

"Yeah, right."

By the time I reach the same level as the world champion squash player, I've also become very comfortable in the lead section of the Barbershop chorus. For no reason whatsoever, I get to thinking that if ever Ernest didn't turn-up for a gig, we'd have a huge problem on our hands, as we don't appear to have a substitute, so I decide to take it upon myself to secretly develop a stand-up routine of my own, just in case. I timed it perfectly, as it's not long before I'm called into action when we put on a show in the Totley College auditorium.

The Dore and Totley areas are perhaps the poshest neighbourhoods in the whole of Sheffield, and the local population is made-up of retired lawyers, bankers, managing directors, medical and business consultants, and a variety of very rich and well respected professionals, none of whom I imagine, will have ever heard of Pitsmoor or Parkwood Springs. So, as we start arriving at the pub just up the road from the college entrance, John mentions we have a problem. Apparently, Ernest has gone down with a dose of laryngitis, so we don't have a compere.

He's taken aback when I offer to step in, and asks if I've ever done a stand-up routine before, as I'll need to have the confidence to crack jokes to an audience full of strangers. I tell him I've been preparing for an opportunity such as this, and I have an act ready for this very occasion. I also advise that whilst I've never done anything like it, I'd be much more confident with doing a stand-up comedy routine than I would be in either singing solo or as the lead singer in a barbershop quartet.

I just hope I'm right for once in my life!

To my amazement John tells me the job's mine, so I ask exactly who it is we're entertaining tonight. He has no idea, but he thinks it'll probably be either some students or maybe the canteen and housekeeping staff.

As we're getting into our stage gear in the changing room, a guy comes in from the auditorium to check if we're ready to go on. I'm standing nearest to the door and I tell him we'll be ready in two minutes, so he nods and smiles before returning to his seat. Then John takes the chorus through the usual vocal warm-up routine, whilst I mentally run through the list of gags I've prepared for an audience such as this. The man comes in again to ask if we're ready, so as the compere is always last onto the stage, I hold the door open to let the rest of the guys file through and into the auditorium, and as they file past, the guy whispers to tell me he's relieved that we were ready to go, as the vicar has just about run out of things to say.

"The vicar? What's the vicar doing in there?" I enquire with some trepidation.

"He's telling jokes," comes the reply.

"If the vicar's in there telling jokes, then who are we singing to."

"It's the Dore and Totley Retired Residents Association."

Oh dear, oh dear. That's not what I want to hear, but I guess it's too late now.

As always, the chorus goes straight into the usual couple of opening songs, the first being what's known as a 'gut-buster' and the second a 'tear-jerker'. A very warm and enthusiastic around of applause follows and now it's my turn. The lads have never had me fronting the show before, so no doubt there's a number of very worried Barbershoppers standing right behind me at the moment.

"Well hello. It's great to be back here in Pitsmo…., sorry Parkwood Spri….." I pretend to glance over my shoulder to ask one of the chorus where we are.

"Totley. Yeah, Totley. That's the place," I smile to the sound of laughter.

"I apologise for my head not being in the right place right now, but just before two o'clock this morning I became the father of a beautiful five and a half pound bouncing baby girl."

That little opener brings a huge round of applause and a rousing number of cheers and well wishes.

"The trouble is that the wife will go absolutely up the wall when she finds out," I frown, as a huge burst of laughter and applause erupts from the audience.

Once I come to the end of my first spot, the chorus belts out another couple of songs, and it takes about an hour for us to get through a dozen Barbershop renditions and my list if increasingly risky jokes. Then in my last spot, I have a joke about a man and his wife who are going to a fancy dress party dressed as a bull and a cow. The gag has a rather naughty ending, so I tone it down a bit and substitute the usual punchline with something less offensive.

The audience is still in raptures when I deliver the toned-down punchline, and they're still applauding when the chorus goes into the final couple of songs. We then leave the auditorium to a huge round of applause, and as we file back into the changing room, each of my fellow singers offers me a congratulatory handshake. John is already over the moon, and tells me we need to sort out something with Ernest, so we can both do our bit in future shows, but as he's the real comedian around here, I suggest we just leave things as they are and I'll just step in as and when necessary.

As we're just about to leave the dressing room, one of the audience members comes in and asks if he can have a word with me in private. That sounds a tad worrying, but nevertheless I agree to accompany him back into the almost empty auditorium. As we head into the now half empty auditorium, I almost jump out of my skin when yet another round of applause and shouts of 'Bravo, Bravo' ring out from the remaining members of the audience. It gets even better when my new companion rests his arm over my shoulder and tells me that the residents association has been coming to shows like this for many years, but ours is the best they've ever seen. Not only that, but according to him I'm possibly the best stand-up comic they've ever come across, and there's just one other thing he would like me to know. He goes on to tell me he has an even funnier ending for the bull and cow joke, and I'm completely flabbergasted when he tells me the punchline I'd considered to be just a bit to too naughty

Meanwhile, I receive an invitation to become a member of the Northern General Hospital's Social Club Committee, which is entirely unexpected as I don't drink these days. During the run-up to Christmas, the Barbershop chorus will be visiting a number of wards to sing a load of seasonal songs to the elderly patients, and with that in mind, I'm asked if I can get the lads to put on a show in the social club as part of a fundraising evening for the Special Care Baby Unit. The club will lay on a buffet and a few crates of ale in return for our services, and I'm delighted to say that the free grub and booze seals the deal.

Mum, Dad and Ar Reet are all also working at the hospital now. Pa is a porter-cum-driver, Mother is a domestic services assistant and Ar Reet works in the hospital shop. Sadly, Mum is the only one of the family planning to be in the audience, and she'll be accompanied by her colleague, Jean. I don't know exactly how the evening has been advertised around the hospital, but tickets for the show completely sell out within a couple of days of going on sale, and as I'll probably know virtually everyone in the audience, John tells me there'll be no holds barred, so I can give them a stand-up comedy routine they'll never forget.

Well, what comedian could turn down an opportunity like that?

The place is packed to the rafters when we walk in and step up onto the risers, and as I follow the now sixty strong chorus, I glance around the room to notice almost every eye is on me, the hospital's assistant catering manager-cum top notch comedian. I can't remember ever being as nervous as I am right now, but I'm very well prepared, so it's not a problem.

We go into the familiar routine of singing a couple of songs followed by a few minutes of stand-up, until we've gone through our respective repertoires. The chorus is brilliant and I'm having the time of my life at the front of the stage, going through huge catalogue of non-stop filth, swearing, racist and religious gags and sexist jokes that would leave some people utterly disgusted. By the end of the show, we've raised more than three thousand quid for the SCBU, and that wasn't all down to the Barbershop singing and the gutter-level comic. During a short break in the performance, one of the hospital porters offers to help raise a bit of extra cash by downing a yard of raw eggs. Yep, thirty nine raw eggs, each cracked into a yard of ale glass, right up to the brim, and he downs the lot in one go.

Yuk!!!! That's even more disgusting than any of the jokes I have up my sleeve.

The following day I'm treated like royalty wherever I go at the hospital but as always, I don't let it go to my head.

And if you believe that, then you'll probably also believe you can plait fog!

With my ego back under control by the end of the day, pop to Ecclesfield for the weekly session of cribbage with Pa. Even before I arrive at 116 Cross Hill, I know he'll already be ready and waiting with pack of cards and crib board on the kitchen table, and Ma will be parked-up in the front room watching early evening TV.

"Hi Dad. How's tricks?" I enquire as I plonk myself down beside him at the table.

"I'm fine but your Mother wants a word."

"What? Ma wants a word? She hasn't had a word with me since I was fifteen. What's up?"

"You'll see. I'll put the kettle on while you're in there. You'll need a drink by the time she's done."

I pop my head round the front room door.

"Hi Mum. You OK?"

"Sit down," Ma demands with a hint of malice.

"Why, what's up?"

"What's up? What's up?" she spits. "Just sit down and shut it. I'll tell you what's up. You're a disgrace, that's what's up, and I'm ashamed of you. What the bloody hell were you thinking of last night?" she demands.

"What are you going on about?"

"What am I going on about? I'm on about you and the jokes you were telling up on that stage."

"Why? What was wrong with them? Didn't you enjoy the show?"

"Enjoy it? You're a disgrace. The singing was OK, but you were disgusting. I couldn't believe the filth that was coming out of your mouth, and where did you learn to swear like that? You've never heard language like that in this house!

"Mum, I've been a chef for over fifteen years and I'm nearly thirty now. Where do you think I learned to swear like that? What's wrong with you?"

"What's wrong with me? It's what's wrong with you I'm worried about. It's not that long since you were thinking of being a Methodist lay preacher. I couldn't believe it when you started telling all those religious jokes, and if that wasn't bad enough, I was sitting with my friend Jean and the Hospital Chaplain, John Browning. I didn't know where to put my face. Have you any idea what it's like to be sitting next to a man of God and listening to the stuff you were churning out?"

"Was John laughing?" I ask.

"Yes, but that's not the point."

"But that's exactly the point, Mum. I know the chaplain, and I know he'd have found it hilarious. He knows me very well and he's fully aware of my beliefs. He knows that everything he heard was just an act, and he would have been delighted that with my input to the evening, we raised several grand for the SCBU."

"I don't care. I'm more concerned about bumping into him again any time soon. I'll have to start wearing a bag over my head so he won't know it's me coming down the corridor.

This ain't good!

"And another thing," moans Ma. " It's a bloody good job my friend Jean is losing her sight. She was sitting on the other side of me, and half way through all the filth and the swearing, she leaned over to tell me the comedian looked like you. I suggested she must be due another eye test, as the comedian looks nothing like our Eric and anyway, he wouldn't dream of saying things like that."

Dad's almost in tears of laughter as Ma slams the front room door shut behind me. He thrashes me at cribbage, so he's the champion for this week, but I'm not particularly disappointed on this occasion, especially when he tells me his colleagues at the Northern General had a great night last night and every one of them thought I was brilliant.

The ego's having a busy time lately!

I hadn't realised that a very popular Jamaican guy by the name of Tommy, who works in the Orthodontics Department lives just up the road from me, and both he and his gorgeous wife decide to drop by one evening to offer their congratulations on the stand-up comedy act, and especially the racist jokes. They knew straight away that I was actually having a pop at racists, and with that in mind they invite me to a party in the Pitsmoor area. I'm told the guest list will be made up of a couple of dozen West Indian men and their English wives, so perhaps I might know some of them from when I was a kid back on Oborne Street. I haven't done much partying since overdoing the Newcastle Brown Ale, Sweet Martini and the Gin and Dubonnet, so I guess I'm not prepared for the sound of Reggae music blasting out from the front window as we stroll down Burngreave Road.

Then as we we head into the hallway, the staircase appears to be a bit foggy for some reason, but I don't have the time to figure out why, because almost every single one of the guests comes over to introduce themselves to me. Several of the guys offer me a fag they've recently rolled-up, but as I gave up smoking when I was seven I gratefully decline.

Once I've made everyone's acquaintance, I stroll past a shedload of booze, most of which I've never heard of, and when I spot a large and lonely-looking bottle Coca Cola, I decide to adopt for myself.

I thoroughly enjoy the company and listening to the music during the next two or three hours, so as I've consumed nothing but Coca Cola for the entire evening, I just can't understand why I'm starting to feel as high as a kite. I decide to offer my apologies to Tommy and Marie and a few of our fellow guests, and then I make my weary way home. For some unknown reason, by the time I reach the bottom-end of Barnsley Road, I can barely stay on my feet, so I take a bit of a breather before staggering the last few yards to Horndean Road. Then, with front door safely secured, I head straight to bed for a solid twelve hours sleep.

I've never seen or touched any kind of recreational drugs in my entire life, but it turns out there's the teeniest little possibility I could be wrong. When I next bump into Tommy, I tell him of my being high as a kite and the sudden bout of dizziness, followed by a complete and utter loss of the ability to walk. I can't believe it when he tells me the fags I was offered at the party most certainly weren't Park Drive Tipped, and that whatever was wrapped up in the cigarette papers was responsible for the fog on the staircase.

Hallmark of Harmony are now in the Barbershop Northern Championships at the Miner's Holiday Camp in Skegness, so we must be pretty good by all accounts. We're instructed not to or drink before the chorus has to do its bit, because that would adversely affect the quality of the singing, but it doesn't concern us as we're due on stage in the early afternoon. Our rendition of The Barbershop Strut appears to knock the judges for six, and the following tear-jerker wraps it up, so we don't have long to wait before the judges declare us as this years champions. We haven't quite finished yet though, as the winners are required to take top billing on the Afterglow Show, so we have to come back down to earth and get our act together for later in the evening.

Unfortunately in the midst of all the celebrations going on around me, it seems to have slipped my mind that I'm 'on the wagon' these days, and as I've had nothing to eat or drink since breakfast, I'm afraid I don't have much to report about the Afterglow, because although my body was on the stage, it wasn't accompanied by what little brain I have.

I can only apologise, as no doubt you believed me when I told you that my 'bit of a blip' was over. What's that? No you didn't believe me? Well thanks a bunch!

The entrance door to each room throughout the holiday camp, has a huge star-shaped notice stuck on it, complete with the name of the occupant and the chorus he belongs to, and the name of the section he sings in, namely lead, bass, baritone or tenor. I can only assume I wasn't completely pickled by the time I left the celebrations to make my way up the staircase and somehow managed to find my first floor room, which overlooks the reception desk.

My head is still pounding when I quietly stroll into the huge dining room for breakfast. I almost jump out of my skin as I approach the breakfast buffet, when some fifty guests suddenly jump to their feet and start clapping and cheering. I feel quite humbled by the fact that fellow singers from numerous other choruses offer such a warm welcome to each of the champions as they arrive for breakfast. I can only smile and nod in acknowledgement, and offer a little wave of gratitude as I reach for the orange juice. By the time I park myself at the table next to my mate Chris, I'm almost in tears, but of course, I'm just about to come crashing back down to earth, when I ask him if everyone else had been greeted in the same way.

"It wasn't due to you being a member of the winning chorus, says Chris. "It's down to what you did around two o'clock this morning."

"Two o'clock this morning? Why, what happened?"

"Don't you remember?" he asks, as I start to get just a tad worried.

"No, I don't remember and I'm beginning to think it might be better if I don't find out, either," I reply, as several complete strangers smile and pat me on the shoulder as they file out of the dining room.

"Three guys from Manchester's Rainy City Chorus were on the lookout for a lead singer to join them in an informal song or two. When they reached your room door, they spotted the star on your room door and the note that said you're a lead singer with Hallmark of Harmony. They dragged you out of bed and onto the balcony above reception. Then, as everybody else started filing out of the bar when it closed a couple of minutes later at two o'clock, the four of you leaned over the balcony above our heads and belted out your version of I'll Take You Home Kathleen. No doubt you'd have brought your pyjamas if you'd have known that was going to happen thirty feet above the rest of us."

I guess it could have been even more embarrassing if it had been a freezing cold night in the middle of January. I don't think I'll mention it to Ma!

The chorus now has a sing-out to do for the South Yorkshire County Councillors Annual Dinner Dance at Doncaster Racecourse Exhibition Centre, and I'll be the compere throughout the entire gig. We're hoping to get some sponsorship from the various councils, and if we're successful the money will go towards funding a trip to Phoenix, Arizona to perform at an international Barbershop convention.

As she'll be in the audience, I call my cousin Maureen to ask what I can and can't get away with in my stand-up routine. She tells me not to take the pee out of political party leaders but I the audience will love it if I take a pop at individual councillors, so she give me a list of names and details of the committees they sit on. It then takes me a few days to sort out my routine.

I'm looking forward to this!

There must be more than two or three hundred in the audience. The men are dressed to the nines, whilst the ladies are decked out in evening gowns, and there are mayoral chains and stuff like that along virtually every row of seats.

It's the usual routine of a couple of songs followed by five minutes of stand-up comedy. The guys behind me are at their usual height of vocal excellence, and then I start off with several of my most popular cheeky gags. It's not long before I start on the newly created routine of jokes about individual councillors and their committees, and to my surprise the applause is absolutely deafening.

By now, I'm getting just a wee bit carried away by the rapturous response to the comedy routine, so I'm completely shell-shocked when a guy on the front row, who is clearly one of the top brass in the world of South Yorkshire politics, stands up and waves his arms into the air to bring the show to a halt. Then he climbs up onto the stage and grabs my wrist, as he beckons towards a guy standing right at the back of the auditorium to instruct him to come forward. My immediate thought is that this must be one of the councillors I've just been taking a pop at, and he's about to have me thrown out, so it comes a great relief to find it's a press photographer heading our way, and the guy holding my wrist wants to have a photograph of the pair of us standing together on the stage.

Phew! That's a relief!

We eventually we get through the first half, then during the interval John tells me it's very noticeable that whilst the audience are enjoying the singing, there's no doubt they're more interested in my stand-up routine than the vocals, so I'm free to move onto the filth and swearing if I wish. I duly oblige.

The guys lined up behind me are required to at least maintain a permanent smile on their faces throughout my routine, but as they've never heard these particular gags before, they've been howling with laughter as each punchline is delivered. Then, halfway through the second half of the show, I go into one of my often-used and very naughty sexist gags about an exotic dancer. Within a couple of seconds of starting the joke, I can hear whispers of panic coming from the risers.

"Oh God, not this one."

"Move onto the next gag. Quick."

"They won't like what's coming!"

"Can't somebody shut him up?"

I can hear them but it's already too late to stop, and as I deliver the punchline a deadly silence spreads all the way around the room. There's not a single smile to be seen, but there are a few looks of utter disgust coming from the female members of the audience. Then I notice a number of middle-aged ladies standing up and looking down angrily into their partner's faces, and a few seconds later the audience starts filing out towards the exit door. Eventually we're left with about twenty single male councillors staring blankly towards the stage. I just don't know what to do but luckily, John steps forward, turns his back on what is now the skeleton of an audience and mimes to the guys to prepare for the final song.

I have no words to say as we arrive back in the changing room and worse still, I barely sleep a wink for the next two or three nights. I feel so bad that I decide to resign from compering when I attend next Tuesday's rehearsals. I mention it to Chris, who without my knowledge, decides to inform our Musical Director. I don't really have the heart for singing during the first half of rehearsal, and it's noticeable that not a single member of the chorus approaches me to discuss the recent show. I'm beginning to think I need to bring my Barbershop singing and stand-up comedy act to an immediate end, especially as I've let so many friends down, due to my ego and unbelievable stupidity.

Then, as I sit quietly alone in the corner of the rehearsal room during the half time break, John, asks the chorus members to gather round as he has something important to announce. He goes on to explain that Eric feels like he let everyone down at the recent sing-out in Doncaster, and is now considering whether he should step down from compering. I can feel the tears already starting to form in my eyes, but then we hear that in the Musical Director's opinion, and in the opinion of each section leader, the show will go down in Barbershop folklore, and regardless of what some members of the audience thought, Eric's stand-up routine was brilliant. John asks for a round of applause and three cheers for me, and he well and truly receives gets it. I end the evening with bruising to my shoulders, due to receiving so many slaps on the back from my friends, so I decide to continue with the stand-up act and Barbershop singing.

Sheffield's Hallmark of Harmony. It doesn't get any better than this!

Chapter Eleven

Counting The Losses

It's not long before promotion comes my way again, when I become Catering Manager at Sheffield Children's Hospital. It's another great place to work, so with that, and all the fun and enjoyment of the barbershop singing and everything that goes with it, my life is simply coasting along for a change.

Yes, you're right. I'm about to back down to earth with a bump. A very large one!

It all kicks off in January 1984 with the passing of aunt Marian, shortly after she suffered a stroke at home in Creswell. It's the family's first loss since Grandma Winnie's passing back in 1971, and there's even more bad news to come, when uncle Eddie calls early on Friday morning on the 10th of February, to say Grandpa Reg has unexpectedly suffered a stroke, and is now gravely ill at home in the bungalow on Dover Street that he and Winnie moved into shortly after he retired, so Mum and Dad drop everything and head to straight to Creswell to stay with him.

During the afternoon, Reg's GP calls round to check-up on him, and he advises Mum and Dad to prepare for the worst, as Grandpa is now in a deep coma and is unlikely to survive the weekend. I suppose it's no great surprise that Reg being Reg, he somehow manages to prove the GP wrong and somehow survives the weekend. The first I hear of it, is when Dad calls me early on Monday morning. I arrive at Grandpa's just before noon, having picked-up Ar Reet on the way. She's now about five months pregnant, so she has enough on her plate right now, but as we both thinks the world of Reg, we can only hope we're not too late.

Uncle Eddie is already there, and both he and Mum have been popping into the bedroom every few minutes to check if Reg is still with us, but although he's still hanging on, his breathing is clearly shallower as time passes by. It's heartbreaking to see our hero like this, but we're just relieved to be able to sit with him and hold his hand.

Cousins Trevor, Neil, Peter, Christine and Sylvia start to arrive by late afternoon, and by six o'clock, the entire Cope side of the family is together for the first time since we lost Grandma Winnie. Once everyone has been brought up to speed, Mum and Eddie pop back into the bedroom to find Reg taking his final few breaths as he peacefully passes away.

It's 13th February, and Rita's twenty fifth birthday.

Regardless of how many years go by, I'll always miss our hero. God Bless Him.

As Reg's funeral arrangements are being planned, a member of the local British Legion arrives to seek permission for his coffin to be draped with the Union Flag, and for a bugler to play The Last Post at the end of the service at Brampton Crematorium in Chesterfield. Permission is duly granted, and the old comrade goes into some detail about Grandpa's role during the Great War, highlighting the fact that thousands of soldiers never returned home from the trenches, but Reg was one of the lucky ones.

It goes without saying that the entire family is struggling with the sad loss, and Dad is very concerned about the effect it appears to be having on Rita. On the day of the funeral, he asks if I would stay at the bungalow and look after her, whilst the rest of the family attend the committal. That results in the pair of us missing out on the opportunity to say our final farewells to the great man with the rest of the family, and it also means I haven't attended the funeral of any of my grandparents. That's remained with me ever since, as I feel I've somehow let the side down.

We're still mourning Reg's passing several weeks later, when I decide to pop over to Ecclesfield on my way home from the Children's Hospital. Pa hasn't called me during the weekend to arrange our weekly cribbage match, and that's unusual to say the least. As you already know, it's always him who greets me when I arrive, but on this occasion it's Ma, so perhaps the fallout from the stand-up routine at the Northern General has been forgotten, I hope.

"Hi Mum. Where's Dad?"

"He's been in bed since Saturday morning. He has a chest infection and he's not well at all. The doctor should be here soon," replies Mum worriedly.

I go straight upstairs, and I'm shocked to find him looking so poorly. I've never known him to be ill, but there's no doubt something is very wrong.

"Hi Dad. How are you feeling?"

It's clearly a bit of a struggle for him to pull himself together enough to come up with a reply.

"Bloody awful," comes the pained reply. "I've never felt this bad in my life. I think I've picked up a nasty chest infection. I picked your Mum up from Bingo on Friday night, but I was struggling to breath. It got worse during the weekend, so I haven't been out of bed for nearly three days now," he tells me as we hear Ma and the GP heading up the stairs.

We leave the doctor to examine him, and once we're back in the kitchen, Ma tells me that during the night he woke up several times with a burning sensation in his chest, and was finding it even more difficult to breath. I got worse during the night, and at one point Dad he woke her from her sleep as he thought he was dying.

A few minutes later, the doctor comes back down to advise Mum he's called for an ambulance. It's already on its way and will take him to the Northern General Hospital, as the ECG check he just had, show he's suffered several heart attacks during the last seventy two hours. Unbelievably, moments after the doctor departs, Pa appears at the bottom of the stairs. He's decided that if he's going to be taken to the Northern General, then Mum needs to sort out some 'snap' for him, as he's not going to be eating the rubbish they serve to the patients in there.

So whilst she starts on the picnic, Pa decides to go out onto the street to wait for the ambulance, and he returns two minutes later with a couple of ambulancemen and a wheelchair in tow.

"Hey, you shouldn't be doing that," says the leading paramedic as he spots Ma standing at the table with a loaf of bread in her hand. "You shouldn't be on your feet in your condition, so let me help you into the wheelchair," he kindly suggests.

"It's not me you're taking to the Northern General, it's that daft sod who just met you outside. He's the one who's had the heart attacks, not me," she replies to a rather confused paramedic.

"Come on Cliff, get in the chair before we end up needing a stretcher," says the second paramedic, who now realises he's already bumped into Pa a few times at the hospital.

"OK, but you're not going to wheel me into the ward in that thing."

He never would do as he was told!

"Cliff, you know it's more than my job's worth to let you walk into the hospital, so don't be daft. You could keel over any second, and then me and my mate here will be in deep trouble, so will you just plonk your backside into the wheelchair, and then we can be on our way.

Then once Pa is safely inside the ambulance and gripping the picnic hamper Ma just positioned in his lap, the three of them set off for the hospital, accompanied by a few blue lights and a siren. Unfortunately, Ma only made him enough sandwiches to see him through the next couple of days, so I can only assume he's not a happy chappie during the next two weeks, whilst being laid-up on the surgical ward. He probably feels even more annoyed, when he's told he can only go home if he promises to do absolutely nothing until he's given the go ahead by a doctor to do some very light exercise. As I mentioned earlier, Pa has never been ill in his life, so doing naff-all for the next few weeks simply isn't on his wish list.

Of course, Dad doesn't stay in bed and spends every day on the front room sofa, but he does misbehave on one occasion, when he decides to run the mop over the kitchen floor. He manages to lift the mop bucket from the cellar-head and hump it into the sink before filling it up with hot water. Unfortunately, when he attempts to heave the bucket and its contents back out of the sink, the sudden violent pain that shoots across his chest forces him to drop the lot onto the floor. I understand Ma had a few choice words to say when she arrived back from the local shop, to find a new paddling pool in the kitchen and Pa sprawled out on the floor next to it, completely breathless and looking very grey and pasty. I don't think the doctor was very impressed either, when Ma called the surgery to request an emergency visit due the outcome of Pa's misbehaviour.

Well, we blokes ever do as we're told, do we?

Rita gives birth to Christopher in June, and Pa really appreciates being chauffeured to my sister's so he can spend some time holding his new grandson in his arms. Then right out of the blue during the drive back to Ecclesfield one evening, he reveals that until he had the recent heart attacks he'd ever given a thought to the future. He tells me that if anything ever happened to Mum, he'd be completely lost without her, although it's now a racing certainty that he'll be the first to leave this world. If that does turn out to be the case, he asks me to make sure Mum is OK, and that I'll always be there if ever my kid sister needs me.

Looking back, I think it's the only promise I ever made to him.

Our cribbage sessions have been twice weekly since Pa's been in poor health, but he still manages to get to be the champion more often than me. He unexpectedly calls me on the morning of Sunday 22nd July to ask if I fancy an extra cribbage session later this afternoon. Mum will knock-up our favourite tea time meal consisting of a few rounds of ham sandwiches and a dish of trifle, whilst we sit in the garden for the third crib championship match in the last seven days. By the time I arrive, Pa is ready and waiting in the garden, with cards, crib board and a couple of mugs of tea on the table. I pop straight into the kitchen to say hello to Ma and to bring out the tea time treat. I can't help noticing the worried look on her face as she tells me that Dad's been acting a bit strange all day.

"I don't know what's up with him, but he just won't leave me alone. He's been putting his round me all day long, and telling me how much he loves me and how grateful he is for the way I've looked after him during the last three months. He's never been that soppy in all the years we've been together, so I don't know why he keeps telling me now. Keep an eye in him will you, and let me know if he says anything unusual to you."

As I head out into the garden, I simply suggest he might have finally realised how much she's done for him over the years, so it could be his way of showing his love and appreciation.

As always, the games are very close and competitive, and I could happily sit here all night playing cribbage. I just can't believe my ears when, with the scores standing at one set apiece Pa suggests we call it a day, as he'd like me to take him to Ar Reet's so he can spend a few minutes with her and baby Christopher.

"Are you kidding?" I ask in amazement. "We've won one set each so far, and during the last quarter of a century, we've never finished a match without playing a deciding set so that one of us gets to be crowned Champion."

"I know, so let's just say we're both champions," he suggests with a huge smile as he gently taps the back of my hand. "There's no need to tell Mum, as I only want to see Chris and make sure Rita's OK, so we won't be gone long.

If only that was the case.

When we arrive outside Rita's, I help Dad out of the car and tell him I'll go and fill up the fuel tank, and he promises to be ready and waiting for the return journey by the time I get back. A little over a quarter of an hour later, I'm pulling up outside Ar Reet's just as she comes hurtling out of the house towards me with the baby in her arms. There are tears streaming down her cheeks as she approaches the car.

"Quick! Hurry up! Dad's on the dining room floor," she screams. "He said he felt a bit dizzy, but when he told me he hadn't got his tablets with him, I told him to sit down on one of the dining room chairs. He collapsed onto the floor before he got to the chair, so I've called for an ambulance, and it'll be here any minute now."

I race inside to find Pa laying motionless on the dining room floor. I do my utmost to bring him round, but there's no response. Then I notice a blue tinge around his mouth, and I realise he's no longer with us. The paramedics arrive and attempt to revive him, and then they fit an oxygen mask over his face, before hoisting him onto the stretcher and out to the waiting ambulance, so I tell Rita to stay put whilst I head back to Ecclesfield to tell Mum. She's in the garden clearing away the remnants of the sarnies and trifle, and as I step onto the grass she glances towards me with an increasingly worried look on her face.

"Where's your Dad?"she nervously asks.

I explain what's happened, but I just can't bring myself to tell her we'd lost him before the ambulance arrived. She dashes upstairs and returns a couple of minutes later with a pair of Dad's pyjamas, his bedroom slippers and a few toiletries, but I already know he won't be needing them. Then when we arrive at the Hallamshire Hospital, we're ushered into the A&E visitor's room to be told by a consultant that the paramedic team did everything they possibly could, but unfortunately Dad never regained consciousness and was declared dead shortly afterwards.

We're invited to go into the emergency room to see him, and apart from the blue tinge to his lips, he just looks as though he's fallen asleep. Mum seems to take it reasonably well, but I'm struggling when it comes to telling Rita. It gets no easier the next morning, when I call in at the Northern General CSSD Department to let the boss know his porter-driver won't be coming back. The moment they see me heading into the office, the rest of his colleagues have a good idea what's happened, so I'm quite touched by the countless words of comfort and condolence I receive on my way back out.

The funeral service at Hutcliffe Wood Crematorium remains a complete blank to me, especially as I spend most of the time attempting to block everything out. I finally fall apart as I lovingly place my hand onto the coffin lid before heading outside to come face to face with family, friends and Dad's work colleagues.

The next few weeks are horrendous, as I'm left with a huge void that can never be filled, and I'm simply unable to move on because I can't help feeling that in some way he's still with me.

I must admit, the feeling has remained with to this day.

It takes me about three months to get my head around Pa's passing, but by early autumn I'm beginning to get back to some kind of normality. Unfortunately, I just can't face getting up on stage to sing and tell naughty jokes, so it's with huge regret I decide bring the Barbershop singing and stand-up comedy routine to an end. My heart's already been broken a few times this year, and tearing myself away from such a wonderful group of friends doesn't make things any better.

I've remained good friends with Harry from my days at Nether Edge Hospital, and one morning in early October, he asks if Mick could do a pre-MOT check on his Renault car. Mick suggests I take the car to him on Friday and he'll sort it out during the weekend, so it'll be ready for collection on Monday. Harry is very well organised at home, so when I return the car early on Monday afternoon, I'm quite surprised to notice four bottles of milk standing on the doorstep, knowing he only has a single pint delivered each morning.

There's no answer when I ring the doorbell, and neither is there one when I peer through the letterbox and call to him. I'm becoming very concerned now, as I can see at least half a dozen newspapers and several unopened items of mail laying on the floor on the other side of the door, so I decide to knock on his neighbour's door.

"Hi. I'm Eric, one of Harry's friends. I wondered if you've seen him lately?"

"I haven't seen him all weekend," he replies. "His car hasn't been on the drive for a few days either, so I assume he's gone away."

"He hasn't gone away. I've had his car since Friday, as it needed some work doing on it, and he knows I'm bringing it back today," I explain with growing concern.

The neighbour notices the bottles of milk on Harry's doorstep, and assures me he always takes the milk inside as soon as it's been delivered. With that in mind, and the fact that there's loads of unopened mail piling up inside, I concerned that Harry might have been taken ill and may not be able to get out of bed. Neither of us has a key to the house, so the only alternative is to call 999.

A policeman arrives in less than ten minutes, and once I've explained my concerns, he has no doubt that the best course of action is for him to to smash one of the small panes of glass in the front door and then to reach in to grab the key and unlock the door from the inside.

Once inside, the policeman suggests I wait downstairs whilst he goes up to check the bedrooms and bathroom. I get the shock of my life when I stroll into the kitchen to find Harry sitting upright in the fireplace with his back against tiles. His spectacles are hanging from one ear and down the side of his face, and his mouth is wide open, as if he's just taking a huge intake of breath. Without going into further detail, it's perfectly clear he's passed away and must have been sitting here for quite some time.

I'll be glad when this year comes to an end.

The Children's is a brilliant hospital to work in, especially as I regularly get to meet patients when the Education Liaison officer brings them along to the kitchen for the occasional chocolate treat. Linda and a number of the nurses were pleased to hear of my past association with the Methodist Church, and they've already invited to join them on a number of occasions when they visit the Spiritualist Church just around the corner from the hospital. It doesn't particularly appeal to me for some reason, so I always politely decline and tell them I've already made other arrangements.

One day in November, Linda tells me the gang are planning to book seats at the City Hall for an evening with the very well known and highly regarded medium, Doris Stokes. I've always found that kind of thing to be just a bit too weird and scary, but for some unknown reason I find myself accepting the invitation on this occasion.

I just can't help myself, can I?

The performance is a sell-out, and as we take our seats, I can't help noticing that the entire audience appears to be very relaxed. A few minutes later, and without fanfare, Doris calmly and quietly strolls onto the stage. I guess I was expecting her to be accompanied by some kind of spooky music and shadowy lighting, but there's no sign of either. Doris takes hold of the microphone as she smiles and waves to several hundred admirers.

She comes across as being very friendly and reassuring, and goes on to explain to anyone who's never seen her before, there's absolutely nothing to worry about. It's just an evening of chatting, although most of the conversations will be between her and people the rest of us can't see. She promises that in the event of someone 'from the other side' having a message for anyone in the audience, one of the stage crew will come over with a microphone, so we can all hear the recipient's response.

I'm beginning to wish I was on the other side right now. The other side of town to be exact!

Doris soon begins to make contact, although each incoming message starts off pretty weak, before gradually becoming clearer, and when someone 'from the other side' does gets through, she repeats the message to the audience, before asking if it means anything to anyone. It usually takes her a bit of time to extract as many details as possible from the contact, but I notice she never asks for any information from the message recipient until they've indicated that the message is for them,

I'm still not convinced, as this could be no more than a well-rehearsed act, and the message recipients could simply be actors playing their part whilst being seated amongst real members of the audience.

Nevertheless, each contact begins to fade away after a while, as the next incoming message starts to come through.

"I have a little boy here, and his name is Dean," claims Doris. "He's saying something about the Prince of Wales. Does any of that ring a bell with anyone? He's clearly not the Prince of Wales, so I don't know what that's all about. Wait! Is there a pub called the Prince of Wales somewhere in Sheffield?"

"There's a Prince of Wales Road," someone in the audience shouts out.

Doris continues the conversation with her contact from the other side.

"Hello, Dean. Did you live on Prince of Wales Road?" she asks.

To everyone's surprise, before Doris has time to go any further, a lady sitting on the same row as us, stands up and starts waving her hand frantically in the air.

"It's my Dean you're talking to. It's my son, Dean," the lady shouts as the guy with the microphone starts to close in on her. "We live on Prince of Wales Road

"Thank you, my love," says Doris. "Please don't worry. Everything's OK. Dean is now showing me the number 7. Do you live at number 7, or perhaps he was 7 years old when he passed away?"

"No," replies the lady. "We don't live at number 7 and he wasn't seven when we lost him. I think he might be telling you he passed away seven weeks ago today."

At this point one of nurses leans over towards me and Linda to tell us she recognises the lady. Apparently, the nurse looked after her son, Dean when he was in the Children's Hospital suffering with leukaemia. He passed away nearly two months ago.

Doris continues once again.

"Dean is asking me let you know he's OK and he wasn't in any pain when he was taken away." He wants you to know he's got a really nice haircut and has learned how to play the guitar. Does that mean anything to you?" asks Doris as the lady is almost overcome with emotion.

"He had lovely hair, but he lost it when he started having chemotherapy, so we promised him that when it grew back we'd let him have it styled. We bought him a guitar for his birthday just before he went into hospital, and we promised he could have lessons when he came home, but he never did," explains the lady to gasps from the audience.

"Well his hair and his guitar playing are all fine now, but he's worried about you and says that you need to throw away the blue jumper you have in the wardrobe, because it's upsetting you. What's all that about?"

I must admit I'm intrigued right now, especially as one of the nurses knew Dean and remembers his mother. This is gripping stuff!

"His favourite colour was blue, so we bought him a blue jumper, but he never had the chance to wear it," Dean's Mum continues. "When he passed away, we sorted out all his toys and clothes and gave them to charity, but I kept the jumper and put it into the wardrobe. Every day when I think about him, I take it out of the wardrobe and cry into it," she explains as almost every member of the audience begins to fall apart, and that includes me.

"Well," says Doris sympathetically. "Dean says you shouldn't do that because he's fine and he doesn't like to see you cry," she says as the message begins to fade.

By the time Doris returns from the interval, the audience is absolutely spellbound as she gets the second half underway. She soon makes contact with someone else from the other side, but in the middle of the cross examination, she suddenly starts laughing.

"Oh, I'm really sorry," says Doris. "There's someone else trying to get through now, and he's obviously not a very patient man. He's not very tall either, and he has jet black hair. He just keeps whistling, although it's completely out of tune," Doris explains before politely asking him to bear with her for a little while longer

"It's OK, love. I'll get to you in a minute. Just hang on for a bit longer."

My first thought is that this sounds very much like Dad. He wasn't very patient and he was only five feet tall. He also had jet black hair in his early years, and he was a rubbish whistler. Anyway, after bit of an overlap of incoming and outgoing messages, Doris finally gets round to her new contact.

"This little man is asking if Robert is here. Not Rob, Robbie or Bob. He's specifically asking for Robert. Does that mean anything to anyone?" enquires Doris as she looks around the audience.

Well it certainly means something to me, and in the unlikely event you've read this nonsense right from the beginning, it'll also no doubt mean something to you, as Robert, not Rob, Robbie of Bob, was one of Pa's brothers. Oh heck!

Doris gets back into her stride once again, and I start to feel a hint of panic as she strolls across the stage, whilst casually glancing up towards survey the balcony, just where we happen to be sitting. She catches my eye once or twice, but I just remain glued to my seat in total silence.

"I can't work this out," claims Doris. "He's now showing me a hill with a cross on it. Not like a cross in a multiplication sum, but more of a biblical cross. I'm also seeing the numbers one and six repeatedly flashing past my eyes, so it could be either of those numbers, or the number sixteen, sixty one or something else with those digits in it. Can anybody explain what it might be?"

I lean towards Linda to tell her that Ma and Pa lived at 116 Cross Hill in Ecclesfield, so as far as I'm concerned right now, there's absolutely no doubt as to who it is that Doris has at the other end of the line. She continues once again.

"Goodness me I'm seeing a rather quaint little village," Doris continues. "It's not in Sheffield, but it isn't far away. It has a coal mine and I think there's also a well somewhere in the village," says Doris, whilst looking directly at me for a couple of seconds before turning away and strolling back across the stage.

"There's no need to be worried if you think the message is for you," she says, without looking back.

I tell Linda I was born in the coal mining village of Creswell, about twenty miles from Sheffield, but there's absolutely no way I can accept the message, even though I know for certain that Pa has popped in to say hello.

I've always regretted not accepting the message, but at the same time I've always believed Dad was doing his very best to let me know everything was OK. I think it's time to move on.

One evening just before Easter, I'm hit by a massive sharp pain in my back. It feels as though my insides are attempting to burst out and there's absolutely nothing I can do other than press the palm of my hand onto the flesh to try to ease the pain. That doesn't work and the pain just gets worse, so now I have no alternative but to call for an ambulance. By the time it arrives, I'm already thinking I could soon be bumping into Pa again, so hopefully they play cribbage up there, especially as we still have a deciding set to sort out.

Following a detailed examination in the A&E Department, I'm told I have a nasty case of viral pneumonia, which may be partly due to the cough I've been unable to shake off during the last two or three months. I must take a complete rest, and make an appointment for a check up with my GP in a fortnight's time. It's actually another six weeks before I'm allowed back to work, but in the meantime, apart from finally getting back to good health for the first time in months, there's another benefit coming my unplanned holiday.

During that time, the World Snooker Championship takes place at Sheffield's Crucible Theatre, and I have nothing better to do than to sit on front of the TV, and watch every shot played during the three weeks of the tournament, right up to the point where Dennis Taylor beats Steve Davis by potting the black ball in the deciding frame.

So I guess I couldn't have timed the pneumonia any better than that, could I?

During the holiday, I pick up a book about the basics of playing snooker, written by the losing finalist. I have plenty of time to study every page, so with that and having watched so much snooker on telly, by the time I start playing again, I can't help noticing the vast improvement in my game.

I'm not suggesting I'm now in a position to be giving Steve or Dennis any cause for concern though. I was absolutely rubbish before I had pneumonia, but now I'm not quite so hopeless.

Meanwhile, the Government has decided that competitive tendering for NHS catering services is the way forward, so at some point in the near future I'll need to get the Children's Hospital catering services ready to compete with private sector organisations. Quality Management appears to have become a top priority, so I decide that's what I should be focussing on. I become very interested in the quality side of things, and it's not long before I become qualified Internal ISO 9000 Quality Systems Auditor, and having written the tendering documents myself, when the services are put out for tender, it's a really warm feeling for the in-house services to be awarded the catering contract.

I don't suppose it does the old ego any harm either, and I think that with all the losses I've been counting up recently, that's the first win I've had for ages.

Chapter Twelve

Living With The Village People

There's absolutely no doubt in my mind that the recent success has now resulted in me going through yet another 'iffy' interview, and I've ended up becoming Catering Manager at Middlewood Hospital, a psychiatric unit dating back to Victorian times. Unlike all the other hospitals I've worked in during the last few years, Middlewood is more like a village in its own right.

The main building stands majestically overlooking the extensive grounds, and is home to less than half of the two thousand patients the hospital accommodated around a century ago. The site has been developed over the years, and the patients now have access to their very own social club complete with cafe, library and clothing boutique. There's even a work area shop which provides job opportunities for the more able patients to earn a few quid.

I already know my assistant catering manager, Roger. He's been working here since God was a lad, and during my first morning in the role he takes me on the obligatory grand tour of the hospital and its facilities. There are no 'secure' wards these days, so the patients are more or less free to stroll around the place at will. It feels quite odd to be bumping into patients walking along the main corridor, and I wasn't expecting Roger to know everyone of them by name. I guess I'm going to have to find plenty of time to interact with them if I'm going to get know them as well as Roger does, because right now I don't know a single one of them and the don't know me.

But as you might expect by now, I'm just about to find out I'm mistaken.

As we head outside on our way to a unit at the bottom of the long drive leading down to Middlewood Road, I suggest to Roger that from now on we should refer to the patients as 'residents'. He thinks it's a good idea, as this is where many of them have spent most of their lives, and calling them residents may be seen as an indication of our respect for them.

On our way back up the drive, I'm glancing through the notes I've made during the tour, when Roger grabs me by the arm.

"Oh here's Nora heading our way. I'll introduce you to her."

I almost wet myself when I look up to see my old sparring partner Pond Street Nora plodding towards us. I can't believe my life could be at risk on my first day in the job. As it's now more than fifteen years since she cornered us in the cafe, perhaps I won't need to make a run for it at this point, although I'm still in a bit of a quandary when Nora comes to a stop as Roger blocks her on the pavement.

"Hello Nora,"Roger beams. "I want you to meet Eric, our new catering manager."

I'm trembling almost as much as Nora as she looks down at me. I can feel her bulging eyes scanning my face, and then suddenly her demeanour changes. The trembling comes to an abrupt halt, and the look in her eyes tell me she's almost at the point of recognising me and recalling all the horrible abuse that me and my Parkwood Springs mates regularly gave her all those years ago. Her huge right hand slowly emerges from the bag and then she places it over her left forearm. I can see her left index finger beginning to shake and point in my direction.

I think I should have made an early exit when I had the opportunity, but maybe it's a bit too late for that now!

"Hello Nora. Nice to meet you. Catch you later," I splutter as I force Roger's hand away from my arm and head up the drive and back to relative safety in the office.

As I glance back over my shoulder, I can see that Nora is watching me, and the look of vague recognition has already drastically changed to one of pure hatred. Then when Roger arrives and parks himself behind his desk and I explain the history between me and Nora, he confidently reassures me that she's completely harmless these days. I'm not quite so sure about that, and as we stroll into the social club, I'm already wondering if it would be seen as a bad career move if I were to resign less than four hours after starting the new job.

I feel even more ashamed now than I was when I was a kid when I realised just how unbelievably disgraceful we'd been towards Nora. I've no doubt whatsoever that if the world had understood as much about mental health issues as they do now, then nobody would ever have been subjected to the kind of abuse we thought was funny. Unfortunately, this turned out to be the very last time me and Nora ever bumped into each other, so I never had another opportunity to apologise. Perhaps we might meet again someday but in the meantime, all I can say right now is God bless you Nora, may you rest in peace.

The residents' social club looks very interesting, especially the snooker room, which is home to a pair of full-size snooker tables, where charge nurse Amir is already enjoying a little practice session. He lives with his wife Zara and their two daughters, Maryam and Ayesha, and in a surprisingly light-hearted manner, he suggests that should indicate they're a family of Muslims. Amir then assures me that his religion is the very reason he finds it so easy to show the utmost respect to everyone, especially the hospital residents.

There's no doubt I could get on very well with Amir, so when he tells me he was subjected to a degree of racism when he lived in Lincolnshire, I decide to reassure him with regard to my own religious views and my time living among and working with non-white colleagues. Then with that done, we can look forward to a great friendship.

My new friend decides to show me around the social club, where I meet the other members of the nursing team and a couple of ladies who will be working for me in the club's cafe. Then he introduces me to a customer sitting at a table with a mug of tea pressed against his lips, and it turns out that he also works for me. Amir explains that Willy's mother gave birth to him outside wedlock, so the rest of the family had the pair of them shut away in what was then called the West Riding Asylum. He's now lived here for more than sixty years, earns a bit of pocket money by weighing out ingredients and loading and unloading the huge ovens in the bakery section of the main kitchen. Anyway, at the end of the tour, me and Amir decide to have a snooker session tomorrow evening.

The moment I step through the club door, Willy comes straight over to me, almost dragging an extremely heavy-looking shopping bag along on the floor behind him.

"Hi Willy. How are you today?" I enquire somewhat uneasily, as I've yet to have a conversation with any of the residents.

"Hello Boocock. I'm fine," comes the reply. "Do you want to buy some sugar?"

"Sugar? How much is it?"

"It's a shilling a bag. I've got some flour and butter and some sultanas as well, if you want some," boasts Willy as he opens the shopping bag to reveal more grub than Ma brings home from the weekly 'big shop'.

"No thanks, mate. Do you take orders for stuff?"

"Yeah. No problem. I can get whatever you want, so just let me know."

"OK, I'll bear it in mind. Thanks."

I decide to have a quiet word with the baker first thing tomorrow morning, and I'm completely stunned when he tells me he's fully aware of what's going on, but it keeps Willy happy, so it's OK as far as he's concerned

Regardless of that little hiccup, I really enjoy the snooker challenge. I'm also delighted that me and Amir are getting on so well, and it turns out to be the start of long-standing friendship I'll treasure forever.

The week before Easter, we receive a delivery of 36 cases of Cadbury's Cream Eggs, just enough to hand out at least a couple of treats to each resident. I hand the store room key to the driver, and then he humps six cases at a time out of the back of his van, around the corner of the building and into the store room. When he eventually calls into my office to return the key, he tells me the boxes have been positioned in six stacks of six cases on the shelving, and asks me pop back into the store room with him to check and sign for the delivery. I'm glad I didn't sign the delivery note without checking, as he appears to have miscounted and there are actually only five stacks of six cases, so he's left us with almost three hundred eggs short.

"That's impossible," claims the driver. "Me and my boss counted them in, and I just counted them out as I transferred them into the store."

"That may well be the case, but you'll understand I can't sign for something we haven't received," I reply with a noticeable degree of authority.

"Yeah, I understand," he replies as he countersigns the delivery note amendment, before heading back to the depot with a very confused look on his face.

Ten minutes later, as I'm walking along the main corridor, one of Willy's fellow residents, Frank, throws his arm across my chest as I make a vain attempt to push the corridor door open to continue my journey.

"Hey up, Boocock. Do you want to buy a few little Easter eggs?"

I'm sure I already know what Frank has in his shopping bag.

"I don't suppose they're Cadbury's Creme Eggs, are they? They're my favourites," I lie.

"Yes they are. You can have as many as you want. I've got hundreds."

It seems I was right for once.

"I'll take the lot then, so bring them to my office and don't tell anybody. How much are they anyway?

"They're only little, so they're tuppence each."

"Okey dokey. I'll see you in a bit."

Surprise, surprise! In less than five minutes I'm the new owner of two hundred and eighty eight Cadbury's Creme Eggs, but poor old Frank is now being manhandled into Matron's office for a bit of a telling off.

Life just doesn't get any better than this.

Me and Amir are getting on like a house on fire, and he absolutely loves the thought of being best friends with somebody he considers to be a senior manager. I even visit him and his wife and daughters during one of their short breaks on the east coast, and I have to say they're an absolutely wonderful family. I decide not to accompany them on their next holiday though, as Mauritius is just a bit too far away. However I do agree to pick them up from Heathrow Airport when they return.

Then when his parents fly over to pay them a visit a few months later, I offer to return to Heathrow with Amir to greet them and bring them back to Sheffield. As we head out of the arrivals hall, Amir's Dad presents me with a beautiful hand-carved model sailing ship, which I'm told has been parked on his knee all the way from Mauritius.

It takes a few minutes to get the car out of the car park, due to the tears still affecting my sight, but please don't tell anyone, as I'm not actually that soft. OK?

The hospital has a team competing in the Sheffield Churches Snooker League, and we take several residents along with us to games at various churches and the Salvation Army Hostel in the city centre. It's lovely to be involved in making the residents of 'Middlewood Hospital Village' feel just like normal people.

One evening whilst Amir is spending a few days in Skegness, we have an in-house staff versus residents snooker tournament, and I'm honoured to be captain of the staff team, which includes the hospital general manager, a psychiatrist and the hospital chaplain. I've been drawn to play against a very tall muscular West Indian resident by the name of Malcolm, a guy I've never bumped into before. Whilst we're waiting our turn to play, I invite Malcolm to have a coffee and sandwich with me, and he gratefully accepts. He's a really nice, well spoken middle aged man, who could very easily be mistaken for a male nurse. Malcolm tells me he spent more than ten years in the hospital, before being moved out into a warden-controlled hostel in the Foxhill area, just a couple of miles from Middlewood, but it's nice to be back for the evening and he's looking forward to the game.

It's an unwritten rule that we mustn't let a resident win a game of snooker, just because he resides in a psychiatric hospital. If he thinks he's a better player than he actually is, he'll more than likely agree to play someone for money when he gets shipped out into the community, and he's bound to come unstuck sooner or later. I have mixed feelings when I thrash Malcolm three games to nil, but my new friend takes the defeat very calmly, and I treat him to a mug of tea and a wedge of chocolate cake whilst we watch the final match.

At the end of the tournament, which I'm delighted say was easily won by the staff team, I offer to give Malcolm a lift back to the hostel, which he willingly accepts. En route a few minutes later, he asks if I'd like to have a look around the hostel, but although it seems like a good idea from a professional point of view, I politely decline due to it now being late in the evening, and I don't wish to disturb any of his fellow residents. We shake hands as he steps out of the car, and before I drive off, we agree to meet again some time in the future for a rematch.

I've been in bed for over an our when the phone rings. It's Amir, and he's clearly in a state of panic. Apparently, he called the hospital chaplain to ask how the snooker match went, and he was pleased to know the staff were the victors on this occasion. The chaplain also mentioned that I'd given Malcolm a real thrashing, but he'd taken it very well and I'd given him a lift back to the hostel.

From what I'm now being told, Amir went into a blind panic at this point, because I wouldn't know that the last thing I should ever do, is to go into the hostel with Malcolm, especially as it's late evening and there's a possibility that no one else would be a round at this time. He asks if I'm OK, and whether or not I accompanied Malcolm into the hostel. I assure him I'm absolutely fine, and that due to the time, I turned down the invitation to have a look around the place.

"That was lucky," gasps a very relieved Amir. "He's been in psychiatric care for so long, because of his nasty habit of using a wet towel to strangle anybody who upset him, and as you gave him a bit of a hammering at snooker, you might have just earned yourself a place on his hit list."

I didn't get much sleep that night!

The elderly residents have a dining room as their disposal, and it makes a refreshing change for them to enjoy meals away from the ward environment. The catering team is very well organised and disciplined, and just like the nurses, they make sure every resident is properly looked after, so there's minimum nursing presence whilst meals are being served. Unfortunately, due to the age and general health of the diners, some occasionally suffer from the odd problem with incontinence. It's a most unpleasant task of course, but the food service team is expected to clean up any mess immediately, without causing embarrassment to the resident. The cleaning up task is delegated equally across the team, so none of them has any greater responsibility than any other colleague.

Slap bang in the middle of today's lunchtime service, the dining room supervisor bursts into my office to tell me that one of the female residents has had a bout of severe incontinence. She goes on to tell me that Grace, one of our West Indian food service team members who has been delegated responsibility for maintaining the dining room in a clean and hygienic condition today, is refusing to carry out her responsibilities. I go straight into the dining room and tell Grace to accompany me back to the office, where I'm about to have the biggest bust-up ever with a member of staff.

"Grace, I understand it's an awful task, but you know the rules and it's your delegated responsibility today, to keep the area clean, so get back in there and sort it out before somebody has a real accident."

"You can't make me do it," Grace venomously responds. "I'm not cleaning up white shit any more. Not for you, not for the patients and not for anybody else."

"Well I'm giving you a choice. You either do the job, just like the rest of your colleagues do, or you get your coat on and clear off home, but if that's the option you choose to take, then don't bother coming back. Do you understand?"

Grace storms out of the office, hurling a few obscenities in my direction as she makes her way to the staff changing room to collect her coat.

"There'll be some trouble coming your way now", says the dining room supervisor. "That woman is trouble, but nobody's ever had the guts to take her on."

A few days later, I'm in discussion with Clive, the Human Resources Manager and Jackie, our local Trades Union shop steward. Grace's solicitor has written to Clive, with a copy being sent to Jackie, advising that I'm being taken to a Race Relations tribunal for my act of racial discrimination against Grace. Clive is new to his post, and as neither he nor the hospital has ever had to deal with this kind of problem before, he finds it most interesting when Jackie goes on to tell us she dislikes Grace, as she's in and out of her office regularly, accusing everybody and their grandmother of racism, and that she's nothing but a pain in the ass.

Clive and Jackie appear to be more than a little surprised when I suggest they don't get too concerned about the accusation, and as I head back to my office, I casually ask Clive to let me know when the date of the tribunal has been decided. A couple of weeks later, the three of us arrive at the tribunal to find Grace and her husband ready and waiting. I'm quite surprised when the husband comes over to shake hands with the three of us, whilst his wife remains seated with a face like a bumble bee chewing a wasp. We head into the office where the case is to be heard by a West Indian lawyer.

He runs through the details of the accusation and then invites Grace to give her side of the story. The anger and hatred builds-up like a volcano getting ready to erupt. At one point, she appears to forget where she is, and states categorically that she couldn't give a damn about the patients, so no matter what happens she's never going to clean up white shit again. The lawyer's chin almost hits his desk at this point, and then he hands over to me. I explain what happened in the residents' dining room, and then I play my ace card. I pull out a few photographs, followed by several sealed envelopes, before stepping toward the lawyer.

"This is a photo of me and my best friend Amir, the senior nurse who manages the patients' social club at the hospital, and here's a photo of me and Amir with his wife and daughters in Skegness. The next one is my favourite though, as it's a photo that Amir took of me and his Dad and the hand-carved sailing ship the old man made for me, and then carried on his lap all the way from Mauritius to Heathrow Airport."

"Next, there's a photo of me with my Ma and Pa and our family friend, Ahmed Mumtaz and his wife and kids, and you'll notice Mum's outfit is Indian-style. You probably know Ahmed, as he's now a Justice of the Peace, and he and his wife also own Millhouses Post Office. Next is Tommy, my friend who works in the Orthodontics Department at the Northern General, and the photo shows me with him and his family enjoying a Sunday lunch together. Finally, here's a pile of letters-cum-references from the people in the photographs, which hopefully will throw some doubt on Grace's accusation."

As I head back to my seat, I can't help noticing the smiles appearing on Clive and Jackie's faces, as the lawyer studies the photographs and letters of support. I also can't help noticing the look on Grace's husband's face as he glances in her direction, as the lawyer relays his verdict to his audience.

"Having given great consideration to what's been said here today, and to the evidence presented by the accused, there's absolutely no doubt in my mind whatsoever, that we have only one racist in this room, and that's you, Grace. I'm well aware that racism exists throughout the world, and it needs to be stamped out, but I have to say you're the most bigoted human being I've ever had the displeasure to meet in my entire life. I strongly urge you to apologise to Mr Boocock, and perhaps to your husband as well. Not only have you wasted everyone's time, you've also brought into question Mr Boocock's integrity, not only as a manager, but also as a man of honour and the highest personal values."

Grace crawls toward the exit door with head almost hanging down to her knees, with husband in tow. He nods and smiles towards me, Clive and Jean as he heads through the door, just moments before world war three breaks out in the corridor. As we're about to depart, the lawyer asks Clive and Jackie if they could give him a couple of minutes to have a word with me in private.

He tells me we've met before, but it was at a party of one his friends.

Apparently he can never remember much about the parties he goes to, due to the effect of all the rather sweet smelling smoke his friends are expelling all night long. However, he does know that he wouldn't want his Orthodontic friend Tommy to be pulling out any of my teeth when he's been at a party with him. Then as we shake hands as I depart, he assures me I won't have any more problems with Grace, although by the sound of what's going on in the corridor right now, I think she might already be having a few problems with her old man.

Until now, I had no idea how much trouble Grace had caused the catering team since she joined them, so now she's no longer on the scene, there's already a few celebrations going on by the time I arrive the following morning. Amir is also thrilled to bits when I pop into the club during the evening to give him the good news, but whilst we're playing a few frames of snooker, I can't help noticing that one of the older residents appears to be watching me very closely.

"What's Joe looking at?" I ask Amir. "He's always hanging around the table when we're playing snooker."

"He'll just be trying to work out whether or not he thinks he can beat you," replies Amir. "He's a bit of a con-artist, and he'll be looking to figure out a way of cheating you out of some cash."

"How long has he been a resident?" I ask somewhat puzzled.

"About forty years, I think. He had a bit of a breakdown during the war and ended up in here."

"So what's the con?" I ask with interest.

"Once he thinks he can beat you, he'll offer to play you for money, and then he'll swindle you before you realise what's happening."

"Yeah, but we're only allowed to play them for ten pence or for the price of a cup of tea, so it's no big deal," I suggest.

"It's different with Joe. He won't take you on for less then a quid, but that's OK. He has to learn the hard way, as when they move him back out into the community, he's likely to try it on against somebody who won't be too pleased if they get scammed," explains Amir. "Just be careful if he asks you to play. He might have been in here for half of his life, but he's not daft."

We carry on with our game whilst Joe continues to weigh me up. Amir miscues when he attempts to pot the final black, leaving it standing precariously over the edge of the pocket at one end of the table, whilst the cue ball ends up at the far end of the table. It's a tricky shot but if I can pot the black then I'll win the frame, but just I start preparing for the shot I notice that Joe is now crouching behind the black ball staring intensely down the table at me.

As I draw the cue back to line up the shot, I try to ignore the smirking face that's now half hidden behind the black, but the very moment I ram the cue forward, the false teeth shoot from Joe's mouth, and with his tongue somehow controlling them, they start spinning around like the propeller on a speedboat. The cue almost rips the cloth as the cue ball flies up into the air, way over the black, and onto the floor close to Joe's left shoe.

I don't know why you're laughing. It's not funny, and I just lost the bloody game!

It's no surprise when Joe approaches me the following Monday, when I'm having an hour's practice session whilst Amir takes a couple of well-earned rest days.

"Tharra good player thee, tharra good player. Does tha fancy a game?"

"Yeah, why not. Are we playing for ten pence or for a cup of tea?" I ask in the knowledge that we won't be playing for either.

"Nah, bugger that. Let's mek it a quid."

"OK then, a quid it is," I reply with feigned surprise, as I set the balls up ready.

From what Amir tells me, Joe's a pretty good player, so I'm delighted when not only do I go one frame up, I've also hammered him by fifty eight points.

"Tharra good player thee, tharra good player. Let's av another game?"

"Yeah, that's fine by me?"

"Double or now't and a quid on't side" Joe asserts.

"What?" I ask with pretend confusion.

"Well if we just play for double or now't, if I win t'game we'll av won a quid apiece, so it'll av bin a waste o' time. On t'other hand, if we play for double or now't and a quid on t'side, then one of us'll av won some money."

"Yeah, yeah, whatever you want is fine by me," I reply.

Half an hour later, we've won one game each and I can't believe I'm handing over a quid. The old fart has conned me, just as Amir told me he would. The crafty old sod made me think I was the better player in the first game, and then when we've upped the ante, he turns out to be a much better player than he led me to believe. I'm still not a happy chappie when I arrive for work the following morning.

"What's up?" asks Roger, as I slam a mug of tea down onto my desk.

"Nothing, why?"

"I can tell by the look on your face and the puddle of tea on your desk that something's wrong?"

"I got conned at snooker last night by one of the residents who's been in here since the war," I squeak. "We won one game each, but ended up losing a quid. I don't care about the money, but I can't believe I let one of the residents turn me over."

"Don't tell me Joe's still at it after all these years," smirks Roger.

He interrupted my next practice session and surprise, surprise, he suggests we have a game for a quid. I'm out for revenge this time and just as I expected, I paste him by scoring ninety seven points to his thirty four.

"Tharra good player, thee. Tharra good player."

I've been waiting for this.

"Yeah, yeah! Don't give me all that rubbish, Joe. Just get the balls set back up and before you ask, yes, we'll be playing for double or now't and a quid on't side. But you won't be conning me this time, you old goat."

"I dunno what tha means, Boocock. It's thee t'break."

I play my socks off but I still end up getting stuffed for the second time, so another quid ends up in his grubby hand.

“I know what you were doing last night,” smiles Roger the next morning, as I almost take the office door off its hinges as I arrive.

“Leave it, leave I,” I suggest.

Joe tries it on again on Wednesday evening, but this time I manage to win both the first and second frames and now he owes me three quid.

“Tharra goo….”

“Yes, yes I know all that, so what happens now?” I ask triumphantly.

“I owe thee three quid, don’t I?”

“You certainly do. One for the first frame and two for the second.”

“OK. So let’s just av one more game then. Double or now’t and three quid on’t side,” Joe suggests as he lines the balls up. If I win this one tha’ll owe me three quid, but if thar wins it I’ll owe thee nine quid. Is that raight?”

“Yeah, that’s ‘raight’, I gleam as I break off.

The Lord be praised! I stuff him out of sight for the third game in a row.

“Tharra good player, thee. Tharra good player. I’ll sort thee winnings out and bring t’cash tomorrow.”

“You won last night then?” asks Roger when I arrive smiling the next morning.

“Oh yes! Oh yes! I thrashed the crafty old sod three frames to nil, so I’m absolutely buzzing.”

Later in the morning, whilst Roger is taking his daily stroll around the wards, the Hospital General Manager, Alan Gregory pops into the office to ask if I’ll be around next Thursday, as he has some news about the future of the hospital. The moment he departs, my secretary dashes in with some unexpected news.

"Ooh, that was close," she says. "That bloke you've been playing snooker with, has just been in to hand over your nine quid winnings. I didn't think you'd want him hanging around whilst the hospital boss was in your office, so I told him you were busy right now, so you'd see him when you're next in the social club."

I decide to leave it for a couple of days, and when I stroll into the social club around lunch time on Saturday, I'm greeted by Amir. He thinks the story is hilarious, but I explain that I don't want Joe's money, I just wanted my pride back. Amir is still laughing when we notice Joe heading our way.

"I an't seen thee forra day or two, Boocock. I think I owe thee nine quid, so if I gi' thee this tenner, can tha gimme a quid change?"

"I don't want your money, Joe. I just wanted to get my own back."

"Tha what? Tha dun't want thee winnings then?"

"No, I don't, so let that be a lesson to be remembered when you're back out in the community."

"Well if tha dun't want thee money, I'll keep it me sen. Tharra good player though, tharra good player," he claims as he heads out and down the drive.

Me and Amir get started on our snooker match, and as we come towards the end of the fifth frame, Joe strolls back into the club and heads towards us.

"Look at this lot, Boocock" gleams Joe, as he pulls out a huge wad of cash from his jacket pocket. "I've just been in t'bookies an' put them winnings tha din't want, on a couple of 'orses. Av cum back wi seventy quid in me pocket, so that weren't bad, worrit?"

Right now I'm not sure whether I love or hate my life, thanks to Joe!

No, that's not true. I really love being at Middlewood Hospital, in fact I could happily stick around here until I retire.

Yeah, I should be so lucky!

We've all known for quite some time that the hospital has been earmarked for closure during the next few years, but my boss, Peter has a plan that could possibly save the catering services, but it would mean that some very difficult decisions would have to be made.

Before arriving at Middlewood, Peter was General Manager at a hospital in Gloucestershire, where the catering services introduced the cook-chill system, similar to the food production technique used by airline catering companies. In his view, the system could provide a lifeline for our own catering services when the hospital finally shuts-up shop. It sounds very interesting so I decide to give it some thought. Without doubt our food hygiene standards would have to be first class, but that won't be a problem with the team we have at Middlewood, but the issue of greatest issue of concern is that we would have to make almost half of the kitchen brigade redundant, and that really would be a big ask. Then it occurs to me that companies producing food for airlines must be preparing thousands of meals a day, so with proper planning and the necessary level of investment, we could take over the nearby soon to be vacated local health authority central purchasing building, and turn it into a cook-chill production unit for all the hospitals in the Sheffield area and even the whole of the Trent Region.

Hell fire! I could get a knighthood for this!

The sky's the limit, and Peter agrees, but the first and potentially most explosive issue is how to get rid of half of Middlewood's kitchen brigade, and potentially all of the kitchen staff in about a dozen Sheffield hospitals and goodness knows how many across the Trent region, even though it would save NHS countless millions in the long term.

I present the plan to the Middlewood team, and I'm absolutely shell-shocked when they agree to it and to the redundancies, so in return I promise to be the first to depart if the plan ends up being binned by the powers that be.

I guess I probably won't be around here much longer then!

In the meantime, Peter somehow finds the money to turn our kitchen into a small cook-chill production unit just for Middlewood Hospital, and we're up and running within a couple of months. We've even managed to create roles for the displaced staff, so now the residents have a host or hostess to serve the meals on each ward.

I'm walking on air when the routine patient feedback report lands on my desk, as the food quality and service has apparently already reached an all-time high. Of course, I soon head back down to earth when I'm told the system hasn't a prayer of being extended anywhere else, due to the fallout the health authority would get from making so many staff redundant.

I now have no alternative other than to call the team together to break the news, and it means they'll all be out of work when the hospital finally closes down. I express my heartfelt thanks to the team for all the support I've received since I arrived on the scene, but the only thing I can do now is to resign as promised, even though the hospital still has a few years of life left.

Heartbroken doesn't even come close to explaining how I feel right now!

There are loads of management jobs on the market right now, and I think I'm now experienced and qualified enough to be a District Catering Manager in the NHS. I know I can't hang around doing nothing forever, so I decide to apply for the first such position I become aware of, and that just happens to be in Bassetlaw. I haven't the faintest idea where that is, but after a little bit of research, it turns out to be pretty close to home.

Sadly, I've heard nothing from Bassetlaw since I mailed my application almost a month ago, so I just carry on looking out for other opportunities. Then out of the blue, I receive a call from the District Personnel Director for Bassetlaw Hospitals, who apologises for the late reply to my application and invites me to attend for an interview a week on Friday. I spend the next ten days getting myself clued-up on all the stuff that comes with the District Catering Manager role, and by the time I arrive in Worksop, I'm feeling pretty confident, however it soon becomes apparent that the panel isn't particularly bothered about all that rubbish, because right now their biggest problem is the quality of food and lack of leadership.

Chapter Thirteen

Everybody Loves Quality Street

I think I've been in this position once or twice before, and on this occasion several management colleagues have already suggested I should steer well clear of Bassetlaw Hospital, as it's catering reputation is just a joke, but I can't do that for a couple of reasons. Firstly, it would be a step up as far as my career is concerned and secondly, if the catering services reputation is so bad, it would be a great opportunity to make a name for myself if I can it into one of the best.

That's exactly why I'm now sitting in front of the hospital's Chief Executive, Human Resources Manager and the General Services Manager. There are also a couple of very well known and highly respected local ladies on the interview panel, but I really don't understand why that would earn them a say in the appointment of the District Catering Manager. Anyway, everything appears to be going rather well as far as the three senior managers are concerned, and they're clearly very impressed with my CV. Then one of the ladies pipes up.

"We have a Catering Committee at Bassetlaw Hospital, which reviews any comments and complaints received from by patients and staff, and one of our biggest problems seems to be that the toast served to patients is always soggy. What would you do to rectify the problem?" she lamely enquires.

A glance towards the senior management trio suggests they're thinking just what I'm thinking right now. Is that really a question to be asking a potential District Catering Manager? They should be asking about things such as my organisational skills, budgetary control, quality assurance, food safety compliance and a whole load of other boring stuff, but this is not the time to be discussing soggy toast.

My response isn't meant to offend anyone, but with hindsight I guess it could have resulted in an earlier than expected end to the interview.

"If that's the only problem you have around here, then I suggest you forget about bringing in a new District Catering Manager, and just send somebody out to go and buy a couple of new toasters for each ward."

The three senior managers peer down at their interview notes, clearly struggling to stay in control as I dig myself an even bigger hole.

"I can only assume that somebody in the main kitchen makes the toast around half past six in the morning and stacks it into warm containers with lids on. Then the containers will be loaded into heated trolleys, where they'll sit for another hour until the hospital porters turn up to start shipping breakfast out to the wards. Then the trolleys will stand for another half hour, until somebody on the ward finally gets round to slapping the toast onto plates and handing it to the patients."

"I suppose that could well be what happens," she replies as I continue blundering my way forward.

"Well, I'm sorry to tell you there's absolutely no way known to man, that you can keep a shedload of toast in those conditions without it steaming itself to death. In my vast experience there are only two ways you can solve the problem, and as I've already suggested the best thing to do is buy a couple of toasters for each ward and have somebody around to make the toast just before the breakfast service begins.

"OK, so what's the second option," asks the lady with the toast problem.

"Stop serving toast" I suggest somewhat sarcastically.

She's clearly lost this particular battle, but she decides to have another go.

"During another Catering Committee meeting, numerous complaints about the gravy being lumpy had been made by patients several days earlier, so what would you do about that?" she asks.

Oh, for pity's sake. Is this for real?

I'm doing my utmost to avoid making things any worse than they are already, but my reply leaves the entire panel in fits of laughter.

"Oh my God! I just hope you're not going to tell me next, that somebody out there is pouring lumpy gravy onto the soggy toast. There's no wonder the complaints are piling up."

"It wouldn't have surprised me if something like that was happening," she smiles. "By the way, do you have a Catering Committee at your hospital?"

I think this is what's known as make or break time.

"Absolutely not," I reply emphatically.

"Why is that?" she asks.

"I've no wish to offend the panel, so please bear in mind that the purpose of this interview is twofold. Firstly, it gives you the opportunity to find out everything you need to know about me, and whether or not you think I'd be the best fit for the District Catering Manager's job. Secondly, it will also give me the opportunity to figure out whether or not I fancy working here."

I suppose I could be mistaken of course, but I get the feeling the panel are suddenly becoming even more interested now.

"There's no point in worrying about soggy toast and lumpy gravy that was served last week, because it's too late to do anything about it. My job would be to get a system in place to make sure nothing leaves the kitchen that you wouldn't happily serve to your mother. The catering team would design the system with me and then they would take individual and joint responsibility for what they do, including checking that all the food is of the highest quality before being shipped out to the wards. It's as simple as that," I state emphatically.

"Sounds good to me," claims the General Services Manager as I continue.

"Might I ask, do you have a Domestic Services Committee, a Linen and Laundry Committee, a Transport and Portering Committee, or an Engineering Committee?"

"No, just a Catering Committee," the General Services Manager states.

"Then why pick on Catering?" I ask a very surprised panel.

"I've no idea," he replies. "I've never given it a thought."

"Then I'll tell you why. We all think we know how to cook, but cooking for a family of four isn't the same as cooking three meals a day for several hundred patients, whilst giving them several options to choose from."

I don't doubt your Catering Committee is made up of well-meaning people, but I very much doubt that any of them has the faintest idea of what that entails," I suggest, whilst checking out exactly where the exit door is.

Well, I'm the chairman of our committee," claims the soggy toast lady.

"Yes, I thought you might be," I reply with a knowing smile, "But I have to tell you with the greatest respect, that in the extremely unlikely event you were to offer me the job, one of my top priorities would be to have your committee disbanded, because its very existence would be an insult to me and to every member of my team. I very much doubt that's something you wanted to hear, but as I mentioned earlier, you need to know all about me and how I would operate if I were to be managing the catering services, so I need to be honest with you."

I'd been told the interview was likely to last for at least ninety minutes and possibly more, but as I head to the exit door a glance at my wristwatch tells me I've only been in there for just over thirty minutes.

It's a pity I blew it, but they needed to know exactly what they would be letting themselves in for if they offered me the job. Don't you agree?

Anyway, it was nice to visit Robin Hood country for a change, so I decide to spend the weekend cycling around Sherwood Forest and nearby Clumber Park, and by the time I arrive home late on Sunday evening I've finally managed to put the disastrous interview to the back of my mind.

I can't believe it when I receive a call from Chief Executive Munro Donald late on a Sunday evening. It turns out that he's been trying to contact me since Saturday morning, and it isn't to tell me I made a complete mess of the interview. Apparently, I impressed the panel so much that they came to a unanimous decision in selecting me for the job, and the soggy toast lady was the first to cast her vote.

Well I can't turn that down, can I?

It's good to know that the catering team are fully on board with my plans, and we soon get to grips with turning things round. They most certainly aren't expecting to be given complete ownership of everything they do, and they're utterly amazed to hear that as far as I'm concerned my job title means almost nothing to me.

If they think about it, my experience in the industry totals up to about twenty years, but the team has about five hundred years between them. With that in mind, I'll do my utmost to earn they're respect through my own respect for them as individuals and as a team.

Their response is absolutely magnificent and it gets even better when I tell them tat from today, we no longer have a staff canteen as that gives the impression of a cheap and tatty old place to dine in. It will now be called the staff restaurant, and I jokingly apologise for making the decision without discussing it with them, and I assure them it will be the last time that happens. I know it's a bit risky, but as long as we comply with things like food safety standards, health and safety regulations, budgetary controls and things like, it won't be long before everybody starts to notice the improvements we're making as a team.

We're absolutely buzzing a month later, when we realise that our team effort has resulted in a significant increase in patient and customer satisfaction, whilst complaints are now almost at zero level. That's never happened before, so I make a point of congratulating the team and assuring them that it's down to us all singing from the same hymn sheet.

Now that's what I call a result!

During my second Catering Committee meeting, the soggy toast lady announces that the quality of catering services has improved beyond all expectations during the two months since my arrival. She goes on to explain that during my interview, I promised that if I was offered the District Catering Manager's position I would make it my top priority to get rid of the committee, and it was that statement which resulted in her being the first member of the interview panel to suggest I should be offered the job. According to her, the sheer professionalism and enthusiasm the team has shown in bringing the catering services to such a high standard, has been nothing but incredible, and it's abundantly clear that the committee is no longer required, and so this will be the last ever meeting.

That's fantastic, but as always, I won't let it go to my head!

The team goes wild when I tell them the good news and assure them it's all down to the effort each and every one of us has put into improving the quality of everything we do. My next little stunt turns out to be a real winner.

Head Chef June pops into my office one morning, and tells me that Veda, the lady who's been washing the pots for the last thirty years has gone off sick. She asks if I would mind taking over as head chef for the day, and then she'll look after all the washing up. I point out that running the kitchen is her job, so she can carry on as normal and I'll do the pot washing for the day.

Head Chef June pops into my office one morning, and tells me that Veda, the lady who's been washing the pots for the last thirty years has gone off sick. She asks if I would mind taking over as head chef for the day, and then she'll look after all the washing up. I point out that running the kitchen is her job, so she can carry on as normal and I'll do the pot washing for the day.

"You can't do the washing up, you're the District Catering Manager," she replies.

"Nonsense," I reply. "I told you the day I started work here that's just a job title and it means nothing to me. I'll be doing the washing up, so let's get cracking."

I've heard that Veda hasn't had a very good life, so I decide to give her a little surprise. I send her a message telling her to get dressed-up and be at work by six o'clock when she returns to work next Monday, as I'm taking her out for the day.

"Where are we going?" Veda enquires as she arrives back at work.

"I'm taking you to Earl's Court in London. There's a huge catering exhibition called Hotelympia there next week, so me and you will be there."

"London? I've never been there before. But I'm only the pot washer, so why me?" she asks with a somewhat puzzled look on her face.

"Only the pot washer? What do you mean, you're ONLY the pot washer?" I ask with pretend dismay. "As far as they're concerned at Hotelympia you're the Deputy District Catering Manager, and that's what it'll say on the name badge I've ordered for you. So make sure you bring a couple of carried bags with you, as you'll be bringing loads of goodies back from the catering supplier stands."

I explain that if the District Catering Manager doesn't to turn up for a week it won't cause any problems, apart from there being a mountain of paper work on my desk when I return. On the other hand, if the pot washer doesn't turn up we'll be up the creek without a paddle. We won't have anybody to wash all the used crockery cutlery when it arrive back from the wards, so there'll be no point in the cooks preparing any more meals, because there'll be nothing to serve it on and nothing for the patients to eat it with. So as there'll be no food for the patients, they'll all be sent home and the hospital will have to shut down, all because there's nobody around to wash the pots.

"So tell me, who's the most important person around here? The District Catering Manager or the pot washer?" Me or you?

Nice one Booey! I think I just made a new friend.

What she doesn't know, is that I've also booked return tickets on the Master Cutler from Sheffield's Midland Station, and neither does she know we'll be having breakfast in the dining car on the journey to London, and dinner on the way back. Veda reckons it's like being a member of the Royal Family, and it gets even better when, after spending four hours in the exhibition centre, we take a taxi to Trafalgar Square and make our way down Pall Mall to Buckingham Palace and on to the Houses of Parliament. Another taxi ride takes us to Harrod's for afternoon tea brings the most enjoyable day of her life to an end, apart from the evening dinner on the Master Cutler.

What a winner and a wonderful day all round!

Meanwhile, the Government is now making 'quality' a major factor in the delivery of NHS support services. Fortunately, there are no problems now as far as our catering services are concerned, but there are some areas of concern in other support services. Actually, it's not just about the quality of services, it's also about financial management and control, competitiveness, and value for money, so almost everything across the board appears to be under review.

I love Quality Street, so it might be worth considering a change of career.

There were three hospitals in the Bassetlaw district when I arrived, but now there's only one, Bassetlaw District General. It crosses my mind that even though we only have one hospital, we still have several District Managers in the Support Services Directorate and in my humble view it's time for a change.

I suggest to the Chief Executive Munro Donald, that I be allowed to resign as District Catering Manager, and then the District Domestic Services Manager can add the catering services to her portfolio of responsibilities. She could also take over the Portering Services when the current post holder retires, and her new job title could be Hotel Services Manager. If the idea was adopted, it would save the hospital a small fortune, and it would bring the hotel services much closer together, making quality management and control much easier.

The plan turns out to be a good one according to Munro, and now I'm delighted to be known as the Quality Development Manager, with responsibility for the review and quality improvement of all support services, and for the planning and implementation of quality management and quality control systems. Once again, Munro has given me a free hand to figure out what needs to be done to make sure our support services are of the highest quality. I don't think I can do that, unless I know what other organisations are doing, so perhaps the best thing to do is to go and find out. I decide to join a Quality Club in Pontefract, where people from various industry sectors share their ideas and experiences of quality improvement, management and control, and I also make a point of visiting hospitals across the country to check out what they're doing about such matters.

Life is made much easier when I realise most operational managers in our support services are up for the challenge, and it's not long before we start adopting the ideas I've picked up during my travels. Munro is delighted with the progress I've made so far, especially when we become aware of other hospitals being interested in what we're doing.

Meanwhile, he has to find the money to foot the bill for me to attend various NHS seminars, but due to the recent interest shown by other hospitals in our own quality initiatives, he comes up with a plan of his own. Most seminars are held in the London area, and that means it can be quite expensive for the purchase of tickets, travel and the occasional overnight accommodation.

Bassetlaw is in Nottinghamshire, and is pretty easy to get to from almost anywhere in the country. We're also fortunate to have a very nice Post Graduate Education Centre of its own, with seating for about two hundred people, so Munro suggests we might consider hosting our own seminars. Not only would it cost nothing for us to attend our own seminars, we would also make a profit from the sale of tickets and best of all Bassetlaw Hospital would become recognised as a centre of excellence in NHS quality.

Not only would it cost nothing for me and other local delegates to attend, we would also make a profit from the sale of tickets, but even better from the Chief Executive's point of view, Bassetlaw would soon become a recognised centre of excellence for NHS quality.

Now that's a plan if ever there was one!

Over the coming months, our seminars are a huge success and we really do make a profit whilst becoming known as a centre of excellence. It doesn't do my own reputation any harm either, and it's with that in mind that Munro suggests I come up with some kind of a project proposal that we could use as our bid for an NHS Quality Award.

And that's a challenge if ever there was one!

Munro has always been keen on all things American. He drives a beautiful American convertible automobile, and he also enjoys the working relationship he has his counterpart in the USA's Inova Health organisation, based in Fairfax, Virginia. I take all that into account, and as I've been spending a great deal of time comparing the management of quality in our support services with those in other hospitals and organisations across the country, I take all that into account and come up with finally come up with a plan.

Leave it! Leave it!

Our bid for the award will be entitled Robin Hood Meets Uncle Sam, and it will be a benchmarking project based upon me and four members of the support services team travelling to Virginia to spend a week with our counterparts in the Inova Healthcare organisation, to compare our respective quality standards, ideas and initiatives with the aim of identifying further quality improvement opportunities for both parties. With me at the helm it's no great surprise when Robin Hood Meets Uncle Sam is declared the winner, and Munro is over the moon when he receives official notification. He's even more pleased in the knowledge that having already decided that the cost of our trip would be met from the profits we've made from our seminars, somebody else is now going to foot the bill.

I think Munro is beginning to love Quality Street as well!

A few weeks later, me and Robin Hood's Merry Men arrive at Uncle Sam's Dulles Airport in Washington DC early on Sunday afternoon, and it's just a short taxi ride to the motel in Tyson's Corner. Apart from myself we have our Domestic Services Manager Betty and Sue, a domestic assistant, Terry who's a porter, an engineer called Dave, and our head chef June. They'll be spending the week working with their respective counterparts, whilst I'll be wandering around all over the place pretending to know something about quality management and assurance.

None of us have ever invaded the States before, so we have absolutely no idea how anything's done in this neck of the woods, and I don't just mean in healthcare, so after unpacking, we decide to take a stroll around down-town Washington DC before it gets dark, and it's not long before we find ourselves heading down Pennsylvania Avenue towards the White House. Dave is walking ahead of the rest of us, and is busy taking photographs of President Clinton's pad just across the road. I'm happily taking in the sights a few steps behind him the rest of the gang are lagging even further behind, due to them having stopped at several hawker stalls to pick up things like American flags, tee-shirts, baseball caps and a multitude of other cheap-tack souvenirs.

It's early evening by the time we close in on the White House gates, and I can see a line of red and blue lights heading down the drive. There's an intersection just a couple of hundred yards further along Pennsylvania Avenue, and a pedestrian crossing at the end of each road leading to it. A policeman is clearly visible sitting side-saddle on his motorbike on the opposite end of each pedestrian crossing, and as I approach the intersection I can only assume they've suddenly received some kind of signal or instruction, because every single one of them suddenly cocks his leg over the handlebars, kickstarts his motorbike and drives it over the edge of the side walk and into the road. The oncoming traffic is brought to a standstill in a matter of seconds, and then each cop steps back onto the side walk.

As I come within touching distance of the policeman directly in front of me, I can't help noticing he's fully kitted-out with crash helmet and sun-glasses, and he has a handgun buttoned-up in a holster underneath his leather jacket. I'm within touching distance as he suddenly stretches out his arms as he raises them to shoulder height, then he spins around to face the crowd gathering behind him and starts yelling instructions to the pedestrians.

"You sir, stay right where you are. You ma'am get behind me. You sir, don't move," and on it goes until the world comes to a complete and utter standstill.

I'm standing right behind the policeman, but Dave is still about twenty yards away taking photographs via his very expensive Nikon camera. A quick glance over my shoulder tells me my other colleagues are about another thirty yards to my rear, and appear to be examining the bags of souvenirs they've just bought. By now the red and blue lights are approaching the White House gates leading out and onto Pennsylvania Avenue.

It turns out to be a convoy of some sort, led by four motorcycle police out-riders with red and blue lights on their handlebars, followed by a huge black limousine with blacked-out windows. Behind that is a second limousine closely followed by an ambulance, yet another limousine with blacked-out windows and finally four more motorcycle police outriders bringing up the rear. I doesn't take long to figure out that umpteen protection guys with pistols at the ready will be hiding in first limousine, President Clinton will be taking a ride in the second, with his personal ambulance-cum-operating theatre in tow just in case, and the final limo will be carrying the rest of his protection squad.

I can't believe we've only been in the States for just over four hours, and here we are with President Bill Clinton in our midst. This calls for a photo, but as I don't have a camera I turn and peer over the top of the gathering crowd and start waving my arms around to catch Terry's attention, once he lifts his head up from his bag of flags, tee-shirts and baseball caps.

"Terry! "The President's in the second car. Can you get a shot from there?" I stupidly yell without thinking.

The cop clearly doesn't have the same grasp of the English language as me, and it takes less than two seconds for him to lower his arms, spin round, unbutton the holster, whip out the gun, poke the end of the barrel straight onto my forehead and finally click back the safety catch. Believe me when I tell you this is not a very good position to be in, especially as his face is devoid of any expression whatsoever. He remains completely silent for a few seconds, whilst gradually increasing the pressure of the gun on my forehead.

"Sir, are you from the United Kingdom," he calmly enquires whilst I'm desperately trying to remember if I'm carrying any clean underwear in my back pocket.

"Er, yes I am," I stutter.

"Sir, how long have you been in the US of A?

"Err, hmm, err about four hours, I think.""Sir, you probably won't make five," he growls. "Sir, some advice. Whilst ever you're in the United States of America NEVER use the words 'president' and 'shot' in the same sentence. Sir, do you understand?"

Right now I'm more concerned about making sure I remain in control of the severe bout of incontinence I think I'm about to experience. Luckily, after what feels like an eternity the policeman finally rams the gun back into its holster just in time, and then Big Bill gives me a friendly wave as he goes by in the direction of Dave and his Nikon camera.

For some reason my legs appear to have turned to jelly and I could do with grabbing hold of the policeman's shoulders for support, although that might not be a good idea right now. It would still be great to get a photograph of the President so soon after our arrival though, so without giving it a thought I stand up onto my tiptoes and peer across the crowd in the hope of catching Dave's eye. I think there's only way I can tell him to take a photograph of the oncoming limousine's passenger without risking life and limb, and that's to mime the instructions in the knowledge that in the event me getting it wrong for a second time, the policeman will probably end up blowing my brains out.

Of course, if my brains were to be splattered all over the pavement there wouldn't be much mess for him to clean up, would there?.

I place my hands flat onto the top of my head before raising them up and down several times to indicate I'm taking about 'the big man'. Then I hold my arms out in front of me and pretend to turn the steering wheel of an invisible car a few times, before sticking two fingers up in the air to indicate the big man is in the second car. Then finally, I point directly towards Dave as I lift an invisible camera to my face and press the button a couple of times. He should now know the President is in the second car and that I need him to take a photograph. Genius! So we only have to wait for Bill to smile and wave to him, and that'll be job done.

If only that was the case!

This is not the time for Dave to run out of film, and it's most unfortunate that his use of the English language appears to be on a par with my own.

"I can't get a shot right now. I've got to reload," he bellows towards me and the deeply suspicious cop, who goes into a spin as he unbuttons his holster once again.

"Sir, is he with you?" he demands as he starts to extract the gun. "Sir, tell me RIGHT NOW. IS THAT GUY WITH YOU? YES OR NO?"

"Yes! Yes! He's with me," I scream with more than a hint of panic. "He's going to take a photograph of the President, but he's run out of film."

I'm somewhat relieved to notice the pistol being slammed back into its holster as the cop shakes is head in total disbelief and turns away. It takes him a little while to calm down before he steps off the side walk and signals to the waiting drivers to let them know they can restart their engines.

"Jeez! Damn Limeys! Friggin' crazy, all of them," he mutters under his breath.

Well he's right about that, especially this one!

I'm glad to get back to the hotel and relative safety. Then, whilst we're discussing our plans for benchmarking project over a drink or three at the bar, I get chatting to a local chap who asks what I think of the USA so far. I tell him what happened earlier on Pennsylvania Avenue and that I'm still in a state of shock, due to almost having my stupid head blown off. I explain that back in the UK, we see the President being interviewed twice a day on the CNN News channel whilst he's jogging around the streets of Washington. There's always one reporter running alongside him and asking a question or two during Big Bill's first jogging session of the day, and then another reporter takes over to ask more questions whilst he's pounding the streets for the second time. I can't understand is why the most protected man on earth can waltz around the streets of Washington without a care in the world twice a day, but I almost get my brains blown out when I just want to take a photograph of him, whilst half of the CIA and the Washington police force are holding his hand.

"Oh, golly no. The President doesn't run around the streets of Washington or anywhere else. He wouldn't last ten minutes. You must be mistaken," comes the disbelieving reply.

"But we watch him jogging twice a day on CNN News and sometimes, you can even see the White House in the background, so he must be doing it."

"Ah, hang on a minute. I think I know what's going on, and it ain't what you think. I suggest you go down to the White House just before noon one day, and hang around for a while. I think you'll soon figure out what really happens," the man smiles as he shakes his head and strolls out into the car park.

I'm intrigued, and I guess you might be as well, so I'll let you know how I get on.

Just before noon on Wednesday, I'm standing on the Pennsylvania Avenue side walk, immediately opposite the White House. There's a CNN News van parked a few yards further along the side walk to my left, and an identical van is parked across the road between the White House gates and the notorious intersection to my right. A reporter is perched on the step of the side door of each van.

Then shortly after noon, the track suited President and another guy, who I assume is a member of his protection squad, appear outside the White House and start walking down the drive. As they stroll through the gates the bodyguard sticks his arm up into the air to beckon to the nearest reporter, who is sitting just a few yards further down the street to his left. The guy trots up to him and Big Bill and then all three of them then step off the side walk and start jogging across the road.

The reporter asks a question as he almost rams the microphone up the President's hooter. He thanks Bill and heads back to the waiting van. Having safely jogged all the way across the road, the President and his mate step onto the side walk close to me, and stroll towards the intersection before bearing right and out of view.

So far the President has only jogged about thirty yards and he's already had his first interview of the day. I think I'm beginning to figure out what's going on.

They reappear a few minutes later and the bodyguard is carrying several small boxes in his arms, each bearing the logo of the Wendy Burger House, which apparently is just around the corner where they disappeared out of sight a few minutes ago, having made the huge effort to jog all the way across the road. They stroll back along the side walk towards me until they're immediately opposite the White House gates. Then just as I'd anticipated the bodyguard signals to the reporter to my left, and within a few seconds the three of them are jogging back across the road.

After a couple of questions the reporter nods his appreciation and heads back to his van, leaving the President and his sidekick to step onto the side walk and stroll back up the White House drive. I'm laughing to myself as I consider the scam I just witnessed. The whole world and his granny are being led to believe the President of the United States spends most of his day keeping fit and healthy by pounding the streets of Washington DC, but all he actually does is jog across the width of the street to collect a Wendy Burger and then jog back.

It's our final day in America I present the results of our Benchmarking project to the senior management team of Inova. I'm delighted to find that we're at least on a par with our hosts when it comes quality management and control, and by the end of the meeting I'm delighted to hear that they're already preparing to implement a number of my initiatives for themselves.

Another job well done, and I've lived to tell the tale. Impressed or what?

Back home, I'm asked to make a number of presentations to various management representatives from across the Trent Region, further enhancing my reputation and that of the hospital. I've delivered countless presentations and staff training sessions to all levels of NHS staff and management over the years, and there's no doubt in my mind that my ever-increasing confidence and skills in public speaking is the result of making sure I'm well prepared in advance, just like I was when I was a bit of a singer and a stand-up comedian.

It's still a surprise to be invited to host my own show on the Bassetlaw Hospital Radio station, and that sounds like something else that could be right up my alley.

Chapter Fourteen

A New Dawn Arising

After a bit of training, mainly in how to use the turntables and microphone, I now have a two-hour slot entitled Heartbeat every Tuesday evening, which sounds to me like an appropriate name for a show on hospital radio. It's a really nice feeling to be popping onto the wards for a quick chat with patients and to ascertain their favourite records so I can dedicate them during the evening.

The show focusses on classic sixties songs and country music, with the emphasis being placed on easy listening. I also enjoy doing some homework on every record I play and that gives me the opportunity to pan-out the chat and bring in the odd-bit of comedy. The feedback from patients and nursing staff is brilliant.

Our brilliant General Services Manager, Paul Nesbitt has left Bassetlaw, so we have a new boss by the name of Brian Gibbs. Meanwhile, it's beginning to look as though all the support services are going to be put out to tender, so Chief Executive Munro decides to bring in a consultancy firm to advise and assist in making sure we'll be competitive in terms of service quality and cost effectiveness.

Philip Russell is the company's Managing Director, and we hit it off from day one. He loves the way I go about my work, and the enjoyment I bring to the job for other members of the support services team. It's also good to know we have similar views on topics such as staff flexibility, multi-tasking, staff ownership and quality management.

He suggests I could do very well if I worked in the private sector, so if ever I fancied a career change I should let him know and he'll find something for me. That comes as a great surprise and a huge compliment, and something I'm totally unprepared for, but having spent the last twenty-odd years in the NHS, I thank him for the offer but I have to turn it down at least for the time being.

So, having come up with so many quality initiatives and having made so many improvements during the last couple of years, Philip and his company are no longer required, but we depart on excellent terms and on the understanding that I'll let him know if I ever change my mind about joining him and his team.

I doubt that will ever happen, but it's a nice thought!

Phil's parting words get me thinking about my life, and I think perhaps it's now time for me to figure out some long-term plans for my future. I cherish the memories I have of my childhood, and since leaving school I've loved my working life, apart from the bit of a blip I went through a while ago. Through the years I've been involved in numerous sports and I've been a barbershop singer and a stand up comedian. Now I have my own hospital radio show. I have an interest in a few things I wouldn't normally talk about such as biblical theories, UFO's and other conspiracies. So with all that going on, it's no surprise that the most important thing that's missing in my life is a loving relationship with a woman I could happily spend the rest of my life with. I've had a number of relationships over the years, but as time goes by I've come to realise that true love is something I've yet to experience, but I just don't know where to start.

Hopefully a quiet word with Him Upstairs might help.

The hospital support services secretarial team ise based in the office block next to mine. Sandra is very outgoing and enjoys a good laugh, so my constant mickey-taking and offensive jokes are always well received. Joyce and Jane are quite reserved although they do have a decent sense of humour. Brian's PA, Dawn is a close friend of Jane and doesn't come across as having a sense of humour that's anywhere close to my own. In fact I have noticed occasionally that when the rest of us are having a good laugh, she just seems to fake the occasional smile whilst continuing to tap away on her computer keyboard. No doubt she'd make a good job of being the headmistress in a posh girls' school, but as I know absolutely nothing about her, I could be wrong.

Surprisingly, as I'm following Dawn up the steps towards the Medical Records office one morning, I can't help noticing what a fabulous pair of legs she has. Then as I overtake and come face to face with her, I realise for the first time that she has the most beautiful eyes which appear to have just a hint of sadness in them. In an instant I know for certain that this is the woman I've been waiting for, but I simply don't have the nerve to say anything because with me being a simple Dee Dah, she's clearly in a totally different league from me. I spend all night thinking about her and my mind is in turmoil by the time I arrive for work the next morning.

The first chance I get to speak to Dawn alone, I ask if she would meet me for a coffee, but without taking her eyes off the computer screen she declines my offer as she doesn't think it would be a good idea for either of us.

Something deep inside tells me I must try again, so I leave it for a few days before asking again. She turns me down for a second time, but my heart still tells me not to give up on her. Then after another few days she turns me down for the third time, and right now I can't help thinking I've never felt as low as this in my entire life and I'm certain that Dawn realises how much her rejection has affected me. Then later that day I hear that she's to have some minor surgery next Monday, which will put her out of action for the next few weeks, and I can't help thinking that by the time she arrives back in her office she'll have probably forgotten I even exist. I can only hope and pray I'm wrong as always.

Unbelievably, my prayers appear to have been answered the following Tuesday, and it turns out to be one of the best days of my life. Whilst I'm waltzing round the hospital picking up playlist requests for my radio show, I pop onto the ward where Dawn is now temporarily in residence. I ask if she has any favourite records she'd like me to play later in the evening. She tells me she does have a favourite song she'd like to hear, so halfway through the show, I announce that a very special lady by the name of Dawn who is currently residing on the surgical ward, has asked me to play 'Spirit In The Sky' by Dr Hook and the Medics.

I'm in no doubt whatsoever that Dawn will already be feeling much better, so as I'm absolutely head over heels in love with her, I decide to make her understand exactly how I feel about her.

"So now that Dr Hook has done his bit for Dawn I'd like to dedicate the next song especially to her, as she's the most beautiful woman I've ever met. The song comes straight from my heart so just for you, Dawn, here's Rod Stewart singing my message, 'Have I Told You Lately That I Love You?'

Yes, I know it's soppy, but who cares?

It's not long before Dawn is on the mend, and whilst neither of us is sure it's a good idea, we take a day out in the Derbyshire Peak District. We have lunch at the Millstone in Hathersage, followed by a stroll around the village and a brief visit to Little John's grave in the grounds of St Michael's Church. We hold hands all along the way, and as I look into her eyes when we get back to the car I can't help thinking it would be wonderful if we could spend more time together. That won't happen of course, but it doesn't mean I won't do everything I can to make her see me in a different light, if only she'd just give me the chance.

Wrong again Booey, but this time I'm pleased about it!

A couple of weeks later we're back in Hathersage having lunch at the George Hotel, and the pudding turns out to be the best ever when Dawn tells me she'd like us to move forward and have a long-term relationship. We decide not to go public just yet, although we agree that in the event of things working out we will always regard today, the 1st June 1996, as being the first real day of our relationship.

What an afternoon this turned out to be!

During the coming weeks we just get closer and closer, and it's now time to break the news to everyone. As my annual performance appraisal with Brian is looming on the horizon, I think that'll be the best time to hit him with something he's not expecting. On the morning of my appraisal Dawn tells Jane that she has a new man in her life, and she wants her to be the first to know. Then, when Jane pops into my office to collect some paperwork, I calmly ask if she's heard anything about the new man in Dawn's life.

"Er, yes. She told me earlier this morning," she replies with some hesitation and a slight look of concern. "But I didn't think anybody else knew about it."

"Well I only know about it because it's me she was talking about."

"What? You're kidding me! You mean you and Dawn are getting together?"

"Exactly," I smile.

"That's brilliant," beams Jane. "Absolutely brilliant." I'm delighted for you both.

"Everybody will know pretty soon, as I'll be telling Brian when I have my appraisal later this afternoon."

"Oh God," she laughs. "He won't know what the hell to do when you hit him with that," Jane chuckles as she walks out of the office.

For some reason, Dawn doesn't want to be around when I hit Brian with the news, so she clears her desk early and heads home for a vodka or three, but if you ever meet her, don't tell her I said that.

As I wait for Brian to invite me into his office, I still have no idea of how I'm going to break the news to him. There's no way I can ask him for a pay increase for all the success I've achieved recently, then tell him I'm getting shacked-up with his PA. Anyway, zero hour arrives and Brian reels off all the usual flannel about how much the hospital appreciates my efforts and whilst I can't be offered a pay rise, he knows I'll continue carrying out my good work with the usual enthusiasm. I'm just sitting here only half listening whilst he leans back in his chair staring out of the window reciting his memorised script. He never once looks me in the eye but I'm glad about that, because all I can think about, is how the hell am I going to tell him the only thing I have any enthusiasm for right now is his PA?

Eventually he gets to the point at which he invites me to make my contribution to the proceedings.

I guess the next few minutes could turn out to be very interesting.

"Well that's all I have to say, so is there anything you'd like to add to the proceedings before we wrap it up?" he asks in the hope the wrapping can commence without delay.

"As a matter of fact there is," I state to Brian's astonishment.

"Oh, is there something we haven't covered," he splutters. "What is it?"

"I just needed to let you know I have a fabulous new woman in my life, so things are about to change for me on a personal level."

"Well I'm delighted for you. Is it anybody I know?" he asks with pretend interest.

"As a matter of fact it is. It's your PA."

Brian almost falls off his chair at this point.

"Dawn? You mean you and Dawn are getting together?" he splutters.

"Yep. Me and Dawn."

"I had no idea. When did you and Dawn first, er, er er? I mean how long have you and Dawn been, er, er, er? I mean does she know?"

"I can't remember when we first er, er, er, so I don't know exactly how long we've been er, er, er. I'm sure she knows we've been er, er, erring, but I'll check when I see her later. In the meantime that's all I wanted say."

I've no idea how Brian managed to drive home to Chesterfield without writing off the car. He was certainly in no state to be driving when he left the office thirty seconds after bringing the appraisal to a close.

During the coming weeks word gets round the hospital, and it isn't long before we move into our first home on Newcastle Avenue in Worksop. I was introduced to Dawn's two sons, Paul and Dave not long after we first got together, and tonight Dave and his girlfriend, together with her Mum and partner are going ten-pin bowling, and they've invited us to join him at the Queen's Road Bowling Alley in Dee Dah Land.

I'm already aware that Dave is very competitive when it comes to things like ten-pin bowling, and he isn't in the habit of losing. Unfortunately on this occasion, it appears to have slipped his mind to ask if I've ever been bowling before. He knows very little about me at this point, apart from me being a Dee Dah of course, so he hasn't a clue about what's going to happen when we get to the bowling alley. I'm delighted to say I don't appear to have lost any of the skills I acquired back in my early teens when me, Cliff Shaw and a few mates were regularly spending several hours a week in the bowling alley back in my early teens. Dave doesn't appear to be too pleased about it though, when he ends up getting annihilated.

"You never told me you'd been bowling before, you Dee Dah git," Dave says with mock horror.

"You never asked, you Worksop weasel," I reply with a large helping of satisfaction.

"You know I'll have to get revenge sooner or later, don't you?" he promises.

"Good luck with that then," I respond as Dave turns to his Mother.

"I think you should ditch the Dee Dah right now, and we'll take you home," he suggests to his Mother with a twinkle in his eye.

Dawn thinks he's joking, but I'm far from convinced.

During our first winter together, I devote every possible moment to expressing my love for Dawn and we become closer than I ever thought possible. As the New Year arrives I still can't believe someone so perfect in every way has chosen me as her soulmate, companion and lover. Happiness such as this just doesn't come around very often, so I can only hope and pray we'll remain together forever, but the bombshell that hits me in February could easily blow my world apart.

"Due to insufficient funding, thirteen loyal, hard working and dedicated members of staff are to be made redundant," comes the announcement from Munro.

Being the Quality Development Manager I probably have the cushiest job around, so I wouldn't be at all surprised if I was at the very top of the redundancy hit list. If that turns out to be the case, I'll be given the usual rubbish about it not being personal, because it's the job that's being made redundant, not me. Well call me Mr Ungrateful if you will, but it is personal and it's personal with a capital 'P'.

We're still waiting to be told exactly who is being kicked out, when out of the blue I receive a call from my old friend Philip Russell. He tells me that the Malaysian Government recently decided to privatise the support services in its 128 hospitals. A local organisation called Faber Medi-Serve has been awarded a contract to provide the Engineering, Bio-Medical Engineering, Linen & Laundry and Cleaning Services to seventy two of the hospitals across Northern Peninsular Malaysia. FMS is required to develop and implement an internationally recognised quality management system.

I'm flattered to receive the offer and it sounds very interesting, but to be honest I haven't a clue where Malaysia is, and all I know about the place is that it has a jungle of some sort. Nevertheless, Philip and I discuss the job in great detail and with potential redundancy looming on the horizon, I accept the offer provided that nothing is said to my boss Brian for the time being, and most important is that the new love of my life agrees to accompany me.

I won't be holding my breath on the second bit!

I know Dawn has no desire whatsoever to go anywhere near an aeroplane, let alone climb aboard one and then spend more than half a day up in the air, so I'm absolutely ecstatic when she unexpectedly agrees to join me.

Meanwhile, everyone has been made aware that those due to be put out of work will be told next Friday, so as the day of reckoning arrives I'm ready and waiting when Dawn calls from her office next door, to say Brian needs to speak to me.

He explains that it isn't personal of course, it's the job that's being made redundant, not me. He tells me he's already in the process of trying to sort out another job he can slot me into, because the hospital really doesn't want to lose me. I tell him not to worry about it as I've gone as far as I can on Quality Street, and I'm sure I'll be able to find similar work elsewhere. All I need him to do is to let me know when my redundancy package is sorted, and then we can part on good terms. Brian is more than a little relieved with my professionalism and understanding.

It only takes a couple of weeks for me to receive formal notification that my redundancy package is sorted, so now I'm back in Brian's office to agree the date of my departure.

It's payback time!

"First of all," says Brian. "The Chief Executive is delighted with the way you've dealt with this most difficult decision, and he's asked me to thank you not just for that, but for everything you've done for Bassetlaw Hospital in recent years".

"Tell him it's been a real pleasure and I've enjoyed every minute."

"I'm still trying to find another job for you, so do you have any thoughts of your own about what you'd like to do in the future?" he asks with absolutely no idea of what he's about to hear.

"You'll be pleased to know my future has been sorted out and I'd like to leave at the end of March," I reply with an 'up yours' look on my face.

"Oh! I had no idea you'd got things sorted, but would you mind staying on until the second week of April and then we can pay you your redundancy money from next year's budget?"

"Yeah, that's no problem," I reply.

"So what are you planning to do when you leave here?"

Here comes the knockout punch!

"Dawn and I are heading off to Kuala Lumpur in Malaysia. I've accepted a job as a Facilities Management Consultant, and we just can't wait."

"You're not going to be working for Philip Russell are you?" enquires Brian with more than a hint of puzzlement.

"Yes I am."

"I knew he was looking for somebody, but I was going to apply."

"Oh, what a shame. Never mind, I'll send you some photos."

So that's it then. Malaysia here we come, but fear not. The Dee Dah might be on his way to the other side of the world, but Pitsmoor and Parkwood Springs will never be forgotten, no matter how much time I spend overseas.

A couple of months, with our personal stuff already on its way to Kuala Lumpur, we take one final glance around the front room of our lovely little home. Then before we find ourselves completely overwhelmed, hold Dawn tightly in my arms and I simply suggest 'we go for it'.

We're about to leave behind everything that means anything to us as we head into the unknown. We also wondering if we'll ever see our home, family and friends again, and we're already have way to Heathrow Airport before either of us is able to speak without bursting into tears.

I never imagined I would ever be doing anything like this, so I can only hope and pray we can look after each other and turn the experience into something wonderful and never to be forgotten.

The flight to Kuala Lumpur takes almost thirteen hours, and as Dawn hates flying, I have a quick word with the hostess as we board the plane. She does her best to persuade Dawn that flying is by far the safest way to travel these days, but she remains unconvinced. The hostess comes up with an idea.

"Once we're up in the air I'll take you to the upper deck. You'll be much closer to God up there and he'll be looking after you," she suggests to no avail.

"Not a chance," Dawn reasons. "At my age I'm already close enough to God as it is, so I prefer not to get any closer than I already am."

I think she may have a point there!

Some twelve hours later we're enjoying breakfast somewhere above the Bay of Bengal, and it's beginning to feel that we're much closer to our new life than to the one we left behind yesterday. Dawn will be relieved to say the least when we start our descent, however we do have a bit of a laugh just before then. There aren't many passengers travelling in Business Class, but there's quite a bit of activity the moment the captain announces the descent will commence within the next few minutes. Whilst the captain is still speaking, several passengers start shuffling around their hand luggage before chucking their bags into the overhead storage compartments. One passenger races into the toilet before the captain instructs everyone to fasten their seatbelts, and another gets down on his hands and knees between his seat and the one in front of him in search of the shoes he took off almost half a day ago.

Then as the captain finally gets to the end of his message, a hostess arrives with an aerosol canister of pest killer. She apologises for any disruption it may cause, but she explains that the BA policy is to spray the interior of the aircraft shortly before landing, just to make sure any unwanted insects don't get the chance to end up in Kuala Lumpur. She promises the spray is harmless, but as it might make some passengers cough if they breathe it in, she suggests we might want to cover our mouths and noses before she starts squirting the pest killer around and then she starts squirting the windows, the inside of the overhead hand luggage compartment and the gangway and gaps between the seats. She keeps squirting until she reaches the front row, some five minutes afters she started. By now the canister is almost empty, so she strolls towards the toilet and gives the canister one final shake before aiming it above the door, just as the occupant opens it from the inside.

As he's been in there for a good five minutes, he clearly hasn't just been taking a pee. You can imagine the embarrassment as he emerges from the loo to come face to face with the hostess spraying an aerosol like crazy above the toilet door. The look of embarrassment changes to one of absolute horror a couple of seconds later, when the man notices most of the passengers are coughing and spluttering into their handkerchiefs, scarves and Kleenex tissues. I'm almost sure he's considering going back inside to flush himself down the bog and out into the clouds.

It's been worth a thirteen hour flight just to witness this!

We're booked into Kuala Lumpur's Legend Hotel for a couple of weeks until we find ourselves a nice apartment. As it's only mid-afternoon when we check in and get unpacked, we decide to pop down to take a peep at the photo exhibition that's taking place on the first floor, and I wish we hadn't bothered.

There's a photograph of an Indian guru who apparently has put himself into a trance and allowed a huge python to swallow him from the feet right up to his neck. The snake's jaws are wide open and the guru's head is sticking out from its mouth. I've never been a fan of snakes and such things, so I'm absolutely horrified by the photograph I'm staring at. Then whilst I remain rooted to the spot, I read through the card underneath the photograph which explains what happened next. Apparently when the guru woke up from his afternoon nap, a couple of his mates grabbed the guru by the neck and started pulling him out from the python's stomach, whilst another two friends grabbed the other end of the snake's body and dragged it in the opposite direction.

Well excuse me, but that's not something I want to know about so I don't think I'll be taking in the rest of the exhibition, thank you very much. And while we're at it, I think we'll also be giving one of the hotel's dining outlets a wide berth. I dread to think what the dish of the day will be in the Monkey Brain Bar, so I think we'll just settle for a 'lite bite' from the room service menu tonight. Good night!

Chapter Fifteen

Paradise Malaysian Style

It's only about 5 miles to the Faber office in Taman Desa, but the traffic jam extends almost all the way. Luckily the taxi driver knows all the short cuts, and the trip takes only about an hour. I know that sounds a long time for a five-mile trip, but apparently it's good going for this time of day in KL, especially as the highway was completely gridlocked when the driver decided to take a detour. He tells me that many children are conceived and born in the traffic jam, and they go on to be educated and married and have children of their own, before going on to live a long life without ever pulling clear of the never ending line of vehicles.

I assume he's joking, but by the look of the traffic around us, I could be wrong.

It feels as though the journey from The Legend Hotel to Faber Towers took almost as long as the flight from Heathrow to Kuala Lumpur, but at long last I get to meet my new boss Desmond Steele. He introduces me to Faber's General Manager of Operations, Mohammad Ali Mohammad Noor known to everyone as Ali, Senior Manager Danny Hamidon, and Gopinath 'Gopi' Pillai the Quality Officer.

Danny invites me to join him in a grand tour of the office to meet the rest of the team, and by the time the introductions are over and done with I seem to have already made a few new friends. I noticed during the tour of the office that quite a few members of the local team refer to me as a 'Mat Salleh' after we've been introduced, so I ask why they would do that.

One of my new colleagues informs me it derives from the term 'mad sailor,' which was conjured-up by the British elite back in the colonial days when describing the drunken boisterous sailors when they disembarked at Malaysian ports. Over the years it's pronunciation evolved into the Malay term 'Mat Salleh,' and became a neutral reference extended to to all white folk, mad, drunken or otherwise.

I like the sound of it, so I decide to adopt the term when making light-hearted comments to both the locals and expatriates.

Bangsar is a beautiful residential area just a few miles from the city centre, and within a couple of weeks of our arrival in Kuala Lumpur we find ourselves checking out of the Legend Hotel as we head to our new home in a condominium complex by the name of Bayu Angkasa, or Waterfall Gardens as we Mat Sallehs would call it.The complex towers stands regally overlooking Taman Bukit Bandaraya or the Park on the Hill Overlooking the City.

The main attraction is the magnificent outdoor pool and adjacent jacuzzi. The waterfall is nothing short of perfection, especially as the silver and gold lighting, positioned amongst the rows of ornamental rocks and potted palms, creates an incredibly romantic ambience of peace and tranquillity. Then standing to the side of the condominium block just a few yards from the pool, the residents have their very own fully equipped gymnasium, squash and badminton courts. Finally, with a spectacular view towards the city centre we have a crazy golf course, just like the ones you'd find back in the UK in places such as Mablethorpe, Skegness and Blackpool, although this one looks just a wee a bit posher in my view.

Great care is clearly taken by the groundsmen and gardeners to ensure the entire complex is maintained in perfect condition for the residents to relax and enjoy, and as it's well away from any busy roads all you can hear when you lounge by the pool, is the sound of the waterfall. It's absolutely wonderful and our Chinese-style ninth floor 2,000 square feet three-bedroomed apartment in this tropical paradise ain't too bad either.

So after a romantic candlelit evening meal on the balcony, we spend the rest of our first evening at Bayu Ankasa taking a walk by the pool and through the beautiful gardens, whilst admiring the incredible views. Then after a drink in the bar, we stroll back to the apartment for an 'early night' in the en-suite master bedroom.

Of course, there just has to be a problem ahead!

We're just into the process of entwining ourselves under the cotton sheetst, when there's a power cut. It wouldn't be a problem back in Dee Dah Land, in fact it would probably make the moment even better, but in Malaysia it means we now have no air conditioning and the evening temperature is above thirty degrees.

I've considered Dawn to be one 'hot' lady since we got together, but this is something completely different!

The apartment soon becomes a steaming oven operating on full blast. We check the electrics but nothing appears to have tripped, then when we open the sliding door of the balcony we realise Bayu Angkasa is in total darkness. Worse still, the view across the city suggests the whole of Kuala Lumpur is without power, so I head down to the security box just inside the entrance to the complex. Unfortunately, nothing's working there either, so I'm advised to simply go back to the apartment and wait until the power comes back on.

Well it doesn't come back on, so we spend the entire night sweating cobs and slapping wet towels and cloths onto our skin, just to keep the heat at bay. It's not until mid-morning on Sunday that the air-con finally clicks back into action, and we can hear the cheers of relief and delight from the dozens of other residents as their apartments begin to cool down at last.

As it turns out, the power cut affected the entire country and it wasn't long afterwards that somebody in charge of the national grid was in a spot of bother. Serves him right for messing-up our romantic evening!

As part of my conditions of employment, Dawn and I are entitled to return business class flights to the UK twice annually, but in view of her dislike of flying, Des has spoken to Philip Russell back in London, and he's agreed that the money it would have cost for our flights can be used for Dawn to accompany me when we start travelling around Malaysia. That won't be happening until early in the New Year, although we do have one trip coming up that we weren't expecting.

According to Des when we arrived, my application for a work permit and Dawn's resident visa application wouldn't take long to process, and then we'll be given resident status by the Immigration Office. We've been our little paradise for two months now, and it turns out that things don't always get sorted as quickly as you might expect.

"Sorry Eric, but I have some bad news for you," says Des as he strolls over to my work station.

"Oh, hell. What's up?"

"I'm afraid you and Dawn have to leave the country today. When you arrived and went through Immigration, your passports were stamped for an eight week stay and your eight weeks expire today. Unfortunately, your work permit and Dawn's resident visa haven't come through yet, so if you're still here at midnight tonight you could both be arrested as illegal immigrants."

"You must be joking!" I reply with great concern

"No I'm not. It's a very serious situation so you've been booked on a flight to Phuket in Thailand this afternoon, so you can spend the week in Patong with all expenses paid and then when you arrive back in Malaysia, Immigration will stamp your passports again. Is that OK?"

"A week in Thailand? Well I suppose it'll be OK if we really have to," I smile.

I make sure I hold on tightly to Dawn until we're on the plane and heading to Thailand, but by the time we reach the pure white clouds at about 10,00 feet, we've already calmed down. A couple of hours later we're waltzing around in the glorious sunshine beaming across Patong beach.

I just can't believe this back street Dee Dah and the love of his life have somehow managed to con their way to a week in Thailand at no cost. Not a bad result!

The waves rolling gently over the sand are topped with a beautiful golden glow as the evening sun sets over the horizon, and as we stroll along arm in arm along the seafront everyone smiles and says hello as they pass by. There's no doubt that the sheer romance of the place brings me and Dawn even closer together, if that's possible, and we absolutely adore every single moment of our short stay on Patong.

I think I could get to like Thailand and its people, and the look on the face strolling next to me suggests Dawn feels exactly the same. At this moment I have absolutely no doubt whatsoever that this won't be our one and only visit to yet another tropical paradise.

I'm feeling on top of the world as I stroll into the office on Monday morning, and now I hear I'll be heading to a city named Kota Kinabalu in the region of Sabah in Borneo next week, where I'll be giving several presentations to local Ministry of Health representatives, hospital directors and Faber's Facilities Managers.

I still can't help wondering how the hell a pleb like me has managed to find himself a job like this but hey ho, I suppose somebody has to do it, so why not me?

It's a couple of hours before we hit the Kota Kinabalu runway, and I'm absolutely overwhelmed when the taxi drops us off at the Tanjung Aru Resort an hour later. If ever there was an exotic place to stay then this is it, and when I compliment the receptionist she explains that the King regularly comes here for his holidays and takes over an entire floor.

Dawn's reaction when we open the door of our suite, is completely off the scale. The balcony has stunning views across the bay and over the South China Sea, with the sacred Mount Kinabalu just a few miles away on the horizon. Romantic just doesn't do the place justice.

Perhaps I should now leave it that, as this is not the sort of book to be used for me to explain exactly how wonderful the rest of the evening went, if you get my drift!

The next morning we're introduced to Zamri, Faber's Regional Manager for Sabah. He's a great guy and a real gentleman, and when Dawn asks about the wildlife out here, he suggests we should stay on for an extra night at the weekend and take a short flight to the eastern side of Borneo to visit the Orangutan Rehabilitation Centre in Sepilok. There's just no way that we can turn down such an offer, so just after breakfast on the morning of our flight, Dawn pops down to the hotel lobby to pick up a few postcards and souvenirs. She's only been gone for a minute or so when I answer a knock on the door and come face to face with a gorgeous little Filipino girl.

"Good morning Hello Mr Elick. I come to bed?" she asks with a beautiful smile.

"Pardon?"

"I come to bed?" she repeats. "I come three times every day."

"Pardon?"

"I turn it back for you?" she states with a gleam in her eye.

"Pardon?"

"Is OK, I do it all the time."

"Lucky old me, but I think we might have our wires crossed. Exactly what is it you're here for and is there a cost for your services?" I stutter.

"No, no. Tanjung Aru pay me to do it when guests need it."

It might have been better right now if Dawn had flown to Tesco's in Worksop!

"I come to bed after breakfast, during afternoon and again after dinner. I make sure bed is neat and tidy, and then I turn back duvet so you only have to get into bed when tired. Is OK?"

Oops! It seems you got it wrong as usual, Booey! I wonder how she'd get on in a Sheffield Hotel if she went around offering her services to all and sundry!

Dawn is ecstatic at the very thought of getting up close to the local wildlife. I'm not sure just how close I want to get to any animal, let alone the big ones that swing all over the place in a tropical jungle. I have no alternative if I want to keep Dawn happy, so I just have to go along with it. Then as we approach the gates of the orangutan rehabilitation centre, I just can't believe I'm actually in a jungle and it's no great surprise that I'm already becoming more than a little apprehensive.

The centre is made up of several huge bamboo buildings set out on the edge of the jungle. We're given a very warm welcome, and after a cool refreshing drink and an overview of the place, we're invited into the adjacent building which houses dozens of photographs of the centre's past and present residents. Apparently, it's illegal to keep baby orangutans as pets regardless of how well they're treated, so a number of photographs show babies being taken back into care and rehabilitated so they can eventually be released back into their natural habitat. Other photographs show orangutans after their rehabilitation when they're taken back to to their families and long lost friends. It really does give your heart strings a massive tug.

There are a few newspaper articles displayed on a noticeboard, which show the apes inflicting revenge on humans who don't give them the respect they deserve. One article describes what we believe to be a rather funny event, when a couple of our fellow humans decided to verbally abuse a group of orangutans, only to find themselves being surrounded by a load more. The wicked humans were then stripped of their clothing and possessions before they escaped to safety, so no doubt the orangutans had a good laugh at their expense once they'd gone.

We're told that once the orangutans have been rehabilitated they're allowed to head back into the jungle whenever they wish, and then they can come back at any time. That's exactly what they do twice a day, at noon and then again at three o'clock when somebody turns up with lunch and afternoon tea. I never knew orangutans could actually tell the time, but I'm just about to find out exactly how they figure out it's dinner time.

Just before noon we're invited to go outside and step onto the wooden platform, which stands just a few yards away and leads straight into the jungle. Apparently the platform leads to the orangutans' dining area about 600 yards into the jungle, so we're advised to stay on it otherwise we would sink into the jungle floor and get stuck in the very soft earth.

As we set off I realise we're the only people heading into the unknown. I often feel just a wee bit uncomfortable when we take a walk around the Derbyshire Peak District, so a stroll into the middle of the Borneo jungle simply isn't my cup of tea.

So as usual I'm clinging tightly to Dawn's hand as we venture forward, but on this occasion it's not due to my affection for her.

As we finally reach the end of platform, we're now on the edge of clearing with a single huge tree right in the middle of it. A bamboo ladder reaches up thirty feet from the jungle floor and into the branches of the tree, where another narrow little platform has been attached all the way around the bark.

Right now I haven't a clue why I agreed to do this, but the moment a massive overhanging shrub some twenty yards ahead of us starts shaking for all it's worth, I suddenly remember exactly why I shouldn't have. My mind is already back at the photo exhibition at the Legend Hotel, and I have this awful feeling in my stomach that we might be about to come face to jaws with a Hissing Sid, just like the one with a liking for Indian gurus.

I might also mention that I'm experiencing the same discomfort in my bowels I felt when I had a policeman's gun stuck to my head on Pennsylvania Avenue.

Anyway, the shrub shaking gets more frantic by the second, and no doubt Sid will be perfectly happy to slither his way down from the trees unnoticed, until he finally decides to make an appearance. We're still twenty yards away when the shrub suddenly stops shaking and starts to open up just above the bamboo handrail of the platform. Within seconds Dawn is jumping ecstatically into the air, as a furry head with huge black eyes peers out from the gap between the leaves and peers in our direction. It's not a snake after all. It's an orangutan and it now decides to jump up onto the handrail and eyeball us.

Dawn decides to run ahead of me to say hello to our new hairy friend, but when my vocal chords finally get back into action I suggest she calms down a bit.

"Whoa! For crying out loud! Slow down will you" I bellow. "This isn't Chester Zoo and there isn't a glass screen between you and Old Hairy Ass. We're in the jungle and this is where it lives. It's the orangutan's territory and you're racing toward it. Have you seen the size of it's arms?" I scream to no avail as Dawn is already within spitting distance of the ape.

The orangutan remains calmly perched on top of the handrail as Dawn approaches. It never bats an eyelid and just continues to peer at her. I'm still fifteen yards away, but by now Dawn and her pal are holding hands and gazing into each others eyes like a pair of long lost lovers.

"Oh, aren't you beautiful. Aren't you gorgeous."

That's Dawn speaking by the way, not the orangutan. So here we are, standing eyeball to eyeball with a fully grown orangutan in the middle of the jungle. How far can you possibly get from Pitsmoor and Parkwood Springs?

After lapping up a couple of minutes of non-stop admiration, the orangutan lifts a hand up to its mouth and starts furiously licking the palm. Then it holds the hand out to Dawn to reveal a large cut across its palm, which has healed. She appears to understand what the ape is suggesting, so without hesitation Dawn takes hold of its hand, licks the fingertips of her free hand and then starts to rub her freshly dampened fingers over her friend's palm to help make it better.

Oh bless!

Now it's my turn, so when the ape places its hand in mine I repeat the treatment and I just can't believe what's happening. The orangutan has now received the magic touch of human love and care from the pair of us, so now it jumps down from the handrail and onto the wooden deck, before calmly taking hold of Dawn's hand again and lead her further into the jungle. I haven't a clue what to do as they approach a bend in the platform that will take them out of sight, but no doubt Dawn will know exactly what to do.

"Booey! What am I supposed to do now?" yells Dawn as she looks back.

"How the hell should I know?" I reply. "If push comes to shove maybe you should try telling it you've got a headache."

Seconds later the two lovers go out of sight. This is a bit worrying but Dawn could well be just a wee bit more concerned than I am. As I approach the bend they come back into sight and yet another orangutan is waiting for me. The new man in Dawn's life turns out not be a man after all, and I almost bump into a little hairy toddler who's waiting for his Mum.

The moment the kid spots his Ma and Dawn strolling hand in hand around the corner, he leaps up onto the platform's handrail and starts showing off by doing something akin to a tightrope walk along it. Then he jumps back onto the platform and does a few forward and backward rolls along the deck.

I'm sick of saying oh bless, but here we go again. Oh bless!

After witnessing that little performance it would be an easy decision to stay here forever, but eventually it's time to say farewell to the trees and our furry friends. We're both in no doubt that this just has to be the best afternoon either of us has ever spent and there's absolutely no way we'll ever have a better one, even if we live for a thousand years.

There's always something happening that brings me back down to earth, and this time it's Des who breaks the bad news to me when I arrive back in the office.

"Sorry mate," he groans. "But when you and Dawn came back from Thailand, your passports only got stamped for four weeks and not the usual eight, so as your work permit and Dawn's resident's permit haven't been sorted….."

"Yeah, yeah. Don't tell me the rest. Where are we going this time?" I ask with a huge helping of frustration.

"Well, I've booked a flight for you to go to Phuket again for a few days, but I thought I'd book a hotel on the opposite side of the hill from Patong, so this time you'll be staying at the Felix Hotel at Karon Point."

"Okey dokey," I moan. "I'll see you next week. Bye."

It's a great relief to find Dawn is buzzing once again when I break the news, so off we go again. They'll never believe this back home and this time our hotel suite is overlooking the Andaman Sea.

I still can't believe we're living a life like this, and neither can I help feeling it's in no small way down to Dawn and to the love and affection we have for each other.

I'll say it one more time. Oh bless!

Another couple of months go by and there's still no sign of my work permit and Dawn's resident's visa, so now yet another overseas trip looms on the horizon.

"My apologies," Des drones. "We still haven't ...."

"Oh for pity's sake Des. Why the hell can't you just get it sorted. I seem to be spending more time in Thailand than I do at my desk," I wail.

"I know, I know. I'm really sorry. How would you fancy a couple of days in Singapore for a change?" he asks as I sit back in my chair and hold my head in my hands to hide the huge smile.

"Yeah, yeah! OK. I'll see you all on Thursday then. Be good!"

Singapore's a nice place, but it's not Thailand. Two nights are enough for us, but at least we can say it's another place we've visited. Unfortunately, I receive a nasty shock when we arrive at the Immigration desk having landed back in Malaysia.

"Sir, I notice you've made several trips out of Malaysia and back during the last few months," he says.

"Yes we have."

"I believe you're doing what you expatriates call 'visa runs' and you're actually working in Malaysia but you don't have a work permit to do so. Is that correct?"

"Yes it is. I'm actually working indirectly for your Ministry of Health and having been here for about five months, I'm still waiting for my work permit and for my fiancee's resident visa to come through," I reply with a little concern.

"I understand sir. This is often the case as processing applications can be very slow however, this will eventually cause you some problems, because if you continue going in and out of the country, Immigration are very likely to worry that you might be carrying drugs or doing something else illegal. Then you could end up being interrogated, body searched and possibly arrested, deported or imprisoned if you are committing any offence. You wouldn't want that, would you?"

"I guess not," I reply.

"Very Well. I will stamp your passport for one month, but you must tell your employer that your work permit application and your fiancee's resident's visa must be sorted out before the stamp expires."

"Thank you. I'll make sure," I promise as we head out into the afternoon sun.

Des is a little shaken when I break the news to him, so he calls in his local 'fixer' and instructs him to get things back on track with Immigration. Then a couple of weeks later, he calls me into the office for a discussion with him and the fixer.

"I'm really sorry, Eric," says Des with sincerity. "We haven't been able to sort things out, so you and Dawn have to visit the Immigration Office tomorrow for an interview with one of the officers."

"I hope you're joking," I spit. "We've been here all this time and we're still being messed about. Thanks a bunch!"

Dawn is worried sick as we head to Immigration, and it doesn't help when we find the officer doesn't appear to particularly like Mat Sallehs and their partners. Without once acknowledging Dawn's existence, the officer explains exactly what the problem is.

"Your work permit isn't a problem, Mr Eric, but as you are not married, Malaysian law say that she cannot be considered as your dependant, and that means she cannot be issued with a resident's visa and she must leave the country and go back to the UK. Do you understand?"

"But back in the UK we're recognised as a common law man and wife," I explain.

"This is a Muslim country, sir, and there is no such thing as a common law man and wife. In Malaysia you are either married or you are not, so as you are not married she must leave the country within the next fourteen days."

"But she is my dependant. We are a couple and she's given up everything to be with me," I point out. "Is there anything we can do to sort this out so we can both stay here?" I beg.

"Yes there is," she says forcefully. "You can get married."

"But we're planning to get married when we go back to the UK."

"That is no good if she wishes to stay in Malaysia," she states very clearly. "The best thing to do is to have a Muslim wedding within the next two weeks."

"But we're not Muslims and our family and friends aren't here," I point out as Dawn appears to be getting ready to either explode.

"That doesn't matter. Just have a Muslim wedding and she will get her resident's visa. You don't need to tell anyone, and then when you finally leave Malaysia you just need to rip up the marriage certificate and throw it down the toilet when you get onto the plane. Nobody in the UK will need to know anything about what you've done, so you can get married again when you arrive back in the UK."

"Are you seriously suggesting we should fraudulently use your religion just so we can get a resident's visa, and then forget it ever happened when we go home? I'm really sorry, but there's absolutely no way I would ever make a promise to your God, knowing I have no intention of keeping it. That's just wrong, so I think the best thing for us to do is to go home," I sigh as Dawn completely falls apart.

Back in the office Des is speechless, but when he gets his voice back he promises he'll do his very best to sort it. I'm absolutely flabbergasted when he hands over my work permit and Dawn's resident's visa three days later, so I ask how he did it.

"Well these things are never easy, but you did yourself a big favour when you told the Immigration Officer you respected the Islamic religion and you wouldn't make a false promise to God, and that opened the door for us to sort things out. Most expats will do just about anything to get themselves a work permit or a resident's visa, but the officer was very impressed with your views and especially with your refusal to act improperly, as that hadn't happened before."

What more could we possibly ask?

Chapter Sixteen

A Few Close Shaves

We're fascinated by the celebrations during Deepavalli, the Hindu Festival of Light. Schoolchildren have designed huge mosaics from multi-coloured grains of rice, and the carnival parades turn the streets of Kuala Lumpur into an extraordinary blaze of colour.

Neither of us have ever witnessed anything like it and now we're approaching our first Christmas in Malaysia. Then on the first Sunday of December, we make our way to the shopping mall next door to the Legend Hotel where we stayed for a couple of weeks when we first arrived in Kuala Lumpur.

The entire place is decorated just as we would expect back home. A large Christmas tree, complete with fairy lights and the usual adornments stands at the entrance to the mall and there's even a giant model of Santa Claus, complete with sledge and Rudolph the Red Nosed Reindeer and his pals behind him. They're also playing traditional Christmas Carols over the public address system, and everything that's happening it's a huge surprise to us. We never expected Christmas to be celebrated in this way in a Muslim country, although we are aware that Malaysia recognises and respects most religions, and that's a huge credit to the country and its wonderful people.

As we stroll further inside the mall, I'm approached by a smiling Chinese gentleman, who asks where we come from. He laughs when I tell him we're from Bayu Angkasa, as he actually meant our country of origin. When Dawn tells him we're from England, he asks what snow actually is and what it feels like. We can tell him what snow is, but it's almost impossible to describe exactly what it feels like, so I simply suggest he locks himself in a freezer for a couple of hours and that'll give him some idea. We haven't given a thought to the fact that Malaysians live with afternoon temperatures of around forty degrees Celsius all year round, but right now in the mall we're up to our knees in artificial snow. I wonder what the locals would do if they were to wake up to realise the car windscreen needs de-icing before they set off for work.

Even though they don't have fireplaces out here, there'll be huge posters hanging from the exterior walls of high-rise buildings for the next few weeks, depicting Santa heading down snow-covered chimneys with sacks of Christmas gifts hanging over his shoulders.

From the day we arrived in KL Dawn has been baking cakes and pastries for me to hand round my expat colleagues. Once they've taken all they want I give the rest to our lovely secretary, Nurul. She then helps herself to as much as she can eat before sharing the rest with the rest of the locals. They enjoy Dawn's baking so much that Ali starts inviting me to meetings that have absolutely nothing to do with me, just so the members of the Faber team are able to grab a load of Dawn's cakes and buns before the meetings commence.

As it's coming up to Christmas, Dawn decides to bake a huge fruit cake for me to hand round. As always my expat colleagues help themselves to a wedge each, and then I hand the rest to Nurul. She devours a couple of huge wedges and then puts the remaining two kilos into her desk drawer. She always appears to be a little more confident than most of the other local female members of the team and occasionally, all you can hear is her voice bellowing out to her friends.

For some reason when she arrives back from lunch today, she's more boisterous than ever. We make every possible attempt to calm her down, but no matter what we say or do she just keeps laughing and jumping around all over the office. We're all very relieved when the day finally comes to an end and Nurul almost sprints toward the lift lobby to head off home without saying a word to anyone.

Over dinner, Dawn asks if the Christmas cake was OK. A look of sheer horror shoots across her face when I tell her the ex-pats loved it, but Nurul ended-up scoffing more than half of it.

"What? I didn't know you were handing cake out to the locals. I thought it was just the expats you were giving it to," Dawn protests.

"I always share whatever you bake with the locals. They love it, especially when I hand the stuff round during meetings."

"You should have told me. I soaked the fruit in a bottle of brandy and then when it came out of the oven, I drizzled another bottle all over the top. So the Christmas cake you've handed round had two bottles of brandy in it and as you well know, the locals aren't allowed alcohol."

"Oh my God! I never expected you to put brandy in the cake? I could be in a lot of trouble now but even worse, how much did all that brandy cost me?"

There's no wonder that Nurul was up in the air all afternoon. Having gobbled her way through half the cake it means she got through a whole bottle of brandy, but being a Muslim she won't have ever had any alcohol before. I can't sleep due to wondering exactly what damage this might have caused. I could be arrested and jailed, kicked out of the country or even worse, because handing brandy out to the locals will no doubt be considered as being a very serious matter, regardless of it being completely unintentional.

I'm not looking forward to tomorrow, assuming of course that the religious police don't come knocking on the door tonight!

Next morning Nurul arrives shortly after the rest of us and she looks dreadful. She normally waltzes in full of life, but not today. She staggers towards her desk, and once seated she manages a few words whilst holding her head into her hands.

"Oh dear," she mumbles. "I'm so ill. My head is going boom, boom, boom."

"Nurul, can I have a quiet word with you in the office?" I ask with some concern. "I think I know what the problem is. You have what we Mat Sallehs call a hangover, and it's because of all the brandy you consumed yesterday."

"Cannot be, Mr Eric. I'm a Muslim so I don't drink alcohol."

"I'm afraid you did yesterday," I whisper as I explain what happened.

Nurul excuses herself and strolls out of the office, and when she arrives back she has some good news for me.

"Everything is OK now, Mr Eric," she says. "I've been told that as I didn't know there was alcohol in the Christmas cake all I have to do is pray for forgiveness every day for the next thirty days. Then as long as I don't die during that time God will forgive me. Also, because you didn't know about the brandy either, nothing is going to happen to you. So everything is OK, but can I ask a favour of you? If Mrs Eric makes another fruit cake, please don't tell me if it has brandy in it, and then I can eat as much as I want because I won't know."

I suppose that'll be OK then, although during the next few weeks I notice that my Malaysian colleagues never ask what's in the cakes I hand around the office. I wonder why that should be?

We spend Boxing Day relaxing by the pool and the sun is scorching hot. It's over thirty five degrees, and it makes it even better when I glance at last week's UK Daily Mail that I picked up from the newsagent's on Christmas Eve. Apparently they've had a few blizzards back home in Dee Dah Land and now the daytime temperature is way below zero.

What a shame!

I've made friends with the very chirpy Chinese-Malay guy who owns the cafe a couple of doors away from our office block in Taman Desa. Yow employs a Chinese chef by the name of Leon and several lovely Indonesian non-English speaking waitresses, who will obviously earn little more than a pittance for their efforts. Early in the new year I pop into the cafe for a Coca Cola.

"Herro Mr Elick," smiles Yow as I arrive. "Is it true you from Ingrand?"

"Hello Yow. Yes it is. I am Ingrish," I confirm with a huge smile.

"Ah so, Mr Elick. We have lestaurants close by that do Ingrish and Western food. We must now do same, but Leon not know how cook Ingrish food. Do you know anything about this, er Ingrish glavy?" asks Yow.

"Of course I do," I reply.

"Oh, Good. You get me lecipe for Ingrish glavy?"

"I can make you some right now, if you want," I state with pride.

"What? You mean you know how to make Ingrish glavy?"

"Sure," I confirm as I head towards the back of the counter and head over to the boiling pan that Leon uses to cook chickens.

So with the aid of a little oil and flour and a few drops of Chinese browning, it's only a couple of minutes before a large bowl of Ingrish glavy is sitting on the table in front of Yow and his team. He then sips a spoonful before calling to his team and instructing them to pick up a spoon each and come over for a tasting session.

"Wow Mr Elick," beams Yow. "Is perfect. Thank you velly much. By the way, do you know about Ingrish feesh and chee?" he enquires hopefully.

"Yeah. I know English fish and chips."

"You know dis, er clispy stuff on outside of feesh?"

"You mean batter."

"Yeah, batter," Yow excitedly replies. You get me lecipe for Ingrish batter?"

"I'll make some if you wish," I reply as the old ego goes into orbit once again.

"What? You can make Ingrish batter?"

"No problem," I reply as I head back behind the counter to sort out the ingredients.

A minute later the duly requested bowl of batter is ready, so I grab a couple of pieces of fish from the fridge. I'm no expert when it comes to seafood but having quickly checked it out, I know for certain it sure ain't North Sea cod. I pick up a few mushrooms, a handful of broccoli florets and finally I slice a large onion into rings. A few minutes later Yow and the team are presented with a huge platter of battered goodies, and he's doing his own version of an Irish jig around the cafe.

"Yes! Yes! Yes!" splutters Yow. "This is it! This is it! Clispy Ingrish batter. The best," he screams with delight.

I stroll back to my table with an unavoidable look of self satisfaction. Then just as I'm about to take a sip of Coke, Yow calls over to me.

"Hey, Mr Elick. How you know to do all this Ingrish cooking?"

"I'm actually a chef," I reply with a wink and a smile.

"What? You Ingrish chef? You want part-time job in Yow's cafe?"

"Thanks but no thanks," I reply with a smile. "I'll tell you what. Why don't I put on a Western Night for my expat friends and the Faber team," I suggest although I don't really know why.

Yow is all ears by now!

"I could sort out a menu of traditional English dishes and give you a list of things you'll need to buy. Then we can sort out the cost per person and we'll advertise the evening around the office. I'll do the cooking and I'll show Leon how to do it. How does that sound?"

"Wow! How much you charge me for doing all that?"

"Nothing," I reply.

"This could be a terrific promotional project for our company," suggests Des when I inform him "I'll ask the International Director if we can foot the bill for all the meals. The locals will love it, and so will the expats. What do you think?"

"Sounds good to me. Let's go for it."

I'm delighted to be told that our International Director, known to me and my expat colleagues as Bob Scratchit, gives us the go ahead. Without doubt it'll be a terrific evening and as the cafe only has seating for forty eight people, it'll be a doddle for me. Dawn is quite a shy kind of person, so it comes as a great surprise when she offers to help out, so that's a perfect end to a perfect day.

Meanwhile I have a few presentations to do in Langkawi. Known to the locals as the Jewel of Kedah, Langkawi is an island and archipelago consisting of ninety nine islands just off the north west coast of Malaysia and close to the Thai border. The hotel Faber have chosen for us is at the top of a hill, and once we've unpacked, we decide to take a stroll down into the town centre for a spot of lunch and a bit of sight seeing. On our way down the hill we notice a few monkeys heading in the same direction as us, about fifty yards away to our left. Of course Dawn wants to stop and see if they'll move a little closer so she can take a photograph, but she knows I'm not particularly keen on getting too close to the local wildlife. I usher her along but when we get about fifty yards further down the hill, I notice another group of apes closing in from the right.

Something doesn't quite feel right for some reason, and then I suddenly hear something like a loud screeching sound, and as look back I get the shock of my life when I see a third gang of monkeys heading down the hill directly behind us.

We stop for few seconds, just so we can figure out what's going on, and we both come the same conclusion. We're being surrounded and it's not by loads of little cuties like the one we met in Borneo recently. Nevertheless, Dawn thinks they're gorgeous and already has the camera on standby. I disagree of course, but right now I don't think I have the time to discuss it with her. I grab hold of her arm and usher her down to the bottom of the hill, gradually picking up speed as we go.

When we finally get to sea level we can't help noticing a huge sculpture of a golden eagle, so we decide to take a breather in a nearby cafe to give us time to calm down and then enjoy the view. I mention to the waitress that we've just avoided being completely surrounded by a small army of monkeys, so she strongly advises us to take a different route back to the hotel. Apparently the apes around here have a nasty habit of ganging-up on tourists and bolting off with anything they can get their hands on.

Yet another close shave!

Western Night is fast approaching and there are a few unexpected problems to sort out. Des put up a poster in the Faber office to advertise the event, but he hadn't taken into account that Malaysians love a bargain. He's offered every member of the Faber team an English meal at no cost, so nobody is going to turn it down, especially when it'll be cooked by good old Mr Eric. As I mentioned earlier, the cafe has limited seating, but no less than one hundred and twenty have booked, so it's beginning to look as though it won't be the doddle I thought it was going to be.

The menu includes traditional fish and chips, halal rump steak with all the trimmings, and a range of omelettes. Dawn will be preparing the apple crumble and custard and the fruit trifles. It's nice to know that my good friend Gopi realises the Indonesian waitresses are going to be working harder than ever, so he's asked the diners to put a tip into the large envelope he's wedged between the salt and pepper pots on each table.

Yow is already closing the shutters as Dawn and I arrive, as he's decided to close early so we can get the preparation done and the place ready for the seven o'clock kick off. The shutters shoot back up at bang on seven as the stampede hits us. It takes less than two minutes for the cafe to become full to capacity, and I notice Faber's new Chief Executive Tajul Azwa Bani Hashim and his management colleagues Ali and Danny are the first group to grab a table by the wall, close to the service counter.

As I'm way down the pecking order, I haven't had the chance to speak to Tajul so far, but I've heard he's a great boss to work for and a real gentleman with a great sense of humour. For the next two hours he sits facing directly towards me, with a huge smile permanently on his face as he watches my performance.

As the onslaught commences I realise I've never been so hot and sweaty in all my life, and the temperature in the cafe just keeps going up throughout the evening. Me and Leon are knocking out a non-stop stream of meals, whilst Dawn doles out the desserts. Food is also being served outside to the diners who were just a bit too late to grab a seat at an inside table, and the air of excitement is amazing. I'm just a tad worried when I start throwing chips at the guests, because it never crossed my mind that they couldn't care less where the chips landed when they returned them. The last thing any of us needs right now is for heaps of potato missiles to land on the new Chief Executive's head.

Amidst all the mayhem I hadn't realised that when Dawn asked one of the waitresses where the returning crockery and cutlery is washed, she was told the cafe isn't big enough to have a wash up area, so the waitresses have to wash everything in a barrel of warm soapy water in the alley at the side of the cafe. So just as we get about halfway through the evening, an unexpected silence spreads across the inside of the cafe as one of the female diners arrives and asks everyone to quieten down.

"I've just seen a Mat Salleh lady doing the washing up in the alley outside," claims the diner. "She's surrounded by about ten piles of dirty plates and dishes, and some boxes of dirty knives, forks and spoons. That sort of work is never done by a Mat Salleh lady, as they consider it to be beneath them. The washing up is always done by the waitresses, so can somebody tell me exactly who it is out there because somebody needs to tell her she shouldn't be doing such demeaning work."

"It's Mrs Eric," Gopi calls out. "They aren't like the usual Mat Sallehs, as they see themselves as being no different from the rest of us, and that makes them very special. Do you know of any other Matt Sallehs and their wives who would be prepared to cook dinner and wash up for so many of us, without being paid anything for their time and effort? No, neither do I, so in that case all I can say is that they deserve medals for what they've done here tonight, and I hope you will let them know how much you appreciate it."

Nice one, Gopi

As the diners depart, every single one of them comes over to offer their sincere thanks to Dawn and I, and so does Yow as he closes the shutters behind us as we say farewell and head back to Bayu Angkasa with a load of cash filled envelopes.

What a fantastic night it's been, and we're not quite finished yet.

The next morning I stroll into the office to be greeted with huge cheers and a round of applause. I'm still on an all time high twenty minutes later, when I receive an unexpected call from Tajul's secretary Odi, to tell me that her boss would like to have a word with me in his top floor office. I'm just a wee bit apprehensive as I've never been that far up the building, and I've most certainly never had a chat with Tajul. I just don't know what I'll be walking into up there.

"Good morning Eric," he says in a smooth English tone that I couldn't even fake. "Please take a seat. Would you like a cup of tea or a coffee?" he enquires as he heads out of the office.

I'm now feeling a little more at ease already, especially as it's a known fact in this part of the world, no matter who you are a Chief Executive simply doesn't make you a drink when you visit his office.

"I just wanted to thank you and Dawn for making last night so special," beams Tajul. "I've worked with dozens of Mat Sallehs over the years, but none of them ever did anything for nothing. You not only almost worked yourselves to a standstill, you also sent staff morale through the roof, and this morning it's all they're talking about. Even the Chairman is singing your praise and believe me, he doesn't do that very often. So thank you for everything."

I assure him it was our pleasure to have been given the chance to make everyone so happy and to make such a difference to the staff morale.

Yes, I know I'm a smarty pants, but surely there's no problem in somebody giving the old ego a quick massage every now and then, is there?

Oh by the way. I found out much later that he didn't make the tea after all, even though he was gone for the best part of five minutes. Apparently he asked Odi to call the office tea lady and tell her to bring a cup of tea up to the top floor, where he'd be waiting for her. So perhaps I'm not quite as important as I thought I was. No surprise there then!

We spend the weekend relaxing by the pool as usual. Life doesn't get better than this, especially when we hear that Dawn's son Dave and his girlfriend have taken up our invitation to join us for a couple of weeks later in the year. I'm feeling so good just now that I haven't given a thought to what usually happens when things are going so well for me, so I guess it shouldn't have come as such a shock when I arrive back at Bayu Angkasa after work on Monday to find Dawn already in bed.

She's been in bed on a number of occasions when I've arrived home, but on this occasion she's there for a completely different reason!

Dawn always looks drop-dead gorgeous, but today she looks absolutely dreadful.

"What the hell is wrong? You look shocking," I worriedly enquire.

"I feel absolutely awful," comes the reply. "I think I've been bitten by a mosquito," she suggests whilst lifting up the duvet and pointing to her thigh.

As I look down I can't help noticing the huge saucer-like white lump on her thigh.

"You could be right," I reply. "Hang on whilst I get the thermometer to take your temperature," I say without realising she has no option but to hang on as she's feeling so weak.

I stick the thermometer into her mouth, but then I can't make-out the reading.

"Give it to me," she demands as she snatches the thermometer out of my hand and holds it in front of her face. "It's normal," she lies before dropping the evidence onto the floor.

'Rubbish!" I snap. "You're as blind as a bat without your specs on, so if I can't read the thermometer there's no way you could. I'm taking you to hospital, and don't argue about it."

Forty minutes later we're sitting in the Emergency Department waiting area at Subang Jaya Hospital. Dawn is sweating profusely and appears to be close to passing out. It's very noisy as a number of children are running around and shouting, whilst the waiting adults endlessly shuffle around on their seats. The incessant heat and humidity doesn't help either, so I make my way back to he reception desk.

"I'm really sorry, but my wife and I have worked for many years in the NHS back in the UK, and I've never seen such a lack of consideration for the people waiting to be seen. I promise we're not trying to push our way to the front of the queue and I'm not asking for any special consideration, but do you have anywhere quiet we could sit until the doctor is available, because if Dawn has to sit in the middle of all the mayhem for much longer, she'll probably end up on the floor.

Just a couple of minutes later we find ourselves sitting quietly in a side room. It's not long before I'm helping Dawn into the consulting room, where we're met by a most understanding doctor who steps out into the waiting room and bellows to the kids and orders them to sit down and be quiet.

Back in the consulting room, the doctor gives Dawn an examination which includes taking a blood sample and checking her blood pressure, heart rate and temperature. The results show that she has some kind of infection that's led to her temperature and blood pressure being slightly above normal, but as it will take a short while for the results of other tests to come back, he suggests I take her home and make sure she keeps warm during the night and takes the medication he's about to prescribe for her.

Within the hour Dawn is fast asleep back in Bayu Angkasa, but not for long. I receive a call from the doctor to say that the blood test confirms she has Dengue Fever and I must bring her back to the hospital immediately.

Dawn is admitted to hospital and I'm advised she'll be very ill for a while, due to the infection attacking her blood cells. Apparently there's no cure for the disease, so all the doctor can do is keep her under observation twenty four hours a day until her body does its best to fight off the infection. I'm also told I can stay with her throughout her stay in hospital, but the doctor suggests that won't do either of us any good, so it might be best for me to carry on working and just visit her every day.

I find it almost impossible to focus on anything else, as Dawn appears to be getting weaker and weaker by the day. It doesn't help that whenever I ask what's happening, I'm simply told she's very ill because she has Dengue Fever. A whole week drags by and Dawn is now comatose, so for the first time since she was admitted, I find myself speaking to a doctor who is prepared and able to give me some answers.

"Mrs Eric is very ill now and she's in a coma. The infection is attacking her blood cells, and if her blood count drops below a certain level, she will start to lose haemorrhage and that will be extremely serious. Her blood count is continuously being recorded, and I have to tell you that if her body is unable to start fighting the disease within the next twenty four hours, she will be in real trouble."

I just can't hold back the tears when I walk into Dawn's private room the next morning. She's looks completely lifeless and I fear the worst. I sit beside the bed and hold her hand in mine, but there's no response whatsoever. Surely God wouldn't take her away from me so soon after we got together, but all I can do is hope and pray she'll somehow pull through. Then within a few minutes of my arrival, the doctor I met yesterday pops into the room to check Dawn's pulse and temperature. She has with her a copy of the graph from yesterday, which clearly shows the steady decrease in Dawn's blood count. I'm then told that the doctor is now waiting for a copy of the graph from this morning's check, so she'll bring it to show me as soon as she receives it. The doctor returns an hour later and lays the graph onto the table.

"Oh that is good news," she claims whilst holding up the graph. "You can clearly see that the line of descent started to level out during the night, so that means she's beginning to fight the infection, although her blood count remains very low.

You just wouldn't believe how relieved I am!

"We need to do another check in two hours, and if the line of descent has levelled out even further then we'll be sure she's on her way back," the doctor promises.

It transpires that God doesn't want her back any time soon, and she comes out of the coma by the following morning. Dawn tells me she wasn't happy when she finally woke up and asked in vain several times for the nurse to bring something for her to vomit into. Eventually she couldn't wait any longer and ended up pebble dashing the wall at the side of the bed.

She's still quite poorly a few days later, but I'm told she can go home as long as I stay with her 24/7 for the next week, as she won't have the strength to do anything for herself. I must also understand it will take quite some time for her to fully recover, so she won't be able to do anything energetic for at least three months.

The closest shave yet, in my view!

Chapter Seventeen

All Good Things Must Come To An End

I can't imagine Dawn sitting around doing nothing for a whole week, nevertheless I do my utmost to look after her and keep her from making things worse. It's nice to spend a few days by the pool, but by the end of the week Dawn is ready to get up and go as Dave and his girlfriend are due to arrive in a few days, so she has a few things to do before they take up temporary residence with us.

Dave is a decent golfer and carries his clubs around with him wherever he goes, so I book a round at the Saujana Golf and Country Club. Sure enough, as they stroll into the arrivals hall, the Slazenger bag is parked on top of the rest of their luggage.

I drop him off at the club a few days later and assure him I'll be waiting in the car park when he's completed the round. He's not a happy chappie as he shuffles out of the clubhouse with clubs in tow. I jokingly suggest he has a face like a bulldog chewing a wasp so he must have been rubbish out on the course.

"Shut it, Dee Dah," he snarls. "I did OK for the first nine holes but I didn't realise just how bloody hot it was going to be out there and I didn't think to bring a barrel of cold water with me. By the time I arrived back in the clubhouse I was soaked in sweat and then when I tried to order a drink, I realised my mouth and throat were bone dry and I couldn't speak. How the hell do you cope in this heat?" he asks.

"Simple! We don't go waltzing around a golf course in the middle of the day and even if we did, we wouldn't be stupid enough to leave the water at home. As Noel Coward once said, only mad dogs and Englishmen go out in the midday sun."

"Cobblers!" says Dave. "Just get me back to the apartment and I'll call my mother and ask her to run me a bath."

"You'd be better off having a shower," I suggest.

"I'm not going to get into the bath, you idiot. I'm going to drink the water."

Well at least he hasn't lost his sense of humour!

I've now booked the four of us into the Felix Hotel at Karon Point in Phuket for a week, so we're off on our travels once again.

I pick up a leaflet from the hotel reception desk and it appears that a group known as The Lady Boys are appearing at a nearby theatre. I've never heard of them, but I still decide to book four seats for the show. Apparently, The Lady Boys are a group of young men who are about halfway to becoming a group of young women. Being an old fashioned Sheffield Dee Dah I find that to be just a little confusing.

The show is a sell out and just as we reach our four very expensive looking armchairs, a barmaid comes over to ask what we would like to drink. I stick with my usual Coca Cola of course, whilst my three companions hit the beer and vodka. I can only manage to get through a couple of pints of Coke in a single evening, but Dave appears to really enjoy the six pints of ale he gets down.

As the curtain goes up a dozen gorgeous Thai girls race onto the stage and start throwing themselves around in time with the music. They're wearing what I can only describe as very sexy, black skimpy underwear complimented with black stockings and high-heeled shoes, and their makeup is fantastic. They go into a terrific dance routine, and when the applause has died down another black-haired beauty steps into view from the side of the stage, and goes into her own routine. Eventually, they all start singing and dancing together and they're simply amazing.

I lean towards Dawn and suggest that it wouldn't really matter if The Lady Boys don't turn up, because the audience love these girls.

"They are The Lady Boys, you idiot," she says with a look of surprise. "We've been watching them since the curtain first went up."

"You're not serious are you?" I reply. "You mean they're men, not women?"

"Of course. That's why they're called The Lady Boys."

"But they absolutely stunningly beautiful, ever single one of them."

"Yes I know they are, so shut up and watch the show," she demands.

The show finally comes to an end and the audience goes wild, especially when one of The Lady Boys invites us all to join them outside the theatre so we can have our photographs taken with them. Having watched that performance I'm even more confused than I was earlier but nevertheless, we decide to join them.

Whilst chatting to two drop-dead gorgeous Lady Boys we're told that each of them is going through a gender change, and they're performing so they can hopefully earn enough money to pay for the medical procedure and to have some money left over for when they get older. Apparently, when they've had the sex-change, they'll become social outcasts when they get old and ugly.

How awful is that?

After a few minutes I notice Dave has his arm tightly wrapped around the naked waist of one of The Lady Boys. He's pulling him/her ever closer whilst he/she lays his/her head on his shoulder and peers up lovingly into his eyes. Dave appears to have forgotten that his girlfriend is standing just a few yards away, but luckily she has her back towards him as she carries on chatting to another Lady Boy.

Dave is standing to my left, between me and his Lady Boy. I think I need to have a word, so I lean towards him as he continues to hold onto his Thai friend.

"You do know that's a bloke you've got your arm round, don't you?" I whisper.

"What?" replies Dave with mock annoyance.

"I'm just asking if you know that's a geezer peering into your eyes."

Dave gives his admirer a smile before turning back to me.

"Of course I know it's a bloke, but I've just got through six pints of ale so I don't care," he snaps before turning his gaze back to you-know-who.

I just hope each one of The Lady Boys finds the love and happiness they're looking for, but right now I'm hoping Dave's girlfriend isn't aware of what's been going on behind her back!

Despite the doctor's warning, a couple of days later the four of us are perched on the back of an elephant, trekking along the top of a hill and dangerously close to a hundred foot drop.

Dawn is wearing a pair of skin-tight tiny shorts and a crop top. I don't know if it's due to the heat or to all the unexpected effort, but by the time the elephant finally takes us back down to the bottom of the hill, she's completely drenched in sweat as the guide comes over to assist her off the animal's back.

"Ooh Ma'am. You look very hot and all that sweat makes it look like you've pee-peed your pants," claims the guide to Dawn's embarrassment.

"Yes, I know," sighs Dawn. "And if you don't hurry up and get me down off this bloody elephant, I'll also end up looking like I've poo-pooed."

Back in Kuala Lumpur Dave has noticed the Bayu Angkasa crazy golf course, so I pop down to collect a couple of golf sticks and balls from the security box. Then as I'm wiping the golf stick handles dry, I just can't believe my eyes when Dave arrives, accompanied by his Slazenger golf bag and about a thousand quidsworth of clubs including putters, irons and something called a Big Bertha which looks like it's used for sending golf balls into orbit.

"What the hell are you bringing that lot for," I ask. "We're only playing a round of crazy golf. We're not in the British Open."

"Do you remember when you slaughtered me at ten-pin bowling?" he asks with a huge grin between his ears. "I told you I'd get my revenge, and today's the day."

"You ratbag! You had no idea I was booking you a round of golf at the Saujana Club. Are telling me you decided to cart all those clubs nine thousand miles just to get revenge on a crazy golf course your mother mentioned in one of her letters?"

"Absolutely, so do you want to tee off first or shall I," he laughs.

"I knew I'd end up hating you. I'll tee off and you can bugger off!

Just in case the dipstick reads this book, I guess I ought to mention that he finally managed to get his revenge. I'm delighted for him, I think!

It's a sad day when Dave and his girlfriend head back to the UK, especially for Dawn, but during the next few months we have a great time going backwards and forwards between Kuala Lumpur and fabulous places such as Sabah and Sarawak in Borneo, the Cameron Highlands, Penang, and almost every town and city in Northern Peninsular Malaysia.

It's been a wonderful experience and we've met and made friends with so many lovely Malaysian people along the way. I just hope they all feel the same way about us.

One morning I pop into the Faber office and notice a sheet of paper pinned to the wall. Written on the paper is the name of each member of the Faber team and at the side of each name is a cross written in red. When I ask Danny what the list is for, it appears that one of our local colleagues has contracted Dengue Fever, and is seriously ill in a nearby hospital, and has had to have a blood transfusion. Apparently in Malaysia, if you receive blood then you, your family or friends are required to donate the same amount between them.

That sounds like a good idea to me, so why don't we do the same back in the UK?

Anyway, almost everyone in the office has been to the hospital with the aim of donating blood on behalf their colleague. The red crosses on the list indicate they've all been turned down for some reason or other, so I decide to give it a try myself. Then without saying a word to anyone, I take a stroll down to the hospital during my lunch break.

"Good afternoon sir," says the smiling receptionist. "How can I help you?"

"Hello. I work nearby for Faber Medi-Serve and I understand that one of my colleagues who is suffering with Dengue Fever, is a patient here and recently had a blood transfusion. I'm here to donate some blood of my own."

"But you're a Mat Salleh. Why would you want to give blood?" she asks.

"Because the blood used in the transfusion has to replaced, so I'd like to help."

The receptionist is clearly confused, so she disappears and returns with a doctor.

"Hello, I understand you wish to donate blood. Is that correct?" asks the doctor.

"That's correct," I reply.

"But Mat Sallehs don't give blood to Malaysians."

"Well this one does!"

"That's very good of you sir, but I don't believe that's ever happened before."

"Well if you don't mind, I'll be delighted to be the first."

"Very well, please follow me," he says.

We head into a consulting room where I'm requested to lie on the couch. Then just as the doctor is about to commence the blood donating procedure, a dozen nurses file in and line up against the wall opposite me.

"I hope it's OK sir," says the doctor. "My nurses have never seen English blood before, so I invited them to come and have a look."

"It's fine by me, but I assure you it won't look any different from what they've seen before. They might also have read somewhere that our Royal family is blue-blooded, but that's not actually true," I joke.

Unfortunately, just as the doctor makes a start, a medical consultant strides into the room.

"Stop, stop," demands the consultant. "You can't take the Mat Salleh's blood. He doesn't meet the blood donor eligibility criteria. When they had the Mad Cow Disease outbreak recently, the Malaysian Government decided not to permit anyone who lived in the UK between 1980 and 1996 to donate blood to our citizens, and Mr Eric has only been here since 1997. I kept the blood.

Perhaps I might have been made a saint if there wasn't a risk of me turning somebody into a mad cow!

We've been living in Kuala Lumpur and working for Faber Medi-Serve for almost two years now, and from the day of our arrival we've always been made to feel welcome not just by Faber, but throughout this wonderful country. I suppose that could be the reason I'm so angry, when Des calls me into his office to inform me that we'll be going out on other business next week, and I'll need to report sick on Monday morning so that Faber will still pay for my services whilst I cheat on them.

"You can't be serious," I snap. "Do you really expect me to cheat on all my friends and colleagues in Faber Medi-Serve? Do you really believe I would even consider doing such a thing?" I ask as I glare into his face. "How about I take a few days leave to come with you, as that won't be cheating, will it?"

"No. You're not taking paid leave. They'll never know you're not really ill because they trust you," Des replies. "Anyway, it's only for a few days."

"I'm sorry Des, but I don't care if it's only for a few minutes. There's absolutely no way I'll ever cheat on Faber or anyone else, so you can forget it. It won't happen now or any other time," I snarl before walking out of the office and almost taking the door off its hinges as I slam it shut.

Dawn is also furious when I arrive back at the apartment and explain what's happened. Just like me, she regards everyone in Faber as friends and wonderful people, so cheating on either them or the company would be unacceptable in every way. No doubt Des realises just how much he's offended me, so during the next few days he noticeably keeps his distance and avoids me like the plague.

It comes as a total surprise when Des asks me to accompany him into his office on Friday morning, but then he introduces me to what I can only describe as the most miserable looking face I've ever seen. It turns out to be Bob Scratchit, the International Director who gave us his approval to do the Western Night at the company's expense.

I think I know what's coming my way.

"Hello Eric. Des called me a few days ago to inform me that you had refused point blank to carry out his instructions, so I thought it best for me to fly to Malaysia and warn you that should you continue to refuse to do what the company demands, then you may come to regret it," Scratchit moans. "As International Director, it's my job to make sure that everything the company and it's employees does overseas is done in accordance with the Board of Directors instructions and expectations. So I'm here to make it clear that you will take sick leave next week and you will accompany Des on other business. Is that clear?"

At this moment I think I'm just about to return to the bit of a blip I had some time ago, because I'm itching to kick the living daylights out of this idiot.

"Yes. That's clear," I state. "Now let me make something clear to you. Nobody insults me in the way you just did, so you can stick your job where the sun don't shine because I'll be heading back to the UK, and then it'll be you who regrets it when Faber find out what's happened."

Walking out on Faber and my colleagues isn't something I ever imagined I would do, but cheating on them just isn't going to happen no matter what.

We have a bit of a miserable time at Bayu Angkasa during the weekend. The last couple of years have been absolutely wonderful and now it's coming to end. I leave it as long as I possibly can, but I have to notify our letting agent back home and ask them to give notice to the tenant living in our house. Our world suddenly appears to be falling apart, but I still have the problem of informing Tajul, Ali and Danny that I won't be around for much longer.

I'm still trying to find the words a week later, when Ali is giving us a little presentation of his plans for the next twelve months, which includes a load of projects he'll be handing over to me. I think that now is the time to break the news, so I ask if I can have a word. I explain that due to unforeseen circumstances, Dawn and I have to return to the UK, so he will need to rethink his plans. I don't think it's a good idea for me to go into detail about what's happened, so I just offer my sincere apologies and best wishes to Faber Medi-Serve and the team. Then I call my boss Philip Russell to explain what's been going on and as it turns out, he doesn't like old misery ass any more than I do, so I'll have a job waiting for me when we arrive home.

But it's not quite over just yet!

We spend quite a romantic evening sitting in the moonlight on our balcony, reminiscing about everything we've grown to love about not only Kuala Lumpur, but Malaysia in general and all the lovely people we've met. We have so much to talk about that we haven't realised how quickly the time has passed by, so by the time we climb into bed the sun is already beginning to rise. Dawn is comatose within minutes, but I just lay awake and keep running everything through my mind over and over again.

I must have dozed off at some point though, because as I turn towards Dawn I notice she has a nasty looking mosquito on her shoulder. She's facing away from me so I don't know whether or not she's still asleep. It doesn't really matter one way or the other, because I have to get rid of the insect before it does her any harm.

It'll be no good just flicking the thing off her shoulder as it'll no doubt come straight back, so I take the only other option I can think of and I slam the palm of my hand down onto the insect and squash it against Dawn's shoulder. That works a treat but I haven't considered the fact that she might now be half awake, and if that is the case, then my hand crashing onto her flesh could come as quite a shock.

And it certainly does!

The moment my palm smashes onto her shoulder, she thanks me with an elbow straight into my teeth.

Thank you very much!

I jump out of bed and sprint into the bathroom to check that I still have a mouthful of teeth. When I arrive back in the bedroom, Dawn is asleep once again. As I turn back towards the door I tread onto something that sounds as though it cracked beneath my foot. It was a huge cockroach but not any more, however its pal is now scuttling around the floor. I race into the kitchen and return with a can of insect killer, then I aim the aerosol at the little swine and spray a huge amount of insect killer all over its body. The cockroach still keeps running around the bedroom floor, so I shoot it another squirt but once again the insect simply ignores it. I continue spraying until the can is almost empty, and when Dawn finally opens her eyes an hour later she asks what the pools of liquid are. I explain that I stepped onto a cockroach and then I killed one of its mates with the can of insect killer.

"Oh, the spray works then, does it," she enquires.

"Actually, no it doesn't," I reply.

"I thought you said you killed it?"

"I did, but not with the aerosol spray. I had to beat it to death with the can."

Later in the day Dawn decides to do the washing. Once the linen basket is empty, she removes the liner that's fastened to the inside in the hope of preventing cockroaches from climbing in amongst our soiled clothes and towels.

That turns out to have been a complete waste of money!

A few seconds later a frightening scream emits from the bathroom, so I sprint inside to see if she's OK. She's OK, but she wasn't prepared for the extended family of cockroaches that appear to have taken up residence at the bottom of the basket, and right now a few them are racing up and down her arm. When she finally calms down a little, Dawn suggests it might be a good idea for us to give the apartment a damn good clean, in the hope that any insects still kicking around will disappear one way or another.

So we spend the next three hours clearing out all the cupboards, wardrobes and cabinets before giving them a good scrub. We also give the windows and doors a thorough going over and once the place is absolutely spotless, we decide to spray a few gallons of insect killer throughout all 2,000 square feet of the apartment and then give the floor a good mopping with disinfectant. Finally, we open all the windows before taking a stroll down to the local shopping mall whilst the place dries out and freshens up.

When we arrive back at the apartment Dawn opens the door, and to our great surprise we can hear somebody inside. We never gave a thought to closing the sliding door leading out onto the balcony before we left, mainly due to us being nine floors up, so now we have three unexpected guests of the hairy kind parked on the sofa in front of the TV.

The monkey on the right is holding onto a bowl of fruit, and has clearly been sampling almost every apple, orange and banana it contains. The one on the left has Dawn's handbag on its knee, and is smearing her lipstick all over its face, neck and head. The monkey sitting between the other two is watching TV. It has the TV remote control in its hand, and is nonchalantly pressing the channel selector every couple of seconds, so now we know where the sound of voices was coming from.

There's no way this could possibly happen back in Dee Dah land! Is there?

When our guests notice us heading towards them, they jump straight off the sofa and disappear over the balcony. Luckily they leave the handbag and TV remote control behind, but the bowl of fruit and Dawn's 'lippie' are never to be seen again.

I just can't believe all this is happening, but I am beginning to wonder if somebody has told the local wildlife that we're leaving Malaysia shortly, and they've decided to pop in to say goodbye. Perhaps not, but you never know, do you?

The next morning I'm late for work, due to four of Bayu Angkasa's security officers blocking my exit from the lift when it arrives on the ground floor. They're struggling to hoist a rather heavy-looking load up from the floor of the lift lobby, just outside the lift door. I'm not sure exactly what it is, but it looks to me like a roll of carpet with an elongated head and four huge legs attached. When they finally manage to lift the roll up, I realise it isn't a carpet after all. Two of the guys are clinging onto the neck of a huge monitor lizard, whilst their companions are desperately hanging onto the other end.

The security officers are really struggling, especially as the lizard is thrashing around like crazy, trying to escape their clutches. I simply can't just stand here and watch the wrestling match, so I have two options. The first is to dive in and grab hold of the lizard and help the men to lift it outside, and then carry it across the road and into the nearby grassy area. For perhaps the first time in my life, I take the second option and climb into the Proton Wira.

Well isn't that what you'd do? And don't lie to me!

At least we won't have to go through all this cockroach, monkey and monitor lizard kind of stuff when we get back to the UK. Well maybe not the monkeys and lizards, but I'm not so sure about the cockroaches.

Once we're packed and ready to go, I realise we're in exactly the same position as we were on the morning of our departure from the UK two years ago, when we glanced around the front room for the final time. So I gently hold Dawn's hand as we take one last look around the apartment, and wonder if we'll ever see Malaysia and all our friends again. Then after a moment of reflection we sadly decide to 'go for it'.

I think Faber Medi-Serve may have somehow found out exactly why I chose to make an early departure from Malaysia, as it's not long before I hear that the company of which Phillip and Bob Scratchit are directors, has lost the contract it had with them. Perhaps someone at a high level in Faber Medi-Serve might consider renaming the company as Faber Medi-Serves You Right For Trying To Cheat Us, but I doubt that will happen even though it sounds good to me.

So we're back in Dee Dah land once again. My life just seems to have been up and down like the back-end of a rocking horse, but I've loved every minute. Well maybe not every single minute, but hey ho, that's life.

Throughout the years, something has always happened to make me think life just couldn't get any better, but then something else heads my way to prove me wrong. I thought I had everything a Dee Dah could possibly need, but the moment Dawn came into my life I realised I had nothing, but her love and devotion changed everything, and it's only now that I realise I really do have everything I could possibly need.

No, I'm not being soppy. I'm simply telling you how it is.

In a similar vein, I never thought anything could top the wonderful experiences Dawn and I enjoyed during our two years in Malaysia, but that also turned out not to be the case. Then, almost a year later, Dawn and I took our marriage vows on 8 April 2000, and that was the day my life actually felt complete, especially as nobody suggested we throw the marriage certificate into the bin whenever it suits us.

I don't think God could have been any happier than me about that!

I decided to write my life story, and I'm delighted I lived long enough to complete it. I'd love to write a second one, but that will very much depend on whether or not My Maker decides to offer me the chance to do a repeat performance at some point in the future.

So finally, and assuming you haven't pulled this book out from the bottom of somebody's dustbin, may I take this opportunity to thank you for sharing the laughs and times of this particular Sheffield Dee Dah, although there's not a hope in hell you've enjoyed reading about it more than I've enjoyed actually living it.

Booey